**FOR
REFERENCE ONLY**

Youth Cultures

0211412

Routledge Advances in Sociology

Youth Cultures

Scenes, Subcultures and Tribes

Edited by
Paul Hodkinson and
Wolfgang Deicke

SWANSEA METROPOLITAN UNIVERSITY

PRIFYSGOL FETROPOLITAN ABERTAWE

Library and Learning Resources
Llyfrgeli ac Adnoddau Dysgu

Class Number/Marc Dosbarth:	305.235 YOU
Barcode/Côd Bar:	0211412
Date/Dyddiad:	Location/Lleoliad:

 Routledge
Taylor & Francis Group
New York   London

Routledge
Taylor & Francis Group
270 Madison Avenue
New York, NY 10016

Routledge
Taylor & Francis Group
2 Park Square
Milton Park, Abingdon
Oxon OX14 4RN

© 2007 by Taylor & Francis Group, LLC
Routledge is an imprint of Taylor & Francis Group, an Informa business

Transferred to Digital Printing 2009

International Standard Book Number-13: 978-0-415-37612-9 (Hardcover)

No part of this book may be reprinted, reproduced, transmitted, or utilized in any form by any electronic, mechanical, or other means, now known or hereafter invented, including photocopying, microfilming, and recording, or in any information storage or retrieval system, without written permission from the publishers.

Trademark Notice: Product or corporate names may be trademarks or registered trademarks, and are used only for identification and explanation without intent to infringe.

Library of Congress Cataloging-in-Publication Data

Youth cultures : scenes, subcultures and tribes / edited by Paul Hodkinson and
    Wolfgang Deicke.
        p. cm. -- (Routledge advances in sociology ; 26)
    Includes bibliographical references and index.
    ISBN 978-0-415-37612-9 (hardback : alk. paper)
    1. Youth--Case studies. 2. Subculture--Case studies. I. Hodkinson, Paul. II.
Deicke, Wolfgang.

HQ796.Y59272 2007
305.23509182'1--dc22   2006031355

ISBN10: 0-415-37612-2 (hbk)
ISBN10: 0-415-80240-7 (pbk)

ISBN13: 978-0-415-37612-9 (hbk)
ISBN13: 978-0-415-80240-6 (pbk)

**Visit the Taylor & Francis Web site at
http://www.taylorandfrancis.com**

**and the Routledge Web site at
http://www.routledge.com**

Contents

Illustrations and Tables

Acknowledgments

The idea for this book originated with the 2003 *Scenes, Subcultures and Tribes: Youth Cultures in the 21st Century* conference, organised by the BSA Youth Study Group at the University of Northampton, U.K. Such was the range and quality of the contributions to that event that an edited collection offering a sense of the broad range of contemporary youth cultural research seemed an obvious next step. Because of this, we would like to thank all those who participated in that conference and the BSA Youth Study group itself, which continues to act as a valuable hub for researchers in this area. Our gratitude also extends to colleagues at Northampton who helped organise the conference.

Thanks also go to all those who were involved as participants in the range of research presented in the book. Most of all, however, we would like to thank all the individual chapter authors featured in the book for their extensive time, energy and patience as well as for their expertise.

1 Youth cultures
A critical outline of key debates

Paul Hodkinson

Youth cultures have been the subject of extensive academic research and writing for many years and scholarship in this area has included some of the most well known studies and theorists within the disciplines of sociology and cultural studies. In the early twenty-first century the cultural patterns and pursuits of adolescents continue to be the subject of intense research and debate. Originally inspired by the intense and fascinating discussions which took place at the 'Scenes, Subcultures and Tribes' international conference (University of Northampton 2003), this book represents an attempt to further inform and invigorate this important area of study. The chapters outline and engage with core areas of debate in relation to a variety of examples of contemporary theory and research. Our aim is to critically assess established approaches to the subject at the same time as demonstrating ways in which we might adapt and move on from them in the study of young people's life-styles in the early twenty-first century. While it is impossible to do justice to the rich and varied range of existing youth cultural research in a single chapter, this introduction provides a context for those which follow by offering a critical discussion of some of the most influential perspectives and points of debate.

YOUTH CULTURE: BETWIXT AND BETWEEN?

There is some level of consensus among theorists that, particularly since the mid-1950s, young people have occupied a period of the life course characterized by a degree of instability and transition. More specifically, adolescence is deemed to have constituted a liminal period of time, during which individuals break free from many of features of childhood without yet fully adopting all of the characteristics associated with being an adult. For pioneering psychologist Stanley Hall, adolescence was a response to the physical or psychological changes encountered during and after puberty. The transition of body and mind to an eventual state of adulthood was deemed, by definition, to be characterized by confusion, trauma and upheaval (Hall 1904). Meanwhile, sociologists understood the transition as one defined by socio-economic and cultural factors. For Talcott Parsons, the development of a distinct 'youth culture' in the United States was closely linked with breaking away from a relationship of dependency with the childhood family and moving towards marriage, parenthood and career (Parsons 1949). 'Youth culture'—dominated by the initial rejection of adulthood responsibilities in favour of 'having a good time'—was a mechanism which enabled young people to deal with the strains of their transition:

> The period of youth in our society is one of considerable strain and insecurity... youth culture has important positive functions in easing the transition from the security of childhood in the family of orientation to that of full adult in marriage and occupational status (Parsons 1949: 101).

Consistent with Parsons's emphasis on transition, the notion of youth culture as a response to the uncertainties of moving between childhood and adulthood has dominated much subsequent thinking on the cultural practices and patterns of young people (P. Cohen 1997). In addition to the relatively general family- and occupation-related factors identified by Parsons, however, emphasis has also been placed upon a variety of social and cultural factors which conspired during the twentieth century to further establish and reinforce very particular forms of adolescence, transition and youth culture. Most obviously perhaps there has been the development of a series of legal classifications associated with different stages of youth, notably the age at which young people can vote, have sex, smoke cigarettes, drink alcohol and drive motorcars. While such legal 'stages' vary between countries and can offer a somewhat confusing assessment of where, exactly, adolescence begins and ends (James 1986), they nevertheless offer points of reference and rites of passage in each context which have become symbolically important to transition processes.

If gradually breaking free from legal restrictions has served symbolically to mark the leaving of childhood, then the expansion of post-compulsory education has served increasingly to delay the onset of full adulthood, both symbolically and practically, through enabling significant amounts of time during which changes might be negotiated and identities developed (Valentine, Skelton, and Chambers 1998). At the same time, general trends towards secularisation alongside the advent of the pill afforded young people moral space for experimentation unknown to previous generations. Lastly—and crucially—in spite of class and ethnic divisions, young people as a whole began from the mid-twentieth century to earn for themselves or to receive from their parents, significantly larger amounts of money than in the past, at a time when they had comparatively few financial responsibilities (Osgerby 2004). Disposable income rose, particularly during the 1950s and 1960s, a period when, as a result of the post-war baby boom, the numbers of young people were also particularly high. The prospect of so sizeable a social group, characterised by comparatively low responsibilities and high spending power, inevitably led to the targeting of young people by expanding culture industries.

Whether in the form of the development of night-time entertainment, of youth music and fashion or youth oriented magazines and television programmes, the increasing relationship between young people and particular kinds of consumption has been a key theme of recent scholarship on youth cultures. As we shall see later in this chapter, many contemporary youth theorists believe that, alongside the decline of traditional elements of belonging such as class and community, this expansion in the role of consumption has rendered young people's already uncertain transitions increasingly characterized by ephemeral and individualized tastes, practices and identities (Furlong and Cartmel 1997). Such perspectives contrast, however, with much of the earlier scholarship on youth cultures, which placed emphasis on socio-economic position in explaining young people's cultural responses to their transitional situation. In contrast to the contemporary emphasis on ephemeral, individualized activities, it was argued by subcultural theorists that significant numbers of young people resolved the uncertainties and marginalities they faced by forming distinct communities which offered belonging, status, normative guidelines and, crucially, a rejection of dominant values.

YOUTH CULTURE AS COLLECTIVE TROUBLE MAKING

The first identifiable body of sociological research on what now might be termed youth cultures was located as part of a drive to understand adolescent crime and deviance among U.S. sociologists in the early to mid-twentieth century.

Delinquency and labelling

An ethnographic research tradition originating at the University of Chicago became famous for its attempts to explain deviant activities such as drug taking, petty crime and gang membership as collective normative behaviour associated with distinct urban social regions, each with their own divergent moral codes (Park 1925). For the likes of Thrasher (1927) and, later, Whyte (1943), youth gangs in economically or ethnically marginalized areas formed part of a defiant collective mentality which had developed among groups of young people within such sites of disadvantage.

Weaving together aspects of Park, Thrasher and Whyte's work with Robert Merton's writings on strain theory, it is perhaps Albert Cohen's introduction to his study of delinquent boys which best summarises the youth subcultural theory with which this U.S. tradition of youth research is frequently associated. Whereas Merton had explained deviant behaviour in terms of the rejection of dominant means or goals at an individual level (1938), Cohen—based at Indiana University—drew upon the Chicago approach in attempting to theorize youthful delinquency as a collective phenomenon (A. Cohen 1955). For Cohen, delinquent subcultures emerged as a result of the 'mutual gravitation' of those who suffered similar 'problems of adjustment' as a result of their adolescence and their disadvantaged background. Such individuals responded to their lack of status or direction by forming alternative sets of collective norms, rituals and values which rendered status-worthy the characteristics, abilities and attitudes they shared (A. Cohen 1955: 65–66). Subsequently, the gaining of status among fellow subcultural participants would be accompanied by a further loss of status within society as a whole. Similarly, Howard Becker argues that the labelling of deviant groups as such served to prevent members from being accepted as members of 'normal' society and to increase their attachment to the subcultural group, whose 'self-justifying rationale' contained 'a general repudiation of conventional moral rules, conventional institutions and the conventional moral world' (Becker 1963: 39).

Understandings of youth cultures in terms of deviancy amplification and labelling were also developed in the context of the United Kingdom—in relation to drug-taking subcultures (Young 1971) and in respect of mass media reporting of violent encounters between mods and rockers (S. Cohen 1972). Stanley Cohen's famous study asserted not only that the sensationalist media labelling of mods and rockers intensified the appeal of such groups to young people, but also that the behaviour of mods and rockers began to resemble the initially exaggerated media caricatures: 'the societal reaction not only increases the deviant's chance of acting at all, it also provides him with his lines and stage directions' (S. Cohen 1972: 137).

Symbolic warfare

The notion of adolescence as a form of collective subcultural rebellion also permeates a separate, though related tradition of theory and research on youth cultures associated with the Centre of Contemporary Cultural Studies (CCCS) at Birmingham University. Consistent with the explosion of youth-oriented culture industries during the 1950s and 1960s, the specific focus in many of the Birmingham studies was upon subcultures based around distinctive music and style; groups such as teds, mods, skinheads, bikers and punks. The interpretations of the CCCS theorists were not uniform, but the prevailing view was that such subcultures represented an enactment of stylistic resistance; a subversive reaction by young people to a contradictory situation in respect of both age and class. In addition to the general uncertainties of youth, subcultural participants are deemed to been caught between the traditional working-class culture of their parents and the hegemonic values of capitalism and consumption (Clarke et al. 1976). In different ways, subcultures are said to have resolved this situation through combining working class consciousness with an embrace of a hedonistic consumption specific to the development in the post-war years of a strong generational 'youth' consciousness. Consistent with this, youth subcultures are regarded as 'a compromise solution between two contradictory needs: the need to create and express autonomy and difference from parents... and the need to maintain the parental identifications which support them' (P. Cohen 1972: 26).

Crucially subcultures were also regarded as a means of winning space and as a form of collective defiance. In particular, Phil Cohen, Clarke and colleagues and Hebdige (1977, 1979) all regarded the creative, active manner in which subcultural styles were assembled to have a particular symbolic importance. Although it is recognized that style subcultures could not have emerged without the development of a youth consumer market, the latter is credited only with the provision of raw materials, subcultural styles having been assembled creatively by working class youth, through a grassroots process of bricolage whereby consumer objects were combined and symbolically transformed (Clarke et al. 1976). Thus, for Hebdige, the symbolic value of scooters, conventional smart clothes, medical drugs and even metal combs were hijacked by mods, who turned such everyday objects into symbols of subcultural hedonism and intimidation—subversive parodies of all that was conventional (Hebdige 1979).

Yet crucially, such symbolic rebellion was not regarded as an antidote to working class marginalisation or as a serious challenge to the fundamental relations of power. Rather, it is argued by Clarke and colleagues that:

> when the post-war subcultures address the problematics of their class experience, they often do so in ways which reproduce the gaps and discrepancies between real negotiations and symbolically displaced 'resolutions'. They 'solve' but in an imaginary way, problems which at the concrete material level remain unresolved (Clarke et al. 1976: 47).

Consistent with the findings of Paul Willis's ethnography of counterschool 'lads', then, cultural rebellion was deemed ultimately to reinforce rather than to resolve the material subordination of working class youth, who, as Willis put it, invariably would go on to get working-class jobs (1977).

Meanwhile, for Hebdige, the symbolic creativity and subversion represented by youth subcultures would ultimately fail even to transform power relations within the culture industry itself. Initially generated by active practices of grassroots appropriation and bricolage, subcultural styles subsequently would be recognized for their profit-making potential, at which point watered down versions would be mass marketed to the general public and the styles would lose their political significance. As Hebdige puts it, 'Youth cultural styles may begin by issuing symbolic challenges, but they must inevitably end by establishing new sets of conventions, by creating new commodities...' (1979: 96).

Discussion

The subcultural approaches originating from Chicago and Birmingham offer invaluable and sophisticated insights, many of which retain significance, and it is because of this that they are given such weight in this chapter. The emphasis by Cohen, Becker and others on alternative value systems, labelling and the amplification of deviance, have currency well beyond the gangs and delinquents they were first used to describe, something demonstrated in the elements of such theory taken on and applied to style- and consumption-based youth groupings by the CCCS and also in more recent studies of youth cultures (e.g. Thornton 1995; Hodkinson 2002). Meanwhile, the CCCS' analysis of the relationship between young people's active consumption practices and the youth consumer industries, and their emphasis on the importance of class position has had an extensive and lasting impact within and beyond the field of youth subcultural studies. Such formulations have served as the primary yardstick against which a range of recent youth cultural research has been outlined (Muggleton 2000; Bennett 2000; Hodkinson 2002; Nayak 2003; Huq 2006; Laughey 2006). Nevertheless, a number of elements of this approach have been subject to criticism.

Some have suggested that the CCCS's interpretation of subcultural styles had more to do with their own neo-Marxist theoretical agenda than with the empirical reality of subcultural participants (Redhead 1990). Paul Willis's work on counter-school 'lads' (1977) and motorbike boys (1978) consisted of in-depth ethnographic research comparable to the approach pioneered by Chicago sociologists, but this sort of methodology did not characterize the work of those with whom the CCCS's work on style subcultures is most commonly associated. The explanations provided by the likes of Phil Cohen, Clarke and colleagues and Hebdige tended to be based upon the theoretically and historically informed textual interpretation of subcultural styles. It is indeed ironic that an account which constituted so important a step in the development of an empirical tradition of work on 'active consumers', largely excluded from its analysis the subjective perspectives and experiences of young mods, skinheads and punks, many of whom, as Hebdige was happy to accept, were unlikely to recognize themselves within his account (1979).

The sophistication of the analysis of Hebdige, Phil Cohen and others is underestimated by Gary Clarke's suggestion that it had emanated from 'a few scant observations of styles and artefacts' (1981: 83). Clarke was surely right, however, to emphasize that such theorists were unable empirically to explain how subcultures emerged or to outline the processes through which young people were recruited to them. One consequence of this, according to Sarah Thornton, is that there is little to corroborate the suggestion that culture industries only became involved in the promotion of subcultures *after* an authentic period during which their style was spontaneously created by young people (1995). A further problem according to Gary Clarke was that, rather than studying the variety of responses of marginalized youth to their apparently contradictory social position, the CCCS took as their starting point the response of the most stylistically spectacular youth—or 'card carrying' subcultural members—and then proceeded to read off class, youth and other factors as the explanation. The result is that the motivations, practices and social backgrounds of subcultural participants were essentialized, while both non-subcultural youth and so called 'part-timers' were either excluded from the analysis or dismissed as dupes of the culture industry (Clarke 1981).

That subcultural theory tended to present an overly fixed impression of the cultural boundaries between groups of young people—and that it has placed emphasis on an untypical deviant or spectacular minority—are criticisms often repeated (Bennett 1999; Muggleton 2000). Sure enough, both the Chicago and CCCS traditions tended to seek out distinctive or deviant minority groups and to place emphasis on collective systems of norms and boundaries rather than to detail the complex positioning and movement of different individuals in relation to these. As a consequence, differential and changing levels of individual commitment were under-played and, according to a more recent article by Phil Cohen, 'the majority of young people who did not take drugs, drop out, run away from home, become wildly promiscuous and engage in street violence or petty crime were pushed to the sidelines of academic concern' (P. Cohen 1997: 194).

Perhaps the most significant group who were excluded from subcultural analysis were young women. Angela McRobbie and Jenny Garber criticized their colleagues in the CCCS for focusing on largely outdoor spectacular subcultural activities, something deemed systematically to have excluded a largely separate female youth culture which, as a result of the specific restrictions and risks faced by teenage girls, was based largely around pop music, magazines and teenage bedrooms (McRobbie and Garber 1976). The cultural activities of ethnic minority youth also were covered only partially by a subcultural theory focused largely on the class resistance of white youth. Although not entirely invisible, the main role for minority youth in the 1970s CCCS accounts were as influences on white subcultures, as targets for racist aggression or as the subjects of media moral panic (Huq 2006; Nayak 2003). Meanwhile, for other theorists, the unrepresentativeness of subcultural theory was a more general problem. Everyday aspects of youth culture across the boundaries of gender, race and class were systematically excluded by a subcultural theory enticed only by the spectacular and deviant (G. Clarke 1981; Frith 1983).

The potential value in recognising and understanding youth who are either stylistically, normatively or criminally 'deviant', and indeed of those strongly committed to clearly demarcated collective groupings, must not be forgotten about amongst all this criticism. Detailed research has continued to demonstrate that some young people do become strongly attached to substantive and distinctive cultural groupings whose particular norms and values dominate their identity and life-style for a period of time (e.g., Thornton 1995; Sardiello 1998; MacDonald 2001; Hodkinson 2002). It is therefore not helpful that, at times, critics of subcultural theory have become so purist as to imply that any study which is focused on spectacular rather than mundane youth activities or that emphasizes the importance of collective values more than individual differences, must automatically be dismissed for being insufficiently critical of the CCCS approach (e.g., Laughey 2006). Nevertheless, it is equally clear that a focus on collective deviance is insufficient in itself to make sense of the complexity of identities, values and practices which make up youth culture and also that significant changes have occurred in society since the 1970s.

FRAGMENTATION, INDIVIDUALIZATION AND UNCERTAINTY?

If the study of youth cultures prior to the 1980s was dominated by socio-economic marginalization and spontaneous subcultural defiance, then in more recent years the field has been awash with the themes of fragmentation, fluidity and consumerism. In this respect, studies of youth culture have been heavily influenced by developments in general social theory. Whether under the guise of the condition of postmodernity (Harvey 1989), 'risk society' (Bauman 2001; Beck 1992) or individualization (Beck and Beck-Gernsheim 2000; Bauman 2001), leading theorists repeatedly have emphasized the breakdown, especially in Western societies, of previous forms of certainty, stability and community alongside the simultaneous expansion and diversification of media and consumer culture. A variety of previous sources of security and direction, including religion, social class, place and the stable nuclear family are argued to have declined in significance, leaving individual biographies increasingly unpredictable and subject to changing tastes, circumstances and choices. In particular, an ever-increasing range of globalized media and consumer goods offer temporary and partial sources of identification to individuals who increasingly lack fixed or stable sources of belonging or direction. Rather than having their lives and identities clearly set out by tradition, ideology or community, then, individuals are deemed to live out DIY identities which are both multiple and ephemeral, while the superficial sources of belonging to which they seek to attach themselves are little more than 'momentary condensations in the ever flowing stream of seductive choices' (Bauman 1992: 24). For Beck, the decline of previous sources of stability and direction renders individual biographies increasingly subject to anxiety and risk (1992).

As set out previously, youth has for some time been regarded as a stage of the life course characterized by uncertainty. Yet, while subcultural theories emphasized the role of underlying factors such as socio-economic position and community as sources of stability and collective defiance in an otherwise liminal period of life, more recent theorists have emphasized the declining significance to youth culture of ascribed factors such as class and of clearly bounded collective groupings. Furlong and Cartmel emphasize that the expanded significance of leisure industries and the increasing length of transitions from childhood to adulthood have led to a situation in which 'traditional sources of social differentiation based on social class and communities are thought to have weakened' and 'young people are seen as attempting to find self-fulfilment and ways of identifying with other young people through their consumption of goods, especially fashion' (Furlong and Cartmel 1997: 61). It is suggested, then, that an already transient age-group may be experiencing the kinds of individualized fluidities described by Bauman, Beck and others in a particularly concentrated fashion.

For David Muggleton (1997), who draws on the postmodern theories of Jameson (1991), Harvey (1989) and others, the centrality of increasingly complex, fluid and diversified culture industries makes it increasingly unlikely that young people will commit themselves to clearly bounded subcultures. Previous boundaries between different collective youth styles are deemed to have become increasingly insignificant by ever-more frantic turnovers of fads and fashions and a general proliferation of commercially marketed styles, most of which disconnected both from distinct groupings and from ascribed characteristics such as class or ethnicity. As a consequence, collective stylistic deviance, rebellion or 'authenticity' are deemed increasingly impossible and their pursuit unfulfilling. Instead, young people each develop eclectic individual portfolios of tastes, interests and social networks, which cut across genres or communities. In a later publication Muggleton accepts that some young people continue to adopt what appear to be collective styles, but emphasizes the liminality, internal diversity and external overlaps of such apparent subcultures, as well as the importance to their participants of individual rather than collective difference (Muggleton 2000).

In addition to the general expansion of culture industries, the onset of digital media are argued by some to have acted as a catalyst for the kinds of fragmentation and instability of identities described by Muggleton and others (Turkle 1995; Castells 2001). Research on young people's personal homepages and their use of social software such as online journals and more recently MySpace.com, for example, has placed emphasis on the significance of such media as individual-centred portals of communication (Chandler and Roberts-Young 1998; Reed 2005). Elsewhere, both Wellman (1997) and Castells (2001) suggest that even ostensibly group-oriented discussion forums lend themselves to the pursuit of 'weak' attachments to multiple groups rather than to the exclusive, stable commitment evoked by traditional notions of community. Other forms of new media, from digital television to mp3 players, also have an apparent orientation to distinct individual portfolios of tastes and interests rather than collective or subcultural styles (Rosen 2004–5; Bull 2005). Mobile phones and iPods tend to be individually owned and controlled, rather than shared between household members, something which also applies to the increasing presence of televisions, games machines or computers within personal bedrooms (Livingstone 2002). As we shall see later, however, the impact of new technologies can be highly contingent upon the context in which they are used and not all theorists are entirely convinced as to their individualising credentials (Osgerby 2004).

Some of those who have emphasized the apparent fluidity and instability of contemporary youth cultures have focused upon the notion of 'neo-tribalism' as a means to make sense of it. While their individual explanations differ somewhat, both Maffesoli (1996) and Bauman (1992) make use of this term to refer to the increasing propensity of loose-knit and ephemeral elective cultural groupings, characterized by partial commitment and porous boundaries. For Andy Bennett, the term's emphasis on individual movement between loosely bounded genres, styles and groups makes neo-tribe preferable to subculture in capturing 'the shifting nature of youth's musical and stylistic preferences and the essential fluidity of youth cultural groups' (1999: 614). Although some have questioned whether 'tribalism'— with its traditional implications of highly committed collective identity—is the most appropriate term to describe such apparently superficial cultural groupings (e.g., Hesmondhalgh, this volume), there is little doubt that the term has gained considerable currency within youth cultural studies.

Another term regarded by some as a more effective tool than subculture to make sense of the music related activities of young people is 'scene'. Although it has a somewhat complex history, the academic use of the term essentially signifies the clustering of musicians or fans around particular focal points, whether these be related to local identity (Shank 1994) or musical genre (Harris 2000: 25). Although the link here to theories of postmodernism and individualisation is not direct, 'scene' is clearly felt to recognise fluidities, overlaps and individual differences in music practices in a way which 'subculture' does not (Peterson and Bennett 2004). Nevertheless, the term is also lauded for its flexibility, including—according to Kahn-Harris (previously Harris)...'everything from tight-knit local music communities to isolated musicians and occasional fans' (Harris 2000: 25). It is easy to see the attraction of such inclusiveness, given the apparent internal complexity and external overlaps of many contemporary youth music cultures, but such imprecision has prompted some to question the value of 'scene' as a theoretical device (Hodkinson 2002; Hesmondhalgh, this volume).

Neo-tribe and scene, discussed at length in David Hesmondhalgh's contribution to this collection, are not the only conceptual focal points for youth cultural theorists influenced by theories of fragmentation and fluidity. Others include 'life-style' (Jenkins 1983; Shields 1992; Chaney 1996; Miles 2000), Bünde (Hetherington 1998) and 'proto-community' (Willis et al. 1990). There are various differences in the use of these terms, but all

tend to be used to describe loosely-knit, overlapping and transitory identifications and in this respect they often are contrasted with subculture.
Meanwhile, for Steve Redhead, 'club culture' is proposed as the concept
'which supplements "subculture" as key to the analysis of the histories
and futures of youth culture' (Redhead 1997: x). Redhead argues that the
fragmentation of audiences and consumer groups had rendered the already
questionable concept of subculture insufficient as a means to understand
youth cultures by the mid-1990s. Meanwhile the increasing centrality of
clubbing to the leisure practices of young people from various backgrounds
prompts Redhead to ask: 'are we now in an age of club rather than subcultures?' (xi). Consistent with Redhead's emphasis, a variety of researchers,
perhaps most notably Thornton (1995) and Malbon (1999), have conducted
detailed and valuable research focused upon club culture as a distinct and
increasingly important element of youth culture (also see Rietveld 1998;
Chatterton and Hollands 2003; St. John 2003; Jackson 2004).

Interestingly, however, while Malbon's interactionist approach leads to a
qualified endorsement of the potential value of 'neo-tribe' as descriptor for
what are deemed temporary, diverse and context-specific unities of clubbing, Thornton's study, for all its criticism of the CCCS, places its emphasis
squarely on the consistent, collective labelling and classification practices
of clubbers and the role of media in constructing a subculture with shared
tastes, ideologies and boundaries (1995). While valuable use is made of
Bourdieu's work on cultural classification and distinction, there is little
doubt that Thornton's work owes a considerable debt to subcultural theorists in the deviance and labelling tradition, such as Becker, Albert Cohen
and Stan Cohen. The same could probably be said of my own study of goth
culture, in which the overall group distinctiveness, commitment, identity
and relative autonomy exhibited by this group were deemed to justify use
of a reworked notion of subculture rather than an emphasis on individualism and fluidity. Drawing upon the work of Thornton and of McRobbie
(1989), as well as an emerging literature on 'virtual communities' (Jones
1995: 1997), I sought particularly to emphasize that, while they may sometimes encourage individual difference, commerce, media and the internet
also have the capacity to be used in a manner which reinforces group commitment and boundaries among young people (Hodkinson 2002, 2003,
2006). While the typicality or otherwise of 'substantive' groupings such as
the goth scene, within what some regard as a largely individualized youth
culture, remains open to question, an emphasis on collective identity, values and systems of status can also be found in other studies (e.g., Sardiello
1998; MacDonald 2001; Brown 2003a), as well as some of the contributions to the present volume.

Studies of the significance of ethnicity and diaspora in youth culture,
meanwhile, have been notable for combining elements of poststructuralist
theory with an emphasis on the continuing significance of factors such as
class, locality and ethnicity. Particular emphasis has been placed on the

shifting, 'hybrid' cultural identities of second and third generation minority youth in countries such as the United Kingdom, constructed through a complex combination of transnational cultural flows and everyday national and local contexts (Hall 1988; Gilroy 1993a; Gillespie 1995; Back 1996). Academic attention, for example, has been devoted to the development of ethnically eclectic cultural forms such as bhangra, whose mixing together of traditional Indian sounds with elements of U.K. dance music is deemed an expression of the complex poststructural identities of its producers and consumers (Back 1996). Emphasis also has been placed upon the localized mixing and fusion of musics and styles initially associated with youth from different ethnic backgrounds. Rupa Huq, for example, outlines the development of post-Bhangra sounds such as 'bhangramuffin' and 'raggastani' which explicitly draw upon the Afro-Caribbean genre of raga music (2006). Huq also emphasizes the tendency for localized Bhangra and post-Bhangra events to attract youth from diverse ethnic backgrounds (2006).

Crucially, at the same time as emphasising some of the fluidities, multiplicities and uncertainties of identity—and hence the partial fragmentation of ethnicities—work on youth and ethnicity has tended to provide a consistent reminder of the continuing stabilities and fixities associated with factors such as socio-economic position and place (e.g., Back 1996; Gillespie 1995). Recent examples of this include Huq's work on the role of localized cultural policy interventions which encourage music making among disadvantaged youth (Huq, this volume) and Nayak's study of extensive significance of locality, class and educational context to the ethnic identities of white youth in the North East of the United Kingdom (2003).

The continuing significance of locality is also something which has been emphasized in a more general sense by some advocates of otherwise individualistic accounts of youth cultures. Andy Bennett, for example, draws upon a range of ethnographic research in asserting that locality continues to act as a relatively stable base for otherwise unstable and transient neo-tribal youth identities:

> If... neo-tribal forms of musicalized expression represent highly fluid and transient modes of collective identity, at the same time they are not so fluid and transient as to cancel out any form of meaningful interaction with the local environments from which they emerge (Bennett 2000: 84).

Consistent with this, some studies have focused specific ethnographic attention on the significance of local contexts to young people's cultural practices and identities. An emphasis on the development of locally or nationally distinct manifestations of global genres, styles and associated cultural practices has been a significant part of this (e.g. Shank 1994; Pilkington 2004; Kahn-Harris 2004; Huq 2006). Such work has been invaluable in demonstrating a subtle and complex balance between globalising factors such as media, commerce, travel and migration on the one hand, and inherited or ascribed elements of local or national contexts on the other.

Unspectacular youth

While their tendency to emphasize individual fluidity and complexity contrasts with the notion of subculture, 'post-subcultural' theorists sometimes have been criticised for continuing to focus on spectacular or deviant youth activities, whether in terms of spectacular dress and music or activities such as skating, graffiti, clubbing or drug-taking (Laughey 2006). In contrast, a growing body of research has sought explicitly to place greater emphasis on the everyday cultural activities of young people. Within the CCCS itself, it was McRobbie and Garber's writings on female youth culture which came closest to doing this (1976). Attempting to explain the absence of teenage girls from subcultural theory, they suggested that rather than joining predominantly street-based and exclusive spectacular subcultures, girls tended to respond to the growth of cultural industries by becoming involved in peer-based activities centred upon the bedroom. Reading magazines, listening to music, collecting and displaying rock or pop posters, trying out makeup or trying on clothes and talking about boys were all regarded as core activities of an everyday and largely unspectacular female youth culture. While this bedroom culture is regarded often as having been linked to the 'teenybopper' phenomenon and, hence, dominated by the idolisation of mass marketed pop stars, the bedroom also is regarded as having been central for the minority of girls involved in rock 'n' roll subcultures such as that of the teddy boys:

> Whereas the response of many boys to the rise of rock 'n' roll was themselves to become active if highly amateur performers... girl participants in this culture became either fans or record collectors and readers of the 'teenage-hero' magazines and love-comics (1976:. 214).

The contemporary relevance of so clear a dividing line between male and female youth cultures has since been questioned, as has the apparent implication that female consumption activities were more 'passive' than those of their male counterparts (Lincoln 2004). At the very least, the range of public cultural activities in which young girls involve themselves appears to have broadened in recent years, though bedroom culture remains highly important, and at the same time, some public spaces and activities remain male dominated (Furlong and Cartmel 1997). Nevertheless, McRobbie and Garber's chapter, alongside subsequent work by McRobbie, represented an important moment both for the development of knowledge about female youth culture and for the turning of the spotlight on the ordinary, everyday activities and settings of young people (McRobbie 2000).

Although rather less focused upon the domestic sphere, Richard Jenkins's investigation of the range of youth 'life-styles' in Belfast also represents a shift away from the previous focus on group-based spectacular or deviant youth activities (1983). Dividing youth within the area into 'lads', 'ordinary kids' and 'citizens' on the basis of a variety of factors, Jenkins emphasizes that only the former group constituted an identifiable deviant group, the other two comprising loosely-knit ordinary networks of friends and couples engaged primarily in mundane everyday activities. Paul Willis and colleagues' work on *Common Culture* also examines ordinary youth cultural activities, but places particular emphasis the everyday use of consumables such as fashion and music (1990). While some of his 1970s CCCS colleagues had contrasted the extreme creativity of spectacular subcultures with over-generalized notions of a passive mainstream, over a decade later, Willis and his colleagues illustrate the 'symbolic creativity' of everyday uses of cultural commodities. Consistent with the work of theorists such as John Fiske, *Common Culture* includes wide-ranging examples of the active use by ordinary young people not only of popular music and fashion but also television programmes, magazines, computers and pubs (Willis et al. 1990). The conclusions of the book in relation to fashion are broadly representative of its author's celebration of young people's cultural consumption in general:

> young people don't just buy passively or uncritically. They always transform the meaning of bought goods, appropriating and recontextualising mass-market styles... they bring their own specific and differentiated grounded aesthetics to bear on consumption, choosing their own colours and matches and personalising their purchases (85).

The book's approach is invaluable in dealing squarely with the cultural politics of ordinary consumption practices and in challenging the active subculture versus passive mainstream dichotomy set up by some variants of CCCS subcultural theory. Nevertheless the rather generalized celebration of youth creativity on offer here also runs the risk of encouraging a rather uncritical endorsement of consumer culture.

More recently, research by Dan Laughey has sought explicitly to focus upon the range of music related activities engaged in by a variety of young people, rather than upon specifically identifiable groups or subcultures (Laughey 2006). Laughey catalogues the music use of his respondents in terms of its intensity, the media outlets and spaces (both public and private) via which consumption takes place, the complex ways in which genres are made sense of and the role of social networks including family and peer groups. On the basis of intensity and breadth of music use, the study divides young people into four categories—clubbers, surfers, exchangers and drifters. The attempt here to recognize and categorize the range of different patterns and networks of cultural activity among young people is a useful development even if some elements of Laughey's typology are a little unclear. Yet the overall explanation of how and why young people become clubbers, surfers, exchangers or drifters, and of the extent of any general patterns based on contextual factors such as class, gender, ethnicity, community and so on are a little undeveloped, save for a general endorsement of 'situational interactionism' and an emphasis on the specificities of the individual contexts of his respondents.

Discussion

It is clear that youth culture has changed significantly from the heyday of the baby boomers in the 1960s. Already significant in those days, the massive subsequent expansion and diversification of youth-oriented culture industries has been of key significance to such change, as has the rapid development of media and new media in recent years. While previous sources of identity such as class, ethnicity and gender have in many cases become less all-important either as sources of influence, belonging or constraint, many young people have indeed looked towards the shifting and unstable spheres of leisure and consumption as the primary focus for their quests for belonging and fulfilment. While for some, such consumption appears to have consisted of committed involvement in groupings characterized by some of the key features outlined in previous subcultural theories, it seems likely that, for the many, youth culture is somewhat less focused upon such commitment to a single grouping, consisting instead of social networks of various complexions, as well individual sets of tastes and interests which to some degree crosscut genres, styles and activities.

Nevertheless, there are some difficulties with the emphasis on such fragmentation, fluidity and individualization within some recent writings on youth cultures. The extent of the desire to oppose and avoid the notion of subculture has tended to mean that 'post-subcultural' (or, as I prefer, 'anti-subcultural') explanations, sometimes do not go far enough beyond demonstrating the inadequacies or over-simplicities of the CCCS and/or the Chicago tradition. Having been developed and justified largely negatively, in opposition to the CCCS version of subculture, for example, the detailed positive implications and applications of concepts such as neo-tribe, scene and club-culture sometimes have been left unclear, as have the elements of difference and overlap between one replacement term and another. Indeed, the apparent competition to coin the best replacement may ultimately have acted as something of an unhelpful distraction, not least because of the confusing number of apparently rather similar concepts on offer. It specifically is important that the desire to avoid the structural determinism and clear-cut collective identities with which subcultural theory was associated does not lead theorists to settle either for under-theorized (and arguably rather obvious) assertions that young people's identities are changeable and complicated, or for sweeping assumptions about electivity, individual distinctiveness and consumer choice.

Even though the extent and character of their influence may have changed, the significance of 'structural' shaping factors on youth cultures must continue to be outlined and understood (Carrington and Wilson 2004). Amongst others, ongoing studies of youth, ethnicity or place have offered consistent reminders of the continuing importance of such factors to many young people's practices, networks and identities. The continuing significance of identifiable youth groupings must also be pursued, in spite of the complexity of individual identities. Collective boundaries are sometimes porous and changeable, and membership may sometimes be partial and temporary, but that ought not to prompt abandonment of efforts by researchers to identify groupings or networks, to explain their emergence and to understand the nature of role they play in young people's lives. Maffesoli's oft-quoted statement that 'it is less a question of belonging to a gang, a family or a community, than of switching from one group to another' (1996: 76) arguably has been rather uncritically adopted by some as a sort of premise for 'post-subcultural' youth research when actually the extent of its appropriateness is far from clear. Meanwhile, the role of new media and technologies in relation to young people's patterns of identity and community continues to be somewhat unclear, with those studies emphasising individualisation or fluidity (e.g., Castells 2001) somewhat balanced by others describing the facilitation by the internet of relatively bounded, committed groupings (e.g., Watson 1997; Hodkinson 2003, 2006). Needless to say, although technologies ought not to be treated as neutral tools, a great deal depends upon the contexts of their use (Kendall 1999), and in this respect more empirical research is needed. Finally, if, in spite of the qualifications above, there is something of a tendency towards increasing fluidity and instability among youth cultures and towards the increasing centrality of commercial goods and services, then, consistent with the theoretical accounts of Beck (1992) and Bauman (2000), youth cultural studies must research and outline the negative as well as the positive consequences of this (Furlong and Cartmel 1997). Theorists must be particularly cautious of celebrating young people's 'liberation' from old categories into a world of active consumption and choice. Serious consideration must be given to the variety of insecurities which accompany so-called 'disembeddedness' and also to the possible commercial manipulation and material exclusion which may result from the cementing of identity, belonging and status to the purchase of consumer goods.

One additional point is worthy of note before I provide a summary of the chapters to come. As well as affecting the patterns of identity of young people, extensive social changes in recent decades also have prompted questions about the distinctiveness or coherence of 'youth' and 'youth culture' themselves. Most notably, while the tendency for youth transitions to begin earlier and end later (Furlong and Cartmel 1997) is rendering youth culture increasingly broad and diverse, activities and life-styles once regarded as the exclusive preserve of 'youth' increasingly are practiced across the range of physical age categories (Bennett, this volume). Whether prompted by the nostalgia of previous occupants of youth culture, by the expansion of commerce or by a more fundamental process of individualization, which has universalized some of the characteristics previously associated only with adolescence, the increasing ubiquity of youthful characteristics and activities presents a crucial challenge to youth cultural studies, which is only starting to be substantially addressed. Clarification of what, exactly, we wish to refer to when we evoke 'youth', and of the extent to which and ways in which physical adolescence retains cultural distinctiveness, must be substantially addressed both in theoretical and empirical terms. In this particular volume, Andy Bennett's contribution offers some valuable initial thoughts in relation to such questions.

AN OUTLINE OF THE CHAPTERS TO COME

The contributions to this book do not, of course, cover the entire range of research and theory which pervades the contemporary study of youth cultures. However, as a collection they build upon the broad debates and discussions briefly outlined here in a variety of different ways, covering extensive ground and taking a range of perspectives on some of the key points of controversy within youth cultures.

The collection begins by addressing some of the questions outlined at the end of the previous section regarding the coherence, makeup and boundaries of contemporary youth culture itself. Reflecting upon both academic and media discourse about youth culture, Andy Bennett asks whether the latter concept continues to have meaningful currency in a time of shifting boundaries and rising uncertainties. Critically discussing media suggestions that young people increasingly take the form of conformist consumers and that older people are increasingly engaging in leisure practices previously regarded as the exclusive territory of youth, Bennett asks whether youth culture denotes an age-specific category or whether it has, or should, become a far more general descriptor denoting particular attitudes or approaches to life.

While Bennett's concern is with the currency and implications of the notion of youth culture itself, the emphasis in David Hesmondhalgh's contribution is with the conceptualisation of youth cultural practices and identities—and more specifically those relating to popular music. In light of the current unpopularity of theories of subculture among many youth cultural theorists, Hesmondhalgh provides a detailed critical discussion of some of the concepts which have been proposed as alternative ways to makes sense of young people's use of popular music. He strongly criticizes recent use of 'neo-tribe', 'scene' and 'subculture' itself, and he rejects the notion that the relationship between popular music and youth culture can be understood through reference to any single term. At the same time, he proposes that, although they only represent partial solutions, the notions of 'genre' and of 'articulation' may have greater explanatory power than subculture, scene or neo-tribe.

If some of the CCCS theorists have been criticized for imposing theoretically driven frameworks upon the practices of young people, then the study of youth cultures in more recent years has been dominated by in-depth ethnographic methods focused, in the best traditions of interpretivism, upon accessing and recounting the experiences of insiders. Bearing this in mind, Rhoda MacRae's chapter considers the particular recent trend for such ethnographic studies to be carried out by so-called 'insider researchers' (Hodkinson 2005). MacRae considers the advantages and disadvantages of different levels and types of 'insider' and 'outsider' research, drawing upon existing literature and reflecting on her own experiences of studying youth club cultures from the initial position of a stranger.

The following three chapters begin the book's case-study-led examination of youth cultures by developing distinctive examinations of power, commerce and politics. Drawing upon recent research of the consumption of t-shirts by metal fans, Andy Brown's focus is upon the much discussed relationship between youth subcultures and commercial culture industries. Brown outlines and revises the cyclical model of grassroots appropriation and commercial incorporation associated with some CCCS theorists. Central to his argument is that, rather than being dominated by the spontaneous or subversive transformation of miscellaneous consumer raw materials, subcultural styles and identities often involve the non-appropriative consumption of objects already encoded with subcultural meanings. According to this view, far from resulting in the decline of subcultural identities, the deliberate commercial marketing of pre-packaged subcultural music and style should be regarded as integral to such communities. Subculture, then, is recast as a collective form of youth activity centred upon niche consumerism, and the metal scene is presented as a longstanding example.

While Brown's concern is with the role of commercial culture industries, Rupa Huq discusses the apparent incorporation of elements of youth music culture by policy makers and educationalists in the United Kingdom and France. Huq refers to research on three cases in which hip hop has been used as a means to educate or pacify young people. While recognising that such projects may be regarded a form of incorporation, Huq defends their legitimacy and value, rejecting what she regards as a tendency for academic analysis of hip hop to centre upon simplistic distinctions between grassroots authenticity and mainstream appropriation. The situation is more complex than this, according to Huq, not only because the projects she describes appeared to enable rather than to constrain youth creativity, but also because by encouraging localized versions of hip hop, they served to challenge the U.S. cultural domination of the genre.

Wolfgang Deicke's contribution also integrates the issues of politics, commerce and resistance. Questioning what he regards as a tendency for youth cultural research to equate 'politics' with only 'progressive' youth activities, and to assume an incompatability of 'commerce' and 'politics', Deicke demonstrates how—through a *'Kulturkampf'* by subcultural means—the far right has been able to achieve positions of near (sub)cultural hegemony in some East German communities. While the successful marketing of styles may strain the exclusive nature and distinctiveness of subcultural identities, he argues that 'diffusion' does not necessarily lead to the (political) 'defusion' of style.

The themes of gender and ethnicity are touched upon in a variety of chapters throughout the book but are particularly important to the contributions of Brill, Mendoza-Denton and Gidley. Dunja Brill's chapter takes as its starting point the tendency noted by theorists such as McRobbie and Frith for youth music cultures to be male-dominated and characterized by dominant ideologies of masculinity. Against this context, Brill examines the operation of gender within the goth scene, a subculture which often is regarded as transgressive with respect to gender, as a result of its stylistic emphasis on femininity and gender ambiguity. Drawing upon her own research on the goth scene, the chapter questions an 'ideology of genderlessness' among subcultural participants, arguing that, while male 'androgyny' is celebrated by the group as a form of subcultural transgression, the same does not apply for females, who are expected to adopt styles of dress which ultimately reinforce traditional notions of femininity.

Norma Mendoza-Denton's chapter also draws upon research of female youth but its core focus is upon ethnicity and language. In particular Mendoza-Denton is concerned with the way in which Latino gang girls used distinctive minority (Spanish) language practices as a means to construct and reinforce affiliations. The chapter describes a number of features of 'anti-languages' which had emerged among gang members in Northern California and which marked out belonging and status. From particular conventions on story-telling, to the use of language games and the circulation of poetry, Mendoza-Denton demonstrates that language conventions operate alongside signifiers such as t-shirts, cars, bandanas and makeup in the construction and performance of clear-cut collective identities.

Ben Gidley's contribution shifts the discussion of ethnicity across the Atlantic to the United Kingdom where, as discussed earlier, there has been a tendency in recent decades to focus upon emergent 'new ethnicities' among second and third generation minority youth. While many studies have focused upon the particular mix of 'host' and 'parental' culture for youth from particular ethnic groups, Gidley examines the apparent emergence of a 'youth multiculture', featuring the development among inner city youth from a variety of backgrounds of cultural signifiers and practices which draw from and combine various ethnic identifiers and fuse local practices with global styles. According to Gidley, ethnic difference remains highly important in some situations, but such difference is increasingly played out and negotiated in spaces characterized by intercultural dialogue.

Consistent with Gidley's emphasis, space and place are of key importance to studies of contemporary youth cultures—both in terms of the availability of venues for cultural activity (space) and larger scale questions about the relationship between local youth practices and national or global mediascapes (Skelton and Valentine 1998). Such questions are addressed particularly directly by two of the contributions to this volume. Stewart Varner's concern is with the availability of non-commercial cultural space to young people in Western societies where territory increasingly is controlled either by commerce or by public policy. Whereas some studies have focused usefully upon the appropriation by young people of public spaces as a response to this (McKay 1998; Rogers 2006), Varner discusses a case study in which a group of young music fans in Pittsburgh set up and operated their own gig venue. Operated as a voluntary democratic cooperative, the Mr. Roboto Project sought to offer a safe space and a non-commercial source of community for youth. While outlining such idealistic aims, Varner asks whether the project should be regarded as a significant progressive intervention or whether, consistent with the views of some non-members in the local music scene, it became a somewhat exclusive space largely confined to the servicing of members of a particular subcultural group.

Pete Webb's contribution, meanwhile, emphasizes the development among young people of place-specific inflections of global genres of music and style. Webb's contribution shares with Ben Gidley a focus on the global style of hip hop, but rather than focusing on inter-ethnic relations, Webb examines the way in which the local music 'milieu' within Bristol appropriated and adapted the style, eventually forming a new genre which was labelled 'trip-hop'. Focusing on key musicians, record labels and venues within the locality as well as the role of the United Kingdom's music press, Webb outlines the development of trip hop and goes on to discuss its subsequent decline as a result of the impact within and outside the locality of an emphasis in the national music industry upon a U.K. version of hip hop focused upon faithfulness to the core stylistic features of the global genre.

The impact of new technologies on youth cultures has in recent years become an issue of particular importance. In this book, it is addressed by three chapters which focus in very different ways on young people's use of computer related technologies. Arguing against claims that the Internet encourages the dissolving of collective boundaries in favour of a proliferation of fluid, multiple and even fictitious selves, Eric Chamberlin shows that young people's use of 'community' websites can facilitate some of the features associated with youth subcultures. Although they were somewhat diverse in terms of their music and style affiliations, users of the 'Pin Up Punks' website Chamberlin investigated displayed strong social bonds, upheld a clear value system and identified strongly both with one another and with the site itself. The chapter suggests that, rather than being regarded as part of a separate 'virtual' world, use of such sites should be understood as something strongly connected with 'real life' identities, something illustrated by the tendency of Pin Up Punks subscribers to meet up and get to know one another face-to-face as well as online.

The significance of off-screen context to young people's uses of the Internet, and to the practical and symbolic significance of the technology to their lives, is even more central to Silvia Ferrero's contribution. Through reference to young people's access to and use of online technologies in two schools in Alghero in Northern Sardinia, Italy, Ferrero raises important questions about optimistic proclamations of the liberatory impact of ICTs for young people. Ferrero reports that young people's access to and use of ICTs was severely restricted by the availability of equipment and controls on its use by schools. She also emphasizes that the specific context of the schools and the general context of their locality prompted feelings of pessimism and disillusionment among young people with respect to such technologies. The chapter serves as an important reminder of the significance of institutional and localized contextual factors to young people's experience of and attitude towards technologies such as the Internet.

In the final chapter of the book, however, we are reminded by Nic Crowe and Simon Bradford that for a significant minority of young people online technologies are utilized regularly as a means to play out of fictional roles in virtual worlds. In the online role-playing environment 'Runescape', identity is highly flexible and users frequently adopt characters whose characteristics and biographies contrast with their own. Nevertheless, Crowe and Bradford argue that, rather than being entirely liberated from their 'real-life' identities, the fictional identities constructed and 'lived' by role-players are continually informed by elements of everyday identity and experience. Meanwhile, at the same time as playing out the roles of their characters, players simultaneously are living out a parallel form of youth identity and belonging as gamers who associate themselves with Runescape, participating in regimes of status and value associated with that community. Even at the heart of the digital revolution, where the trying on and casting off of consciously fictional selves is fairly central to young people's daily existence, then, their identities retain elements of stability, continuity and community.

2   As young as you feel
Youth as a discursive construct

Andy Bennett

In recent years *youth* has become a widely debated and increasingly contested term. Like *culture*, *youth* is now increasingly a discursive construct and, consequently, a term overlain with multiple and, in many cases, conflicting meanings. The meanings now attached to youth reflect a variety of different political, ideological and aesthetic positions. Underlying each of these, however, is a common argument. Thus, the term *youth* is no longer regarded as straightforwardly linked with the condition of being young. Indeed, according to some observers, young people's exclusive claim on the term *youth* has largely disappeared. Such views are grounded in the allegedly apolitical and apathetic outlook of contemporary youth. From this point of view, contemporary youth is seen to be lacking the perceived tendencies towards subversion and resistance deemed to have characterized the youth of previous generations from the 1950s onwards. For others, the exclusive association of youth with the young has become weakened due to the fact that many of the traits once connected with youth are now observed across a far broader age range. To some extent, this is attributed to changing sensibilities relating to ageing and the life course in late modern society. Similarly noted is the shifting demography of audiences for popular musics such as rock, punk and dance. Once defined as 'youth' musics, these genres now attract increasingly multi-generational followings. During the course of this chapter I will consider the significance of these arguments for our understanding of the term *youth* in the context of contemporary society. In the concluding part of the chapter I will assess to what extent youth can still be regarded as a valid conceptual framework for the study and interpretation of cultural practices and collective sensibilities associated with the young.

DISCOURSES OF IDENTITY

The notion of youth, or indeed any other form of social identity, as a discursive construct, is inherently linked to particular changes in the social fabric signalled by the onset of late modernity. Traditionally, identity was considered to be rooted in socio-economic factors, notably class, gender, race, community and occupation. During the late twentieth century, however, deindustrialisation, combined with the transition from work to consumer-centred cultures and the increasing mediatisation of society (see Stevenson 1995) have weakened the influence of such traditional factors and provided a new basis for the formation and articulation of identity. In the context of contemporary society, identities are argued to be reflexively understood, individually managed projects (Chaney 1996). Much of the work focusing on the concept of reflexive identities has sought to examine its implications for individuals' understanding of themselves. Thus, for example, Giddens argues:

> What to do? How to act? Who to be? These are all focal questions for everyone living in the circumstances of late modernity, and ones which, on some level or another, all of us answer, either discursively or through day to day social behaviour....
>
> Everyday choices about what to eat, what to wear, who to socialize with, are all decisions which position ourselves as one kind of person or another (1991: 70, 81).

The effects of late modernity have had a considerable bearing on identity formations across the social strata. Indeed, as we shall see in more detail later, one of the major challenges to youth as the preserve of the young in late modernity results directly from shifting perceptions of and attitudes towards ageing in late modernity as individuals in middle age and later life seek ways of maintaining a youthful appearance and life-style (Featherstone and Hepworth 1991).

It follows that if late modern individuals create discursive constructs concerning themselves and their own identities, they are equally capable of reflecting upon, evaluating and critiquing the identities of others. It is precisely such forms of evaluation and critique that provide the basis for another prominent discursive construct of youth in late modernity—one which threatens to rob the young of their claim to the title of youth altogether. I will focus in more detail on these issues in a moment. In the first instance, however, it is useful to consider the origins of youth as a social category.

THE ORIGINS OF YOUTH

Common understandings and definitions of youth regard it as a twentieth century phenomenon. More specifically, the origins of youth are said to be rooted in socio-economic changes that occurred in the west following the end of the Second World War. This is not an entirely accurate reading as accounts of youth-based groups and gangs that existed prior to the 1950s reveal (see R. Roberts 1971; Pearson 1983, 1994; Fowler 1992). For example, Pearson has famously noted how in the 1600s, young apprentice workers in London were viewed as a shocking spectacle due to their visual appearance and mannerisms. As Pearson observes, the apprentices

> 'were thought of as a separate order or subculture'.... Various attempts were made to regularize the conduct of apprentices, banning them from participation in football games, playing music, or drinking in taverns.... The length of hair was another focus for periodic conflict between the generations, and one typical order of 1603 had required that they should not 'weare their haire long nor locks at their ears like ruffians' (1994: 1166).

A similar example of a pre-twentieth century youth culture is the *Deutsche Jugendbewegung* (German youth movement), a cluster of ideologically diffuse youth groups with the common aim of celebrating youth and marking its place in society. Officially founded in 1913, some of the *Deutsche Jugendbewegung's* core organisations actually date back to the mid-nineteenth century. The movement's emphasis upon patriotism, nature and physical exercise were key to its association with Nazism in the 1920s and 1930s (Laqueur 1984).[1]

Despite the existence of such historical youth cultural formations, however, the post-Second World War period did mark a significant change in the way youth perceived themselves and were, in turn, perceived by others. The combined effects of the post-war baby boom, increasing affluence in the western world, breakthroughs in mass production technologies and the development of consumer industries radically altered the status of young people (Chambers 1985). From the 1950s onwards a range of consumer products appeared that were specifically targeted at youth (Bocock 1993). As a consequence, 'youth' became a significant social category, both economically and culturally. As Shumway observes, the increased spending power of young people gave them an independent status, to the extent that they 'began to identify themselves as a group' (1992: 120). Such self-identification was most stridently manifested through the formation of style-based gangs or 'subcultures'. Early examples of this new style-based phenomenon included teddy boys (so-called because of their appropriation of the Edwardian-era style suit re-introduced during the 1950s), mods and rockers (see Hall and Jefferson 1976). The visually spectacular image of these youth groups helped to mark them off from other social groups and portrayed a sense of cultural distinctiveness. Equally important in this respect were the specific genres of music preferred by these youth cultural groups and the range of other products they consumed; for example, magazines, jewellery, drugs and alcohol.

The formation of youth as both a social category and a cultural form during the post-war years has had important ramifications, culturally speaking. While it would be erroneous to suggest that all young people in every decade since the 1950s have been committed 'youth culturalists' (see Clarke

1981), for those who have, or who have had more than a passing association with a particular youth style, popular music genre, and an attendant
ideological or aesthetic sensibility, their perception of themselves, their
fashion sense, political beliefs, life-style preferences and so on has often
been significantly shaped by their youth experience. To put this in another
way, the cultural project of youth has in many cases metamorphosed into a
template of ideas—and ideals—which many individuals continue to apply
in their adult lives. This, in turn, has seen another transformation in the
cultural properties associated with the term *youth*. Thus, today 'youth' is
often reflexively considered, by those in middle age and older, to be 'a way
of feeling' rather than being necessarily dictated by age. Indeed, for many
'feeling young' is considered more important than actually being young.
Thus, as Ross observes:

> an entire parental generation [is] caught up in the fantasy that they are
> themselves still youthful, or at least more culturally radical, in ways
> once equated with youth, than the youth of today....It is not just Mick
> Jagger and Tina Turner who imagine themselves to be eighteen years
> old and steppin' out; a significant mass of baby boomers partially act
> out this belief in their daily lives (1994: 8).

Ross's account is arguably exaggerated. Indeed, as Hunt observes, while
the pursuit of eternal youth is increasingly common in middle age, there are
still enough middle aged individuals who 'will simply opt to "grow old grace-
fully"' (2005: 183). Nevertheless, Ross's point concerning the baby boom-
er's ideological and cultural colonisation of youth undoubtedly carries some
weight. Evidence of this can be seen in some of the scathing reports on the
'state of youth' written by baby-boomer journalists since the mid-1980s.

THE YOUTH OF 'TODAY'

As Thornton observes, the media 'take a regular interest in youth culture,
which they tend to treat either as a moral outrage or as terrific entertainment' (1994: 182). A particularly strident media discourse concerning
youth has focused on its alleged threat to moral order and social stability.
A succession of post-Second World War youth cultures from the mods and
rockers in the mid-1960s (S. Cohen 1972) to the punks in the late 1970s
(Hebdige 1979; Laing 1985) and ravers during the mid-1980s (Redhead
1993; Thornton 1994) have in turn become a focus for the mass media's
moral panic-making machinery (S. Cohen 1972). In some cases, the effects
of such concentrated media attention have contributed to new forms of
legislation designed to curtail particular forms of youth activity. Thus, the
Criminal Justice and Public Order Act 1994 gave the police special powers
to intervene in or prevent the staging of raves (Redhead 1993). Certainly,

this sensationalized style of media reporting on youth continues to influence public perceptions of youth. For example, in April, 2005, the Blue Water shopping complex in Kent took the decision to ban young people from wearing hooded sweatshirts or 'hoodies', a fashion garment made popular through its central place in hip hop style, alleging that shoppers found the presence of hoodie wearing young people intimidating. This decision was undoubtedly influenced by media reports citing a link between hip hop culture and gun crime.

Increasingly, however, such moral panicking about youth shares the stage with another style of media reporting—one which paints a rather different, if equally damning, portrait of young people. Ironically, in the context of such reports it is the alleged absence of anti-social, resistant and counter-hegemonic traits that is singled out as the 'problem' of youth in contemporary society. Such accounts are primarily the work of forty- to fifty-something journalists, and are informed by particular interpretations of youth, these being grounded in the specific historical and ideological milieus of the journalists themselves. The resultant 'take' on youth culture is then used as a benchmark for the judgement of contemporary youth, who are generally found to be a pale reflection of their predecessors in the sixties and seventies. Consider, for example, the following observation by journalist Emma Forrest in relation to popular youth TV shows of the mid-1990s, such as *The Word*, *The Naked City* and *Passengers*:

> Youth TV is so depressing because it keeps on trying to tell us we have some sort of youth culture when we know that Generation X has created nothing of value at all....What we have to be proud of, according to Channel 4, are men who eat maggots, dykes on bikes and girls who'll sit naked in a tub of baked beans to get on TV (1994: 17).

Forrest goes on to allege the absence of 1990s equivalents of *Oz* magazine[2] and Sid Vicious[3], the use of such cultural icons being intended to reinforce her point concerning the pronounced political awareness of youth in the 1960s and 1970s as compared with the allegedly apolitical and apathetic nature of young people in more recent times. Forrest's sentiments are only a short step from declaring the end of youth culture as a meaningful term, which is precisely what Young tries to convey in a piece entitled 'The Shock of the New' that appeared in the British periodical *New Society*. According to Young:

> The term 'youth culture' is at best, of historical value only, since the customs and mores associated with it have been abandoned by your actual young person....The point is that today's teenager is no longer promiscuous, no longer takes drugs, and rarely goes to pop concerts. He leaves all that to the over-25's....Whatever the image adopted by

teenagers now, it has to have one necessary condition: it must have nothing to do with being a teenager (1985: 246).

Again, in Young's depiction of contemporary youth, a clear cultural bias is evident in that he interprets youth culture from a particular point of view, based on an idealized notion of the past. Accounts such as those proffered by Forrest and Young are typical of the way in which contemporary youth is lambasted by those who claim to know better than young people themselves what being young is all about. In addition to its alleged lack of political awareness, contemporary youth is also regularly criticized for its consumer-centredness, its preference for pre-packaged 'boy' and 'girl' bands, and its obsession with digital distractions, such as video-games and 'texting'. 'Authentic' youth cultures, we are told, are a thing of the past. Youth no longer has the commitment or vision to sustain such forms of allegiance in a world where the focus is upon glitzy ephemera and instant gratification. Even the apparent style mixing of contemporary young people, a phenomenon referred to by Muggleton (2000) as post-subculturalism, has attracted a decidedly negative response on the part of some journalists who regard this trait as an abandonment of once more strongly articulated stylistic allegiances. Thus, describing the crowd in a contemporary dance music club, one journalist observes, 'there is no stylistic cohesion... as there would have been in the (g)olden days of youth culture' (Willis 1993: 8).

FOREVER YOUNG? THE PURSUIT OF YOUTHFULNESS

The weakening association of youth with the young can also be attributed to new sensibilities of ageing that are emerging in western society. Such sensibilities are giving rise to an increasing continuity across the generations in terms of leisure and life-style preferences. As Featherstone and Hepworth observe:

> There is an increasing similarity in modes of presentation of self, gestures and postures, fashions and leisure time pursuits adopted by both parents and their children, and some movement can be seen towards a more informal uni-age style (1991: 372).

According to Featherstone and Hepworth this trend is largely down to an emphasis in late modernity on maintaining a youthful identity and persona in middle age and later life. Due to the increasing availability of consumer products and leisure pursuits aimed specifically at those in middle age and beyond, individuals can now take greater control of the way in which they manage the ageing process. In recent years, a highly lucrative retirement industry has grown up precisely around this desire on the part of those in middle age and later life to look, act and feel young (McHugh 2003). Age then, is no longer a given but something that is open to a process of reflexive engagement and negotiation. Not surprisingly, much of this age 'management' is concentrated upon the surface of the body and its social presentation. As Jackson et al. argue, in the context of late modernity the body is increasingly regarded 'as a project that can only become completed once we have made certain lifestyle choices. How we choose to regulate and present our bodies becomes increasingly open to question in a culture where it is read as an expression of individual identity' (Jackson, Stevenson, and Brooks 2001: 91).

Aligned with the above scenario are changing perceptions of adulthood and nature of adult responsibility. Once acknowledged as the primary years for raising a family and building a career, the period of adult life from the mid-twenties to mid-thirties is increasingly regarded as an extension of one's youth (Du Bois-Reymond 1998). The process of settling down and start-ing a family is often started later in life, an increasing number of women giving birth to their first child in their mid- to late thirties. Other adults choose never to cohabit, marry or raise children at all, opting instead to remain single and enjoy the increased freedom, both socially and economi-cally, that this affords. Again such trends offer possibilities for preserving a youthful identity, in this case by rejecting modes of behaviour traditionally associated with adult life. As Thornton observes:

> This is one reason why youth culture is often attractive to people well beyond their youth. It acts as a buffer against social ageing—not against the dread of getting older, but of resigning oneself to one's position in a highly stratified society (1995: 102).

Continuity across generations can also be seen in patterns of leisure, nota-bly in relation to music. Thus, many of those musics traditionally referred to as 'youth musics', notably punk and metal, now attract an increasingly multi-generational audience. This is perhaps inevitable, given the longevity of these musics and their capacity to attract die-hard audiences who remain loyal for years on end. Significantly, however, electronic dance music styles, such as house and techno, whose histories are far shorter, are showing clear signs of moving in the same direction, spawning a range of sub genres to suit the broadening demography of their audience. Similarly, many DJs and dance party collectives cater primarily for an older clientele.

THE END OF YOUTH?

Thus far this chapter has considered a number of arguments suggesting that youth has ceased to be the exclusive domain of teenagers and early twenty-somethings and become instead a discursive construct that reflects a variety of competing ideas, values and aesthetic sensibilities. Central to this contention is the notion that youth now describes a way of feeling rather than a way of being. Are we then to assume that 'youth' no longer has currency for our specific understanding of young people's social sensibilities and cultural practices? Is it really the case that because anyone, irrespective of age, can make a claim on youth, this has altered the sociological meaning of the term?

There are a number of issues to consider here, and it is perhaps useful to begin by revisiting the contention discussed above that the term *youth* is obsolete due to the failure of contemporary young people to act in ways consistent with conventional understandings of 'youth'. There are, of course, obvious problems with this diagnosis, not least of which is the decidedly nostalgic, not to say rose-tinted, perspective that underpins it. To begin with, the notion that the sixties and seventies were in any way typified by the kind of youth sensibilities identified by journalists such as Forrest and Young (op cit.) is highly spurious. For example, in his semi-autobiographical book about the late sixties and early seventies, *The Last of the Hippies*, C.J. Stone suggests that accounts of the era which emphasize the dominance of hippie style and counter-cultural ideology are heavily romanticized:

> We tend to forget this, that the lives of the vast majority of people were simply untouched by the so-called spirit of the sixties; that most people went through most of the decade hardly knowing what a hippie was, still less interested in what hippies had to say (1999: 21).

In addition to this obsession with nostalgia, however, there are more far reaching issues associated with critiques that either decry young people as undeserving of the title youth or reject youth entirely as an obsolete term. In effect, the 'reality' of youth is being constructed for us, and for young people themselves, by empowered 'outsiders'—journalists and other social observers with access to the 'official' and 'authenticating' channels of the media who use this power to express a particular point of view. The crucial voices missing from these accounts are those of young people. There are obvious parallels here with the subcultural theory of the Birmingham Centre for Contemporary Cultural Studies (CCCS) whose primary method of interpreting the socio-cultural significance of youth cultures was a process of theoretical abstraction drawing on the cultural Marxism of writers such as Gramsci and Althusser (see Hall and Jefferson 1976). This approach also served to relegate the young to the sidelines—their voices being absent for much of the time. However, as Stan Cohen observes, given the lack of empirical evidence to support the claims of CCCS, it is very difficult to ascertain 'what, if any, difference exists between indigenous and sociological explanations' (1987: xvii). A broadly similar criticism could be made of journalists who attempt to explain away the meaning of contemporary youth practices and sensibilities without recourse to the attitudes and outlooks of young people themselves. Where, ultimately, is the evidence that the views expressed in such critical accounts of youth reflect to any degree at all the views, aspirations or anxieties of youth?

In relation to the above point, it is evident in reading accounts lamenting the 'passing' of youth that there is very little understanding, or at least a willingness to accept, the very different socio-economic and cultural circumstances that shape the lifeworlds of young people today, as compared with the 1970s. The promise of full-time employment, and a lifetime of economic security, has been replaced by the precariousness of short-term contracts and 'McJobs' (Desforges 1998). Although this is not a problem confined uniquely to young people, they have been particularly hard hit by post-industrialisation and in many cases face an increasingly elongated transition from education to work (Furlong and Cartmel 1997). Confronted with this void of uncertainty, the 'twenty-four hour' party life-style associated with contemporary dance culture, together with forms of 'risk' behaviour such as drug-taking and sexual promiscuity, could in many ways be regarded as a similarly 'natural' reaction on the part of today's young people as the hippies' counter-cultural ideology and the anarchy of punk were in their time and place. Indeed, in many ways the twenty-four-hour-party life-style and risk-taking behaviours would appear to be a far more 'normalized' form of youth activity, in that they are engaged in by a broad cross-section of contemporary youth, while hippie and punk sensibilities— however radical they appeared at the time—were the preserve of a distinct, if spectacular, minority.

Finally, even if there is evidence to suggest that young people today are less interested in mainstream politics than previously (Kimberlee 2002), the contention that this renders young people as a whole apolitical and apathetic suggests an element of generational myopia among those making such claims. Thus, as Lipsitz observes: 'Contemporary discussions of youth culture seem particularly plagued by memories of the 1960s—as if nothing significant has happened [in subsequent] years' (1994: 17). Indeed, the downturn in young people's interest in mainstream party politics has seen a concomitant rise in their involvement in alternative and single-issue political movements such as Reclaim the Streets (Jordan 1998) and the much publicized anti-World Trade Organisation demonstrations (Smith 2001; Welsh 2000).

Turning now to the second theme discussed above, the transformation of youth into an increasingly 'elastic' concept due to changing perceptions of ageing in late modernity, this notion too has inherent problems. There is no doubt that the leisure habits and, to some extent, cultural sensibilities, of respective generations are more similar now than they were several decades ago. But, given the fact that every westernized generation born since 1945 has been effectively immersed in consumer culture, this is hardly surprising. Whatever our age, as denizens of late modern, consumer-centred society, we now take it for granted that we will be 'catered' for in terms of our leisure and lifestyle preferences—that everything is available to consume.

That said, however, while such cultural shifts in the social fabric may have acted to some degree to bring the generations closer together, there is still enough that keeps them apart. Most notably, youth retains its status as an economically marginal and legally dependent group. Young people below the age of sixteen generally speaking have little access to economic resources other than those provided by their parents/guardians or acquired through low-paid evening or weekend work. Similarly, youth unemployment and trajectories into training schemes or continuing education, result in continuing economic dependency among post-sixteen youth. Moreover, in most European countries, youth do not technically assume full adult rights and responsibilities until the age of eighteen, while in North America the acquisition of full adult status occurs between the ages of nineteen to twenty-one depending on country and region. This has a marked impact on both how youth consume and what they consume, young people's leisure habits often being actively policed by the parent culture. Thus, for example, choice of dress may be closely censored by parents, particularly for young girls, while alcohol and cigarette consumption, although widespread among young people below the legal age, is for obvious reasons generally practiced in clandestine fashion in contrast to adults for whom such consumption is an accepted part of their public life. Even young people's choice of music is sometimes subject to censorship by the parent culture. Indeed, in one celebrated case, such censorship transcended the realm of the private domestic sphere in the shape of the Washington, DC-based Parents Music Resource Center (PMRC). Established in 1985, the central purpose of the PMRC was to censor the lyrics of metal, rap and other popular music styles and raise parental awareness of the potential harm that such lyrics could cause to young listeners (Martin and Segrave 1993).

Notwithstanding such attempts of the parent culture to control youth's leisure and consumption patterns in this way, there are also clear differences between the actual leisure preferences—and leisure competencies—of the young and the old. This is observed, for example, in generational differences in response to new technologies. Bausinger (1984) notes how in every decade of post-war society it is the young who have most readily embraced new forms of media and technology. In our own age this is most clearly observed through the way in which young people take for granted the availability of domestic digital technologies such as computers and mobile phones and have little problem in understanding the operational functions of such devices (Howard 1998). Returning to the theme of music, there are significant differences in terms of patterns of music consumption between different age groups. This is marked by the continuing progression of new genres and subgenres which are primarily marketed to and culturally appropriated by the young. For example, hard-core and extreme metal are essentially 'youth' musics as opposed to musics that are also enjoyed by the majority of middle-aged rock fans, who often claim to find these musics too aggressive and 'unmusical' for their tastes. It seems clear then that the attraction and appeal of new styles in rock and pop music is as age-related as it has always been.

Even among popular music genres such as punk, heavy metal and dance, where audiences are becoming more multi-generational (see Bennett 2006), there are notable differences in the way that fans of different ages respond to the music and its associated visual image. A pertinent example of this is punk. During the late 1970s, when punk was still essentially a 'youth' music, Hebdige (1979) drew attention to the spectacular visual image of the British punk scene, identifying connections between the ripped clothing and body piercing of punk fans and the ensuing socio-economic dislocation of Britain at this time. In recent research on older British punks, who came of age during the original 1970s punk scene, I discovered that many of these fans have consciously toned down their punk image. For these older punks, the necessity to visually display their punk credentials on the surface of the body has given way to a more reflexively understood and articulated form of punk identity:

> rather than commitment being externally communicated though spectacular style, there appears to be a shared understanding among older punks of having 'paid one's dues' in this respect, the proof of commitment residing in the individual's ongoing, but matured, 'punk persona'. In other words, from the point of view of older punks themselves, sustained commitment to punk over time has resulted in them literally absorbing the 'qualities' of true 'punkness', to the extent that these exude from the person rather than the clothing and other items adorning the surface of the body (Bennett 2006: 225).[4]

At the same time, however, it should be noted that older punks were by no means dismissive about the continuing importance of style for younger members of the punk scene. Indeed, many older punks regarded this as a rite of passage and openly championed younger punks for having the courage to display their punk credentials on the surface of the body in this way. Likewise, it was often clear that younger punks welcomed the presence of old punks in the punk scene and felt that this demonstrated the longevity of punk and the credibility of its ethos as something that literally became 'a way of life' for committed followers of punk. Nevertheless, the prevalence of such age-related discussions in punk circles concerning the meaning or not of visual image points to obvious differences in perceptions of punkness between the young and the old.

A final point to be made here relates to the physical differences that separate youth from adulthood. Whilst not wishing to lapse into essentialism, there are in the final analysis limits to what an older body can, in the main, achieve. To be sure, and as this chapter has already considered in some detail, the new sensibilities of ageing that pertain in late modernity have seen many individuals in middle age and later life attempting to 'manage' the ageing process. But even this has certain limitations. It is one thing to retain particular leisure habits, to dress in a youthful way and so on, but quite another to fully cheat the ageing process. The key issue here is the distinction between being *culturally* and *physically* young. Thus, particular levels of music volume, hot and crowded club and venue environments, frenetic dancing rituals and the sheer levels of physical stamina they demand may ultimately present their own obstacles to participation in particular forms of 'youth' activity beyond a certain age. The current dance style referred to as 'moshing' is a pertinent example of this. Moshing, which is chiefly associated with punk and hardcore musics, derives from the original punk 'pogo' dance but involves more violent movements and a greater amount of bodily contact. Participants frequently collide, knocking each other to the floor (see Tsitsos 1999). Although not in itself an exclusionary form—certainly moshing is far less male-centred than the original pogo dance—those involved tend to be primarily teenagers and twenty-somethings. This holds true even in the case of those scenes where audiences are more multi-generational. For example, in the author's own research on older punks, those interviewed talked of 'sticking in the back' of a music venue rather than joining in with the moshing engaged in by young people.

Older punks were similarly reticent to become involved in other current crowd conventions such as stage diving and crowd surfing, and sometimes showed disdain for such activities when they impinged on their personal space (Bennett 2006). Relatedly, while there are clear physical risks for anyone partaking in such activities, their potential effects may be perceived differently according to age. Thus, whereas younger fans generally carry no burden of responsibility, except for themselves, older fans, especially those with work and family commitments, need to consider more carefully the consequences of sustaining an injury through participation in such forms of contemporary concert crowd behaviour. Thus, even as certain distinctions between young and old appear to be dissolving, there is a clear sense in which particular conventions of contemporary youth cultural practice remain, due to the very nature of the activities they involve, dominated by the young.

CONCLUSION

This chapter has examined the transformation of youth from an accepted social category, describing the cultural practices of the young, to a discursive construct expressing an increasingly varied and, in many cases, conflicting range of political and aesthetic sensibilities. Having outlined current debates about the notion of social identity as a reflexively managed project, the chapter then went on to consider the origins of the term *youth* in the mid-twentieth century as both a social category and a cultural form.

It was further noted how, since the 1950s, successive generations have come of age during particular youth cultural eras, this experience remaining with them as they have aged and giving rise to a new construction of youth as an attitudinal sensibility rather than necessarily connected with age. This, in turn, it was illustrated, has given rise to a situation whereby definitions of youth and what it means to be young are generationally contested, as is demonstrated by the wave of media reporting that decries the 'passing' of youth. The chapter then went on to consider how individual articulations of youthfulness into middle age and beyond are further facilitated by the consumer market which actively promotes products, life-styles and leisure practices designed to assist older adults in their quest to continue looking and feeling young.

Attention was then focused on the implications of such challenges to the definition of youth for our understanding of contemporary young people. In the first instance, it was argued that interpretations of contemporary young people condemning them for their lack of political interest and awareness are based on romanticized memories of the sixties and take little account of the socio-economic circumstances in which young people find themselves in today. Additionally, it was suggested that claims of widespread apathy among the young take no account of youth's activities in single issue and radical politics, or their involvement in global demonstrations such as those associated with the anti-capitalist movement.

The final part of the chapter considered the influence of new sensibilities of ageing on definitions of youth. It was argued that, while there are certainly less obvious divisions today in terms of leisure and life-style preferences exhibited across the generations, differences nevertheless remain both in terms of youth's economic marginalisation and legal dependency, and in the responses of the young and old to consumer goods and resultant patterns of taste and leisure. Finally, it was argued that physical differences between the young and the old may also, in the final analysis, create distinctions in cultural practice even in those 'youth' spaces ostensibly characterized by uni-age cultural forms and multi-generational social groupings.

NOTES

1. For a further account of a pre-1950s German youth culture see Peukert's (1983) study of the Wilden Cliquen (wild gangs) of the 1920s.
2. Oz was a leading publication to emerge from the so-called British 'underground' press of the mid- to late 1960s. The magazine carried regular features on socio-political issues of the time (see Fountain 1988).
3. Sid Vicious replaced Glen Matlock as the bassist for the British punk rock band The Sex Pistols in 1977 and was quickly branded by the British media as the archetypal punk. Vicious, who is probably best remembered for his punk rendition of the Frank Sinatra classic 'My Way', died of a heroin overdose in

New York in February, 1979 while on bail awaiting trial for the murder of his former girlfriend Nancy Spungen (see Savage 1992).

4. For a similar account of the fashion sensibilities of older women associated with alternative music scenes see Holland (2004).

3 Recent concepts in youth cultural studies
Critical reflections from the sociology of music

David Hesmondhalgh

The concept of subculture has been criticized a great deal in recent research on youth. Some writers, such as Muggleton and Weinzierl (2003), seem willing to hold on to the notion of subculture in a revised form, but one thing is nearly always made clear: the conception of subculture associated with the Birmingham Centre for Contemporary Cultural Studies (CCCS) is off limits. The critiques of Birmingham subculturalism go back many years and, as is occasionally pointed out, some of the most trenchant and significant came from other researchers who worked in the Centre or who contributed to its publications (this includes writers such as Simon Frith, Angela McRobbie and Graham Murdock). But the backlash really came in the 1990s, when a critical deluge came pouring out of youth cultural studies. In reading academic work published over the last few years in this field, it sometimes feels as though there is some kind of collective obsession with this thing called Birmingham. Amusingly, many of these accounts speak of Birmingham subculturalism as an 'orthodoxy', as a dominant approach to youth culture. Never can an orthodox approach have been so unanimously condemned in the field it purportedly dominates.

As this book and others make clear, a number of terms have emerged as offering new ways of conceiving of collectivities of young people in the wake of these repeated criticisms. The most prominent seem to be *scenes* and *neo-tribes*, but there are reasons to think that these do not offer useful ways forward. In this chapter, I present criticisms of advocates of these terms. But I also argue against returning to the now largely discredited notion of subculture. Scenes, tribes and subcultures have all been associated with the analysis of popular music as well as with youth, and my focus in this piece is mainly, though not exclusively, on the areas of overlap between these two domains.[1] This is because I write as someone whose primary academic interest is in music rather than youth. Nevertheless, I think some of the comments below are relevant to the study of youth generally, because they highlight some of the problematic political assumptions and conceptual haziness surrounding the terms.

TRIBES AND NEO-TRIBALISM, AND LIFE-STYLES TOO

Andy Bennett has argued that 'neo-tribalism', a concept he derives from the French social theorist Michel Maffesoli, via some comments of the British sociologist Kevin Hetherington, provides a much more adequate framework for the study of the cultural relationship between youth, music and style than does the concept of subculture (Bennett 1999: 614). Bennett identifies two main problems in uses of subculture as a framework for studying youth, music and style. One is that the term is used in increasingly contradictory ways. The second is that the 'grounding belief' of the subculturalists, that 'subcultures are subsets of society, or cultures within cultures', overestimates the coherence and fixity of youth groups (1999: 605). The main way in which Bennett wants to move beyond these perceived limitations is to find a term which will capture the 'unstable and shifting cultural affiliations which characterize late modern consumer-based identities' (605). He finds the basis of such a term in Michel Maffesoli's concept of the tribe in his book *The Time of the Tribes* (1996). For Maffesoli, the tribe is 'without the rigidity of the forms of organization with which we are familiar, it refers more to a certain ambience, a state of mind, and is preferably to be expressed through lifestyles that favour appearance and form' (Maffesoli, quoted by Bennett 1999: 605).

For Bennett, fixity and rigidity are associated with the old language of structural Marxism, and its concern with class, whereas the concept of tribes or 'neo-tribalism' offers a recognition of instability and the temporary nature of group affiliation. In my view, this is too polarized a presentation of the alternatives. The CCCS subculturalists may at times have overestimated the boundedness and permanence of the group identities they were studying, but simply to offer instability and temporariness as alternatives doesn't get us very far. We need to know how boundaries are constituted, and how group identity is maintained over time, not simply that such boundaries are fuzzier than various writers have assumed. And confusingly, 'tribes' carries very strong connotations of precisely the kind of fixity and rigidity that Bennett is troubled by in the work of the subculturalists. Indeed, it would be hard to find a concept more imbued with such connotations than 'tribe', which has been generally used to denote a social division of a people, especially a preliterate or ancient people, defined in terms of a common descent and territory. The term has been widely used in dance music culture, but as with a great deal of dance music discourse, it represents a projection of pre-modern symbols onto putatively new phenomena. It would be a great mistake for sociologists to take such projections at face value.

Underlying Bennett's criticisms of subcultural theory is a particular interpretation of the historical development of youth culture and a particular view of personal identity. Bennett offers what he describes as a related concept, life-style, in order to provide a basis for 'a revised understanding of how individual identities are constructed and lived out' (1999: 607). Drawing upon the work of David Chaney, Bennett explains how the concept differs from what he describes as 'structuralist interpretations of social life' (though, in fact, his objection seems more specifically to be to the Marxian elements of subcultural theory). The concept of life-style, according to Bennett,

> regards individuals as active consumers whose choice reflects a self-constructed notion of identity while the latter ['structuralist interpretations of social life'] supposes individuals to be locked into particular "ways of being" which are determined by the conditions of class (1999: 607).

Once again, we have a polarity: the term *life-styles* emphasizes activity and agency, whereas structuralism emphasizes determination and that old devil called class.[2] This is an odd characterisation of some subcultural theory, such as the work of Paul Willis, which was at pains to draw attention to the creative ways in which individuals made use of commodities drawn from consumer society. It is true to say that class underpinned Birmingham CCCS theory as an explanatory factor, and it might be fair to argue that the CCCS subculturalists paid too much attention to class as a factor in understanding individual and collective identity, at the expense of other factors. But it isn't clear that Bennett's emphasis on active consumers 'whose choice reflects a self-constructed notion of identity' (607) is a more satisfactory view of the relationships between consumption and modern personhood. Bennett offers what is in effect a celebration of consumerism. For example, he glosses a passage from Maffesoli as implying 'that a fully developed mass society liberates rather than oppresses individuals by offering avenues for individual expression through a range of commodities and resources which can be worked into particular lifestyle sites and strategies' (1999: 608), and it is very clear that Bennett is endorsing this view. He anticipates the objection that the concept of lifestyle does not pay adequate attention to 'structural issues' (it is not altogether clear what this might mean beyond class) and makes the counter-claim that 'consumerism offers the individual new ways of negotiating such issues' (1999: 607). Tied to this celebration of consumerism is a voluntaristic conception of identity, whereby life-style is defined as a 'freely chosen game' and identity is 'self-constructed' (607). The references to choice help to reveal Bennett's uncritical view of consumerism. But what of the factors that might limit or constrain such choice: poverty, addiction, mental illness, social suffering, marginalisation, disempowerment, unequal access to education, childcare and healthcare, and so on? All such states and processes seem to be consigned by Bennett to the category of 'structural issues', negotiable by self-creating subjects. Bennett's conception of 'the cultural relationship between youth, music and style', which he is trying to theorize, appears to be that youth can do whatever they want with music and style.[3]

How does music fit into Bennett's theory of neo-tribes? Bennett draws on his own fieldwork on urban dance music to elucidate the framework. His claim is that 'musical taste, in keeping with other lifestyle orientations and preferences, is a rather more loosely defined sensibility than has previously been supposed.... Music generates a range of moods and experiences which individuals are able to move freely between' (Bennett 1999: 611). The basis for this claim is that DJs mix different styles into their sets, including pop songs; that clubs offer different musical genres in different rooms; and that young Asians have a variety of tastes, including a liking for western pop as well as the 'Asian' genre of bhangra. Now Bennett might be right to say that some Birmingham subculturalists overly simplified young people's musical affiliations, but the uncontroversial idea that people like different musical genres does not sustain a theory of neo-tribalism, which in Bennett's version, implies that all relations between taste and identity are pretty much contingent, or at least dependent on the whims of individuals. Later, I will draw on recent work on music and identity to argue for a theoretical framework that makes it possible to examine different kinds of relations between taste and musical genre, without losing the idea that collective identity or community can be expressed through music.

Maffesoli's concept of tribes has been taken up elsewhere in the study of youth. A more fleeting and qualified use than Bennett's is to be found in Ben Malbon's research on clubbing. Malbon used Maffesoli's contrast of the fluidity (that word again) of 'contemporary tribal formations' (1998: 280) with that of 'classic tribes' such as the Californian counter-culture. The emphasis is supposedly on the 'flitting between groups' of young people, rather than 'membership per se of a group or community' (208). Echoing these comments in his interesting book, Malbon seemed much more dubious than before about the novelty of such groupings, but he added remarks on how Maffesoli's theory usefully drew attention to 'the here and now, the affectual [sic—this word only seems to exist in translations of, or references to, Maffesoli] and the tactile' (1999: 57). Quite why such a mystifying theoretical apparatus was necessary to get at these admittedly important elements of the clubbing experience Malbon never made clear.

More recently, Paul Sweetman (2004) has approached questions of youth identity by juxtaposing neo-tribalism with 1990s debates about reflexive modernisation, most famously associated with the work of Ulrich Beck and Antony Giddens. Sweetman recognizes important critiques of the notion of the subject used by reflexive modernisation theory, made by writers such as Lois McNay, and to be aware of the limits on our capacity to refashion ourselves, but such critiques are brushed aside. Instead, fieldwork interviewees' claims to individuality are offered as evidence of reflexive modernization. What neo-tribalism adds to this, according to Sweetman, is a complementary engagement 'with the more affectual [sic] or experiential aspects of what an involvement with "subcultural" formations can entail' (Sweetman 2004: 85). Again, the problem here is: why use this particular theoretical formulation to get at these important aspects of the 'formations' under analysis? This is an engagement with affect at such a level of abstraction that the emotions of human subjects are hardly registered at all.

SCENES: A FRUITFULLY MUDDLED CONCEPT?

Does the concept of scene offer more as a new key term for understanding the relations between youth and popular music? In comments on the 1993 conference of the International Association for the Study of Popular Music, Simon Frith observed that '[t]he long domination of IASPM (sociology division) by subcultural theory is over. The central concept now (a fruitfully muddled one) is scene' (Frith 1995: iii).

There are two main sources for the widespread use of the concept of scene in popular music studies. One is an influential article by Will Straw (1991), the other is Barry Shank's book on the 'rock and roll scene' in Austin, Texas (Shank 1994). Straw examined the difference between two ways of accounting for the musical practices within a geographical space (a country, a region, a city, a neighbourhood). He set the notion, prevalent in rock culture, of a stable *community* which engages with a heritage of geographically rooted forms against the idea of a *scene*, which for Straw has the advantage of taking account of 'processes of historical change occurring within a larger international music culture' (Straw 1991: 373). Echoing the emphasis on complexities of the local and the global among cultural geographers such as Doreen Massey, Straw draws attention to the way that local processes are dependent on 'a vast complexity of interconnections' (Massey 1998: 124).

Straw in fact developed his use of the term *scene* from an earlier paper by Barry Shank, and in 1994 Shank produced a substantial study of 'the rock 'n' roll scene in Austin, Texas'. Shank's book treats scene in an equally interesting but very different way, closely linked to a type of cultural studies associated with the journal *Screen* in the 1970s. Shank develops a theory of the positively transformative aspects of rock scenes such as those of Austin, a theory which is based on French psychoanalyst Jacques Lacan's account of how individual subjects attempt to achieve wholeness, mastery and plenitude, but constantly fail to do so. In the context of a scene, this results, in a series of temporary identifications, which create 'a productive anxiety' (Shank 1994: 131), which in turn provides the impetus to participate in a live, face-to-face scene. In Shank's words, 'spectators become fans, fans become musicians, musicians are always already fans' (131). In effect, Shank is celebrating this productive achievement, but unlike other studies of local music-making, is grounding it in a (Lacanian) theory of human subjectivity. For Shank, drawing on the work of feminist theorists Julia Kristeva and Jacqueline Rose (who are themselves indebted to Lacan), a signifying community is produced 'based upon new enunciative possibilities within and among individual subjects' (1994: 133).

Shank's approach is in marked contrast to Straw's in a number of ways. Whereas Straw shows a Bourdieu-an concern with processes of legitimation and the competition for cultural prestige, Shank is working within a framework that draws a contrast between these transformative practices and the dominant or mainstream culture. More fundamentally still, Straw seems to be advocating scene as a word which questions the notion of local community which Shank celebrates, and which Straw associates specifically with the rock genre. In a brilliant comparison of the spatial and temporal dynamics of alternative rock and electronic dance music, Straw (1991: 381) argues that the constantly evolving nature of electronic dance music (at the time he was writing) ensured the 'simultaneous existence of large numbers of local or regional styles', such as Detroit techno, Miami bass, etc. This resulted in an interest in a cosmopolitan transcending of place which allowed electronic dance music to bring together the dispossessed and the marginalized across many places. Rock, according to Straw, had become static, lacking in innovation, and oriented mainly towards the white male musical connoisseur. Shank, by contrast, is a rock advocate. He sees the Austin rock 'n' roll community as a refuge for the alienated and the dispossessed.

My point here is not to adjudicate between these two approaches to the concept of scene, but to point out their pronounced discrepancies, not only in how they read the politics of local music-making, but also—and more importantly— in how they theorize this music-making. Both Shank and Straw borrow this vernacular musical and cultural term and put it to stimulating use, but they do so in widely disparate ways. These differences could of course be read as two sides of a productive dialogue. The problem is that, as noted above, the concept of scene has become very widely used in popular music studies as a result of these two crucial contributions and in many cases, the term has been presented as a superior alternative to 'subculture' (e.g., Harris 2001). But its use has been very ambiguous, or perhaps more accurately, downright confusing. This confusion has been compounded by its further use in popular music studies: sometimes to denote the musical practices in any genre within a particular town or city, as in Shank, sometimes to denote a cultural space that transcends locality, as in Straw's approach. The most important example of this approach is Keith Kahn-Harris's lucid and compelling study of the global extreme metal music scene (2006).

So is this a fruitful ambiguity, or simply a confusion produced out of the over-use of a fashionable term? Will Straw has returned to the notion of scene, and has responded to some criticisms. 'How useful', he asks, 'is a term which designates both the effervescence of our favourite bar and the sum total of all global phenomena surrounding a subgenre of Heavy Metal music?' (Straw 2001: 248). Straw proceeds to defend the term by observing that the concept persists within cultural analysis for a number of reasons. The first is 'the term's efficiency as a default label for cultural unities whose precise boundaries are invisible and elastic' (248). My concern is that this might be evasive. Even if boundaries are invisible or hazy, processes of distinction and definition need to be captured in analysis. Perhaps a perceived elasticity is a result of the very imprecision of the concept itself? The second defence of the term *scene* that Straw offers is that it is 'usefully flexible and anti-essentializing', disengaging phenomena from 'the more fixed and theoretically troubled unities of class or sub-culture (even when it holds out the promise of their eventual rearticulation)' (Straw 2001: 248). The pairing with class is revealing here. For studies of 'scenes' seem to have been mainly confined to the bohemian metropolis. This is true even of Shank, who is rarely clear about the social class of his interviewees (see also Stahl 2001). The rearticulation of scenes to social class seems to be deferred endlessly. Finally, Straw observes that '"scene" seems able to evoke both the cozy intimacy of community and the fluid cosmopolitanism of urban life. To the former, it adds a sense of dynamism; to the latter, a recognition of the inner circles and weighty histories which give each seemingly fluid surface a secret order' (Straw, 2001: 248). But how does the term achieve this metaphorical work? Of course, analytical concepts work via metaphor and association (think of Bourdieu's field, or Habermas's public sphere) but in my view scene has gone beyond the point where such metaphorical associations can aid in the analysis of the spatial dimensions of popular music. The term has been used for too long in too many different and imprecise ways for those involved in popular music studies to be sure that it can register the ambivalences that Straw hopes it will.

BACK TO SUBCULTURES?

The two fashionable concepts, tribes and scenes, posited as replacements for the notion of youth subcultures, are both plagued by difficulties. So should we return to youth subcultures? In his book, *Goth: Identity, Style and Subculture* (2002), Paul Hodkinson, responding to the point made by Bennett and others that the concept of subculture overstates the degree to which young people remain fixed in particular groups, argues that we need to 'differentiate those groupings which are predominantly ephemeral from those which entail far greater levels of commitment, continuity, distinctiveness, or, to put it in general terms, substance' (Hodkinson 2002: 24). And Hodkinson proceeds to offer criteria for understanding such 'substance', including consistent distinctiveness of a group over time, commitment, autonomy from wider social and economic relations, and a sense of like-mindedness with others of the same group (28–33). Subculture, he argues, is still a relevant term for certain groups, such as the goths he studies, who display all these features to a high degree. A number of questions arise.

How typical are these substantive groupings? To what extent have we seen a shift in their numbers and typicality? Are they now mainly nostalgic and highly self-conscious re-creations of a lost era of collectivity? How should we conceive of the more fluid groupings which do not fall into the now more narrowly defined category of subculture? Hodkinson's book is very useful in provoking such questions for the study of youth culture, and in clarifying the notion of stability through the study of one notable remaining spectacular youth style. However, it isn't clear that Hodkinson's book has a great deal to contribute to the sociology of popular music. This is not a fault in Hodkinson's work, insofar as this may well not have been his aim. But it means that his book does not provide any reason for thinking that subculture should be retained as a key concept in thinking about music and youth. Music is just one of a large number of cultural practices which bind together goths, and there are only scattered references to goth music. Hodkinson lays greater (and useful) stress on friendships, goth events, DIY media, clothing and the Internet. There is no real sense of why the goths liked the particular types of musics that they liked, other than their 'darkness' (2002: 47). What musical elements and processes constituted that darkness, and how did they come to be understood in that way? *How* did musical darkness evoke emotions and identities in the private and collective lives of goths? For all its strengths, Hodkinson's book is a reminder that subcultural analysis, including that of the CCCS, was never really about music, it was about youth collectivities that used music, amongst other means, to construct their identities. Only in very rare cases (e.g. Chambers 1976) did the subcultural theorists deal with popular music in any depth at all. By far the most developed account is that of Paul Willis in his analysis of bikers and their preferred music in *Profane Culture* (1978), and it is worth returning briefly to this account to examine its conception of the relationship between music and the social and how this bears on youth/music relations.

Willis's main analytical thrust is to emphasize the creativity and activity of the biker boys in forging connections between pop music and their own lives—and this sits uneasily with criticisms of subculturalism for its over-emphasis on structure, and its downplaying of agency. Willis's account very much fits with the CCCS's attempt to construct a theory of popular culture which would not pathologize that culture or its users. The main way in which Willis does this is to emphasize that the relationship between bikers and their preferred music was much more than 'an arbitrary or random juxtaposition' (Willis 1978: 62). For Willis, the bike boys' musical preferences were based on their identification of 'objective features' of the music which 'could parallel, hold, and develop the security, authenticity and masculinity of the bike culture' (Willis 1978: 63). Willis outlines a framework for analysis of the musical characteristics of the bikers' preferred genre, rock and roll, and he discusses 'its specific ability to hold and retain particular social meanings' (76). Willis concludes by suggesting that the 'dialectic of experience' involved in the biker culture brought about 'very clear basic homologies' between the social group and its music.

The term *homology* is significant here. It derives from the Greek for 'same relation', and was developed in the natural sciences to denote a correspondence in origin and development, but it was adapted in the Marxist sociology of art (see Williams 1977: 103–7). Whereas Marxian sociology used the term to refer to relationships between art and society, Willis uses the term differently, to refer to relationships between collectivities of people, on the one hand, and cultural forms, such as music, on the other. The term has been heavily criticized, and certainly, as the musicologist Richard Middleton has shown, there are problems with the socio-musical analysis that Willis carries out in relation to the term. As Middleton (1990: 159–62) argues, the connection between rock 'n' roll and the rockers is much looser than Willis seems to believe. The music was more diverse than Willis implies; and many other groups were finding pleasure in this music. For Middleton, the quest for homology leads the socio-musical analysis astray.

Middleton's analysis supports the view that subculture should not be revived as a key concept in the analysis of popular music (though it may have its residual uses in the sociology of youth) because it was never a concept of much use to socio-musical analysis anyway. But if the proponents of the various terms under discussion in this article fail to offer adequate theorization of the relationship between musical practice and social process, especially in terms of the collective experience of music, what more promising avenues of investigation might there be?

GENRE AND ARTICULATION

One conclusion to be drawn from my discussion of 'tribe' and 'scene' as alternatives to subculture as key concepts in the sociological analysis of music and youth is that the search for any single overarching master-term is likely to be unsatisfactory. Instead, we need an eclectic array of theoretical tools to investigate the difficult questions towards which the terms *subcultures*, *scenes* and *tribes* direct our attention. Nevertheless, some terms are more useful than others and need to be prioritized. In this section, I want very briefly to examine two concepts, genre and articulation, which encourage us to think about the relationship between symbols and other social entities or processes (see Hesmondhalgh 2005: 32–35 for a fuller discussion).

Genre is a much more satisfactory starting point for a theorization of the relationship between particular social groups and musical styles than are subculture, scene or tribe.[4] However, I am *not* offering genre as an alternative master-concept; I am suggesting that it is a necessary, but by no means sufficient, way in which to think about the relationships between music and the social. It is a term which has been used extensively in media and cultural studies to understand the relationship between production and consumption—an understanding which is a necessary stage in the analysis of music or of youth. The key contribution in this respect has been that of Steve Neale, who broke through the formalism of many literary approaches to genre, to see genres as 'systems of orientations, expectations and conventions', which link text, industry and audience (Neale 1980: 19), rather than as taxonomic lists of texts. In music studies, the term *genre* has been taken up by a number of sociologists of popular music, to understand the importance of categories in making value judgements about music (Frith 1996), for example, or to analyse how genres inform the organization of music companies and the perceptions of audiences (Negus 1999). But most significant of all in the context of this chapter is the potential of the term to provide the basis for a theorized understanding of the relationships between music and the social. Jason Toynbee (2000) has offered a particularly promising account of genre, which challenges some of the tendencies in theoretical discussions of these relationships in the accounts discussed above. In particular, Toynbee draws attention to the *political* importance of the relationship between music and the social, often effaced or submerged in recent work.

Toynbee points out that in popular music, unlike in other media, the link between, in his formulation, groups of texts and social formations, has often been conceived in quasi-political terms as a form of representation: 'Genre is seen to express the collective interest or point of view of a community' (Toynbee 2000: 110). He argues that 'to talk about style as the expression of community does not *necessarily* lead to the abstraction of music's social function' (2000: 111, emphasis added), as long as we recall that communities and genres are complex, and in particular that they are porous to outside influence. Another objection or set of objections, to text-social formation expressivism concerns the way that such communities have been assumed to be subordinate and resistant. Many analysts have pointed to changes in class structure and to the complexities of collective identification involved in modern societies. But for Toynbee, it remains the case that 'class and ethnicity continue to generate communities' (2000: 112)—and we might add that gender and age do too. Toynbee also deals, somewhat later in his discussion of genre, with what is effectively a further criticism of text-social formation expressivism, that modern media technology means that music is distributed far beyond its point of origin, both in time and space, and that this effectively breaks the link between community and style. Toynbee asserts in response that 'musical communities none the less continue to provide the basis for genre markets' (2000: 113), all the more so with the advent of globalization.

However, the concept of genre is not sufficient in itself in the present context. We need a concept that gets at the flexible and varying relationship between the social experience of community, on the one hand, and musical form or style, on the other. The most heavily-criticized aspect of subculturalism's understanding of this relationship is the notion of homology. As we saw earlier, this was an important component of Paul Willis's attempt to understand the role of music in the biker subculture, and this has real problems. Homology is often equated by critics with Birmingham cultural studies, but in fact its use is relatively sparse in the essays collected in the much-maligned *Resistance Through Rituals* collection (Hall and Jefferson 1976) and was in fact criticized by another Birmingham subculturalist, Dick Hebdige (1979), writing from a much more post-structuralist perspective, for its supposed inflexibility and fixity.

Whatever the rights and wrongs of the debate, this suggests the problems of analyses which downplay the internal differences of 'Birmingham' approaches. But my main point here is that in the long run, a much more important element than homology in subculturalism's efforts to theorize the relationship between symbolic practice and social process, formation or experience has been *articulation*—and yet this term is hardly mentioned in the many attacks on CCCS work. Articulation was defined succinctly by Stuart Hall (1996b: 141) as 'the form of the connection that can make a unity of two different elements, under certain conditions. It is a linkage which is not necessary, determined, absolute and essential for all time'. In other words it is used precisely to invoke the difficulty and uncertainty surrounding attempts to link two elements (often, the symbolic realm on the one hand and other social processes on the other). This is a very different 'Birmingham' from the straw figure constantly and tediously invoked in recent youth cultural studies. And the concept is hard to miss. The fullest theoretical CCCS treatment of the link between youth styles and social formation, John Clarke et al.'s introductory essay to *Resistance Through Rituals* (Clarke et al. 1976) discusses the 'double articulation' of working-class youth cultures, firstly, to the culture of their parents, and secondly, to the 'dominant culture' of a changing post-war British society. The concept of articulation has been taken up very widely in cultural studies. In the sociocultural analysis of music, it has most notably been adopted in Richard Middleton's important and influential book, *Studying Popular Music*, where Middleton uses the concept to discuss the complex, mediated relationships between musical forms and practices, on the one hand, and social structure on the other (Middleton 1990: 9). Jason Toynbee builds on this basis and, echoing Middleton, 'dethrones' homology, by making it 'just one kind of link between community and social practice' (2000: 114) alongside a number of other potential articulations: rap, for example, draws on many sources, experiences and mediations besides that of African-American communal life, but nearly always with implicit reference back to the homological relation between music and social group that is central to its meaning.[5]

This goes beyond some important limitations in the work on tribes and scenes. Bennett's account effectively denies the continued relevance of communities based around class, and he seems sceptical about making any link between ethnic groups and musical styles (see his discussion of bhangra, 1999: 612). Meanwhile, as we have seen, the two most influential uses of the term *scene* seem to have opposing views of the politics of community in contemporary popular music. Just as significantly, through his uses of the concepts of genre, articulation and homology, Toynbee offers a *differentiated* approach to the relationship between symbols and other social processes. This is relevant to the study of youth culture as a whole, not just music.

So the term *articulation* is a useful adjunct to genre, for it registers some of the ambivalence and complexity needed to understand the relationship between music and the social. This is worth reflecting upon in the light of criticisms that Birmingham subculturalism theorized the relationship between symbolic forms, such as music and clothing, and other social processes, such as class or generation, too simplistically and deterministically. While some Birmingham studies are more adequately theorized than others, the most lasting theoretical legacy of Birmingham subculturalism for cultural studies has been precisely a stress on complexity and multiple determination. However, this is not to say that the concept of articulation is without its problems, and, as with genre, I am not advocating it as an answer in itself to the formidably difficult question of how to understand the relationships between symbols and society. It too has been used in many different ways and is not theoretically precise. It is a general metaphor for complexity of determination. Nor does the usefulness of articulation mean that we can redeem the term *subculture* for the analysis of music and youth, because that term never really advanced understanding of the relations between the two. But combined with the key concept of genre, the concept of articulation, as a metaphor which holds onto notions of determination while recognising complexity, provides the means to discuss youth-based collectivities in a way that, in my view, is still more promising than the theorizations of scenes and tribes discussed above.

CLOSING REMARKS

This chapter is *not* a defence of Birmingham subculturalism. My aim has been to question the cogency and usefulness of the terms *neo-tribes*, *scenes* and *subcultures*. In fact, there are broader issues underlying these debates, which there is no space to address adequately here but which I would like to signal in closing. One concerns the tensions between different theoretical orientations underlying Birmingham subculturalism and recent critiques of it. This was a Marxist approach, but a particular kind of Marxist approach which sought to break with perceived lacks in traditional Marxian analysis: in particular it sought to avoid reductionist explanations of culture and of popular culture in particular, and to see culture as being itself a powerful force. But what theoretical basis underlies the critiques from within youth cultural studies? These critiques spend little time on their own theoretical foundations, which, ironically, seem often to be a combination of interactionist assumptions with a certain kind of cultural studies approach which developed out of the Birmingham School, one that holds the view that audiences have been 'pathologized', but are creative in their relations with popular culture, and so on. This hotch-potch of neo-Weberian sociology and cultural studies often invokes notions of everyday life and of experience that need quite a bit more theoretical questioning than they are granted. It is rare to find anyone taking the time and trouble to lay out a coherent and rigorous theoretical understanding of the terrain.[6]

A second broad issue underlying recent youth cultural studies work 'after subculture' is its failure to address questions of policy, inequality and power. Not every individual piece of research can or should do this. But when it comes to assessing youth cultural studies as a whole, its lack of engagement, say, with how educational, crime and welfare policy interact with the expressive cultures of young people is extraordinary. In the British context, some of this can perhaps be blamed on the bizarre and longstanding division between sociology and social policy. But some of it seems to derive from the depoliticization of this area of research.[7] It may well be that those sections of youth policy and 'youth transitions' studies (MacDonald and Marsh 2005) that are able to engage adequately with expressive culture might offer a much more promising site for the reinvigoration of youth cultural studies than any further tedious rehashing of how Birmingham subculturalism got it wrong.

NOTES

1. This chapter is a substantially reworked version of an article published as Hesmondhalgh (2005). That piece also included a detailed discussion of the relationship between the study of popular music and the study of youth, and a polemical call for an amicable divorce between the two areas. The emphasis here is more on youth cultural studies in general. My thanks to Johan Fornäs, Keith Kahn-Harris and Brian Longhurst for their comments on that earlier paper.

2. The notion of 'life-styles' has also been taken up by Steven Miles (2000). Once again, the CCCS are the villains, and the concept of life-styles seems to be the basis of Miles's claims that we need to pay (more) attention to youth experience. This is presumably a call that few could disagree with, including many CCCS scholars; everything depends on what is meant by experience.

3. There is no need to take an orthodox Marxist or neo-Marxist position to find such notions troubling; see, for example, Fornas (1995), summarized in Hesmondhalgh (2005).

4. In fact, some of the most useful aspects of Straw and Shank's work concern the operations and temporalities of particular musical genres.

5. See also Born's (2000: 32) claim that 'there is a need to acknowledge that music can variably both construct new identities and reflect existing ones' (32) and her important attempt to categorize various forms music/identity relation.

6. One refreshing exception is a chapter by Peter J. Martin (2004). While I do not share Martin's interactionist perspective (amongst other reasons, because it pays too little attention to the way that human relations are historically formed) his chapter constitutes a serious attempt to think through how best to conceive of collectivities of young people, and this allows a potentially much richer engagement between alternative positions.

7. Muggleton and Weinzierl's collection (2003) rightly attempts to understand the broader political and economic contexts of young people's lives, but in my view its attempt to repoliticize youth cultural studies overstates the actual of young people.

4 'Insider' and 'outsider' issues in youth research

Rhoda MacRae

This chapter examines an increasingly important methodological question within youth research, that of the initial position of researchers vis-à-vis the groups of young people they study. The discussion draws upon well-known sociological work and upon recent youth and music research. It also includes some reflections on the author's own study of dance culture. In contrast to some recent 'insider research' within youth cultural studies, this study involved the ethnographic process of moving from being a 'stranger' among young clubbers to becoming a familiar, well-informed citizen (Schütz 1976). Ultimately, the chapter suggests that the initial subjective positioning of researchers with respect to those they study can be of great significance, but that whatever the extent of their initial proximity or distance, critical reflexivity is vital for understanding and making explicit the full implications of one's position.

So-called insider–outsider distinctions and the methodological issues they raise are important to contemporary youth research, not least because ethnographic studies—including some where the researcher has initial proximity to the respondent group—are an ever more popular method in attempting to understand how young people construct their identities as members of youth cultures. Given this, it is important that youth and music research draws on the existing body of sociological knowledge as well as accounting for the peculiarities of conducting research in this field in attempting to discuss the implications of either an insider or an outsider position for the research process and its outcomes (Bennett 2003). Arguably, the proximity of the researcher to the researched affects all aspects of the research process from gaining access to analysing and writing up data. Yet recently the position of the researcher in relation to the researched has been further complicated by how sociology has reconfigured the meaning of identities, something which suggests that the relationship between researchers and researched is liable to be complex and subject to variation rather than straightforwardly identifiable as an insider or outsider situation.

With the multiplicities of identity being widely recognized within sociology, youth researchers, amongst others, have also begun to reconsider insider–outsider distinctions. Research into the lives of young people suggest that young people's transitions may be extending and fragmenting as changing labour markets and welfare policies affect the pathways into adulthood (Evans and Furlong 1997). There have been suggestions that the increasing time spent on training or education, geographical mobility and delay in forming families, has impinged on many young people's patterns of association and cultural identities (Cieslik 2001). Meanwhile, as discussed elsewhere in this book, young people's patterns of association and cultural participation are also argued by some to have become more ambiguous and transitory (Bennett 1999; Muggleton 2000). If young people's cultural identities and identifications are indeed becoming more fluid, multiple, ambiguous and transitory we need to consider the implications of this for the positioning of those who seek to understand them—and specifically whether the notions of 'insider' and 'outsider' have any relevance or value.

This chapter will first outline some of the sociological work that has explored the methodological impact of insider and outsider positions in relation to the group under study. It will discuss the methodological implications of the researcher's positioning and the way in which this positioning affects the research process. It will then look at these positions in relation to the author's own ethnographic work on the clubbing life-styles of young people. Lastly, it will draw conclusions with respect to the value of the notions of insider and outsider and the implications of such positionings in relation to youth cultural research.

GROUNDING INSIDER–OUTSIDER DEBATES

Ethnographic research provides the context for many of the discussions about insider and outsider positions in social research. The position of researcher in relation to the group under study has been a classical dilemma in qualitative, and particularly, ethnographic research into cultural formations. The social and cultural proximity or distance of the researcher from the researched have been of interest ever since Weber developed the notion of *verstehen*, which translates from German as understanding. Following Weber, interpretivists have argued that the sociologist needs to empathize with the group under study, to try and put themselves in their shoes, in order to gain rich understanding of the motives and values of the study group (Schütz 1970a). The principle of seeking access to insider knowledge and experience—and of attempting to immerse oneself within a given culture in order to achieve this—is of course now a widely practiced approach to social research. The initial position of the researcher with respect to those they would study is a distinct, though related question. In the discussion which follows, I am going to argue that the social and cultural distance between the researcher and the researched in youth research can be understood in terms of three approaches: outsider-in, outsider-out and insider-in.

Outsider-in

The outsider-in approach coheres with classical notions of ethnography and in youth research it is perhaps best characterized by The Chicago School, who embarked on an empirical qualitative sociological project of mapping the social groups living within their city. The Chicago School gave great methodological consideration to how much a researcher can or should participate in the life world of respondents, as well as what impact this participation may have on the respondents and the study process and findings. Park began by outlining a programme for the study of urban life, to explore the 'customs beliefs, social practices and general conceptions of life and manners' through empirical inquiry (1925: 145). Within this, he called for the empirical examination of the racial, cultural, class and vocational segregations that underpinned collective urban life. This agenda was to influence and facilitate many participant observation studies as well as to lay the ground for future studies into social and cultural groups deemed 'other', subterranean to or outside of mainstream society. Importantly, with the notable exception of Nels Anderson (1923), the Chicago researchers themselves did not belong to the groups they studied, they held initial positions as outsiders and there was considerable initial cultural distance between themselves and their respondents. The method advocated by the Chicago School hinged on entering the symbolic lifeworld of others, 'striking a balance between the role of participant—learning the experiential world from within—and the role of observer—analysing it from without' (Rock 2001: 32). Consistent with this, interactionists argue that learning about the lifeworld of others through observation and experience from the initial position of 'stranger' would achieve extensive insight and understanding into the customs, language, beliefs and practices of the group under study. Critical distance was required in order to analyze these fieldwork experiences and observations, something which, it was thought could only be achieved after leaving the field. This meant that much early ethnographic work was conducted from the outside-in, whereby the researcher was a cultural stranger who learnt about the groups' beliefs and practices through observation and left the field to analyse the observational data. These ethnographic enterprises have provided fertile ground for discussing the relations of fieldwork and the methodological impact of participant observation research. Questions about the dichotomy of the insider–outsider distinction were, however, never far away. Notably, Whyte, author of the pioneering study *Street Corner Society* pertinently stated: 'we may agree that no 'outsider' can really know a given culture fully, but then we must ask can any 'insider' know his or her culture?' (1943: 371).

Outsider-out

Some of the groups studied by the Chicago School may have been deemed subcultural in today's vocabulary, but the latter term only began to appear during the 1940s as a means of conceptualizing groups which were deemed to be placed 'outside' mainstream society through their delinquency or deviancy (e.g., A. Cohen 1955). The concept of subculture was also key to the research undertaken by the University of Birmingham's' Centre for Contemporary Cultural Studies (CCCS) during the 1970s. The notion of subcultural groups being 'outside' of and different to other social and cultural groups through clearly distinctive spectacular styles was a theme that ran through much of their work. In contrast to the Chicago tradition, much of the work by the CCCS was characterized by what we might term an 'outsider-out' approach. The ethnographic approach taken by Paul Willis in his studies of motorbike boys and school counter-cultures was methodologically unusual within the CCCS, much of whose work was based upon a combination of Marxist theory and external textual analysis of youth styles (Clarke et al. 1976; Hebdige 1976, 1979). Such theorists have been criticized for their preoccupation with Marxist theories of 'reproduction' and, more significantly here, for paying insufficient empirical attention to the everyday 'insider' experience of young people themselves. With the exception of Willis (1980), the CCCS also had a tendency to leave unexamined the impact of their social distance on the research process or its outcomes. Indeed, the difficulties of this 'outsider-out' approach have informed broader doubts about the value of the subcultural analysis presented by CCCS theorists, which have been argued to present too rigid and fixed a picture of youth groupings and to have over-emphasized their links to class resistance (G. Clarke 1981; Muggleton 1997; Bennett 1999).

Insider in?

Perhaps the area of social science which has most consistently placed the subjectivity of the researcher at the forefront of analysis has been feminism. Feminists drew particular attention to questions of status and power between the researcher and the researched and sometimes presented themselves as conducting a sort of insider-in research (Oakley 1981). As a woman with children, interviewing other women with children, Oakley assumed she had enough commonality to be an insider. However, Oakley was criticised by other feminists for neglecting other crucial differences between herself and her respondents, differences such as social class, status and life experiences. This sparked feminist debates about the complex methodological implications of the relationship between the researcher and the researched, many of which highlighted the importance of recognizing identities as multifaceted (Wax 1971; Roberts 1981; Stanley and Wise 1983; Stacey 1988; Roseneil 1993; Heyl 2001). In a different context, such complexities had also been recognized by Merton, who argued in a general sense that notions of insider and outsider have implicitly one-dimensional ideas about the respondent's identity and status (1972: 22).

Consistent with this emphasis on the complexities of identity in other areas of social science, post-CCCS perspectives on youth culture have suggested that contemporary groupings of young people are more loosely bounded than portrayed by much of the youth research carried out during the 1960s, 1970s and 1980s. It was argued that contemporary youth research needed to take account of what Furlong and Cartmel have called a period of rapid social change (1997). It was suggested that the transitions of young people had been subject to increasing fragmentation, and that cultural associations and patterns of association may also have become more fragmented and multifaceted. During this period of social change, the ethnographic enterprise has continued, and post-CCCS ethnographic research has taken more account of the specific and localized contexts of young peoples' cultural formations. Indeed, ethnographic, feminist and latterly youth culture research has facilitated much discussion about the nature of research relationships (e.g., Oakley 1981; Roseneil 1993; Hall 1994; Bennett, 2003; Hodkinson 2005).

Although cultural groupings may no longer have clear boundaries, and identities are conceived of as multifaceted, Rock, an interactionist, has stated that many ethnographic studies 'turn out to be a social anthropology of one's own kind' (2001: 34). However, research by Hamabata (1986) into Japanese elite and by Song and Parker (1995) into Chinese British young people show that research relationships remain complex and that there are still barriers to overcome even when there exist social, cultural and in their case ethnic proximity. As Hamabata (1986) discovered, being a Japanese American researching Japanese was not enough to be perceived as 'one of them'. He had a Japanese face, he spoke Japanese adequately but his lack of cultural knowledge and inability to act habitually meant he was considered an under-educated or incomplete Japanese (Hamabata 1986). Indeed his ethnic proximity and his lack of cultural knowledge combined at times to be a barrier in developing research relationships (Hamabata 1986).

For others, however, such complexities do not necessarily render the terms *insider* and *outsider* entirely redundant. While taking account of the complex nature of the positioning between the researcher and the researched, Roseneil (1993) is content to use the notion of 'insider research' as a means to describe research situations characterized by social proximity and familiarity. Consistent with Bourdieu's suggestion that 'social proximity and familiarity provides the social conditions of 'non-violent' communication' (1996: 20), some have suggested that more proximate relationships may entail fewer barriers to the research process. Hodkinson (2005), for example, has suggested that being an 'insider researcher' can enable youth ethnographers to participate fully and competently, to communicate more confidently, freely and informally without being preoccupied with the unfamiliar. A proximate relationship, then, may provide fewer barriers to overcome in terms of access and the ability to get quality in-depth data, something particularly relevant for ethnography, which is centrally concerned with experiencing and understanding the contexts of people's lives (Schütz 1976; Hammersley and Atkinson 1995; Heyl 2001).

Nevertheless, Hammersley and Atkinson (1995) suggest that ethnographers need to be intellectually poised between familiarity and strangeness, arguing that there is 'no question of total becoming' and that 'some social and intellectual distance needs to be maintained for the analytical work' (Hammersley and Atkinson 1995: 115). Schütz (1976) has discussed the notion of being a stranger to a culture in some depth. He suggests that 'real members' of social groupings are liable to hold common-sense assumptions and to take for granted various aspects of the world in which they live, something which may mean the 'acculturated stranger' is in a better position to come to a critical understanding of the social world in question (Schütz 1976). He also reminds us that a stranger and a member are not dualistic entities; both can have experiences of being strange within their own cultures. Although not explicitly a methodological piece, Schütz's essay nevertheless illustrates that a stranger can render explicit some of the fundamental presuppositions that shape their vision, many of which are distinctive to that culture (Hammersley and Atkinson 1995: 8–9). Differences—and there will always be differences between the researcher and the researched—can be fruitful, then, and rather than trying to eliminate them we need to make them explicit and account for their impact on the research process. Indeed, whatever their initial position, ethnographers should endeavour to provide a reflexive account of the research relationships, the effects of the researcher on the data and an explicit account of the production of knowledge (Hammersley and Atkinson 1995; Oakley 1998; Skeggs 2001). Consistent with this, the next section provides some brief reflections on my own recent ethnographic research on the clubbing lifestyles of young people. In contrast to number of recent studies, I was not in a position of initial cultural proximity when I began the project; rather, my research took the form of an outsider-in approach.

LEARNING TO DANCE

My interest in clubbing life-styles was focused upon exploring how people became clubbers, what process of identification and differentiation they went through and how and why some people eventually moved away from the club scene. When I began to think about how I was going to go about conducting an ethnographic study which explored such issues I turned to various texts devoted to ethnography. I also looked at the studies that had previously explored youth subcultures, music and social dance, and the specific studies into clubbing and raving. Studies into dance club culture by

Malbon (1999), Pini (1997a), Thornton (1995) and Henderson (1993), only give us a brief overview of the methodological issues they encountered. Pini (1997), Thornton (1995) and Malbon (1999) had all been cultural participants of club culture, though of these Malbon was the only one briefly to address what he regarded as the positive implications of this. Even in this case, however, the detailed implications of 'insider knowledge' were relatively unexplored (Bennett 2003:189). At the time of my study, the texts relating to non-youth ethnography such as those discussed earlier were to prove far more valuable for considering the methodology of the study.

My research was carried out in Scotland, Glasgow and Edinburgh being the main sites for much of the participant observation. Over a period 18 months I attended a number different venues which hosted club nights oriented to various types of dance music including techno, trance, house, hard house as well as those more generic in style. In addition to this I interviewed 25 young people, most of whom lived in Glasgow or Edinburgh, with a small number based in smaller towns around the central belt area. With respect to my own position in relation to my respondents, it was clear that I did not have direct experience of or immediate familiarity with their situation, nor was I similar in age. Meanwhile, the ways in which my gender, class, race and ethnicity was going to impact on the process of research and research relationships was unknown. I was not involved in a clubbing lifestyle, I was not part of a club scene and I did not go clubbing frequently. This meant it was likely that I would not have a great deal of initial cultural proximity to those I was researching. I was hoping to move from the position of being a cultural stranger to becoming familiar, not an 'insider' or expert, but a well-informed citizen (Schütz 1976). It is worth reiterating at this point the use of the terms *insider* and *outsider*, and *insider researcher* should not be seen as absolute. They are terms that attempt to portray the extent of familiarity between a researcher and group of respondents, positions that describe the initial sociocultural proximity between the researcher and the researched (Hodkinson 2005).

At the beginning of the fieldwork process, I utilized all my personal and academic networks to generate key contacts, people who would facilitate my access to club scenes as well as young people who went clubbing. Although it may be easier for those already 'in the know' to generate such contacts, this sampling technique has the same disadvantages. Notably it may have produced a 'network of individuals who are in the social orbit of the key contact' (Forsyth 1997: 67). To offset this I recruited from both key contacts and other respondents, in order to get both a sideways and a downward movement that was part snowballing and part networking (Forsyth 1997: 68). This meant that some respondents were involved in different social and club scenes to those nominating them. For example, one contact worked in a bar and introduced me to customers they knew to be clubbers. I also asked my contacts to put me in touch with people who were not necessarily involved in the same scene as they were, or who had just started clubbing; had not been to university or who they knew from another aspect of their lives such as work. In addition to setting up interviews in this way I joined in other social occasions, drinks at pre-club bars, meeting up for coffee, going to buy records, I was able to access 'off site' clubbing information, learn about the music, the DJs, the various dance club scenes and associated cultural tastes.

Although I was clearly not a clubber or identified with a definitive musical taste and style with regard to dance music, I nevertheless had some things in common with the clubbers I was socialising with and interviewing. I drew on my past experiences of living, socializing and clubbing in Glasgow and Edinburgh, at the same time as emphasising my lack of knowledge about the current scene in order to facilitate discussion. Once introductions had been made and I had been vouched for by key contacts I experienced few problems participating in the social occasion. I found that those I encountered were keen to ask about what aspects of clubbing I interested in as well as how and why I was going to do the research. Many expressed that they were pleased I was not focusing on drug use, something which related to a perception that club culture had been misrepresented through media headlines about Ecstasy. My focus on how they got into clubbing, the details of their clubbing experiences and of their tastes in music and style seemed to generate enthusiasm and to break down any wariness about talking to me. Indeed this focus seemed to prompt an active engagement with the research, with the vast majority of respondents happy to discuss their clubbing experiences at great length. Recorded interviews averaged approximately 70 minutes and I also communicated with most respondents prior to the recorded session. Some respondents I had met whilst socializing in clubs, whilst initial contact with others took the form of e-mails or phone calls focused upon responding to queries and establishing meeting arrangements. I found that this pre-interview contact was important in terms of overcoming potential barriers and establishing an open and constructive research dialogue.

Hodkinson (2005) has suggested that it may be particularly easy for respondents to make exaggerations, omissions, guesses and throwaway statements in the presence of a relatively ignorant 'professional stranger' (Agar 1996). And indeed this did occur during the interactions in which I participated. I heard frequently that clubbing was welcoming of anyone and everyone; that a person's age, race, sexuality or class did not matter, for example. However, these statements conflicted with my fieldwork experience and my initial analysis of the data. Most ethnographers are likely to encounter exaggerated or inaccurate statements and ideological cultural discourses during the course of their work. The researcher can, however, take methodological and analytical steps to minimize, recognize and analyse these. For myself as a 'professional stranger' (Agar 1996), conducting interviews in two phases was useful. It allowed me to reflect at length on the initial data, to look for emerging themes and patterns as well as exaggerations and irregularities. I was also able to use the initial interview data to revise my prompts, omit unnecessary lines of questioning and add more fruitful lines of inquiry. By the second wave of interviews I was more in tune with the differences between the ideological discourses prevalent in the dance club scene at the time and the actual practices of clubbing and being a clubber. I also used comparative and reflective lines of inquiry, which allowed me to probe for any inconsistencies, omissions or exaggerations. Sometimes I returned to points previously made in the context of new information, and this reflecting back allowed me to confirm, challenge or seek elaboration of the respondents' accounts (May 1993: 100). Indeed, to problematize supposed subcultural norms and to explore the tensions between and within accounts is an essential part of the research process.

Fieldwork experiences gave me a grasp of some of the specialized cultural language but I explicitly chose not use this newly acquired knowledge in interviews. I did not want to assume that acting like an insider would afford me legitimacy or ingratiate me to my respondents. Rather, I felt that if I acknowledged the fact 'I was out' then there was better chance that 'I could be let in' (Hamabata 1986: 355). Acting as if I was 'in the know' may have impeded my ability to probe and question any responses that required clarification. It also may have given respondents more opportunity to answer in a superficial and 'you know what I mean' manner; probing for more in-depth responses could then be trickier without causing irritation or offence. Indeed, it was often asking the most apparently obvious questions that provided the richest data. In contrast, those researching from a position characterized by a greater degree of proximity, with shared and presumed cultural knowledge between themselves and the respondent, may find their ability to probe and question responses somewhat constrained. How would the 'insider' researcher 'not know' without losing their credibility or without irritating the respondent? Having a constrained ability to ask the most obvious questions may be a general disadvantage to researching from the 'inside'.

Even though towards the end of the research I had developed a level of cultural competence and knowledge, to pretend to be a clubber would have in my view been insincere and exploitative. Without knowing it I heeded Rosalie Wax's warning that 'perhaps the most egregious error that a fieldworker can commit is to assume that he can win the immediate regard of his hosts by telling them that he wants to "become one of them" or by implying, by word or act, that the fact that they tolerate his presence means that he *is* one of them' (Wax 1971: 47).

CONCLUSION

It is clear that research proximity and distance both entail potential advantages and disadvantages—and also that the positions of researcher and researched are not fixed. We must remind ourselves that to assume that researchers are either insiders *or* outsiders in a simplistic sense is to implicitly assume that people's identities are one-dimensional rather than multifaceted and complex. Whether research takes the form of outsider-out, outsider-in or insider-in, the position of the researcher is liable to remain somewhat fluid and unpredictable according to situation and context. Both insiders and outsiders may have experiences of being a stranger within the cultures they study, and similarly, both may have moments of familiarity (Schütz 1976). It is equally important to recognize that any competent researcher, regardless of their positioning to the group under study, needs to take methodological steps and devise strategies to get closer to the key motivations and meanings of respondents.

It may be that in some cases those working from the outside in are more likely to be misled if they do not critically reflect on the process of fieldwork, and that 'insider researchers' with their personal experience may be better placed to verify accounts and to achieve in-depth understanding (Hodkinson 2005). However, accounts can also be verified through the researchers' ability to problematize claims, to undertake sufficient fieldwork as well as careful analysis of data that achieves depth of understanding. As someone with no initial cultural proximity to the study group I devised ways of probing and clarifying through reflective and comparative questioning; I also interviewed in two phases to allow for a thorough analysis of generative data in an attempt to expose any inconsistencies and possible exaggerations. Meanwhile, although their position may entail certain advantages, insider-researchers may also succumb to a whole variety of problems if they fail to problematize what they see and hear. Through having shared characteristics and experiences they may be more prone to accepting habitual modes of thinking, or not questioning or putting subcultural affiliations and ideologies under reflexive scrutiny. As a consequence, they too must take precautions, whether in terms of devising outsider questions, or attempting in a more general sense to see the familiar as strange and to challenge the taken-for-granted. As Hodkinson (2005) suggests, the enthusiast turned ethnographer must go through something of a transformational process in order to become an effective insider researcher. They must question taken-for-granted attitudes and values and unlearn or objectify the cultural conventions and schemes of interpretation that have become habitual during their involvement.

What seems to be essential in realizing the benefits of the researchers' initial positioning, is their ability to reflect critically on the process of knowledge augmentation. Being methodologically reflexive allows the researcher to consider how the process of research affects the construction of data, as well as the limitations and scope of the study. I suggest that the advantages to being an insider are largely related to access, and that advantages to being an 'outsider' are largely related to making the familiar strange and the implicit explicit. I suggest that quality of understanding is more related to the researchers' ability for critical reflexivity rather than their positioning to the group under study.

Nevertheless, as Hodkinson (2005) has suggested notions of 'insider' and 'outsider', of 'us' and 'them' still have currency albeit in a non-absolute sense and can be used to shed light on research relationships, the research process and the outcomes of that process. The benefits of opening methodologies and researcher subjectivities up to critical examination is useful for those about to embark on ethnographic projects, as well as thinking about the relationship between the wider body of sociological methodological literature to further enhance the study of youth cultural research. What is crucial for those undertaking ethnographic youth and music research, whatever position they begin the ethnography from, is that they attempt to maintain a self-conscious awareness of what is learned, how it has been learned and the social transactions that inform the production of such knowledge (Hammersley and Atkinson 1995:101).

5 Rethinking the subcultural commodity

The case of heavy metal t-shirt culture(s)[1]

Andy Brown

> Is there a dollar to be made off the cult of heavy metal? You bet your Def Leppard t-shirt there is (Gross 1990: 127).

In an Internet survey, conducted by a net-based t-shirt distributor, metal bands accounted for the overall most popular t-shirt across all genres as well as five of the six most popular t-shirts in the metal/rock category (Recordstore 2004; Barnes 2004: 9).[2] Consistent with key elements of my own research, the survey illustrates both the importance of the band t-shirt to the youth culture that surrounds metal music, and the strong consumer demand for commercially produced metal-style t-shirts (not least because more metal t-shirt customers responded than any other type of music fan). These two elements are central to the argument presented in this chapter: that the metal t-shirt is a commercially manufactured and distributed item of clothing that is also high in subcultural value.

According to the classic CCCS account of subcultural formation (Hall and Jefferson 1976; Mungham and Pearson 1976; P. Willis 1978; Hebdige 1979) these two factors of commerce and subcultural value ought to be mutually exclusive. The emphasis placed by the CCCS approach on the creative re-working of the meanings of ordinary commodities, precluded the possibility that such uses could be anticipated by commercial interests or that fashion commodities could offer subcultural style, 'over the counter' (cf. Best 1997). Following Stratton (1985), Cagle (1995: 45) and others, I want to argue that many types of youth culture form around the purchase of commodities and that such commodities can be defined as subcultural to the extent that they promote or make possible the distinctive practices of youth groups. Accordingly, this chapter explores the role that commercially produced 'subcultural' commodities play in the formation of youth cultural identities. Building upon the research of McRobbie (1989, 1994) Thornton (1995) Muggleton (2000) and Hodkinson (2002) into the role of media and commerce in the cultural practices and identities of young people, I examine the youth culture(s) of heavy metal and the specific role that a commercially produced and distributed item, the metal t-shirt, plays in constituting the metal youth 'experience'.

Despite the many faults which have been identified with the CCCS account, it offers a seminal and hugely influential 'cyclical' model of the interaction between youth cultures and media industry cultures, whereby the creativity of radical youth is realized against the conforming designs of commerce and industry, only to be re-appropriated and re-commodified in the next phase of the cycle. In reworking this model I focus particularly on two aspects that are under-theorized in the CCCS account: the range and types of commodities taken up for subcultural adoption and the role of the culture industries in promoting the meanings and uses of such commodities by would-be subculturalists. Focusing on the example of the metal t-shirt, I suggest how this commercially mediated item allows metal youth groups to make subculture-like distinctions between themselves and others by reference to the music categories and music artists 'advertised' via this item of youth clothing. I conclude by suggesting that such commercial interaction should not be regarded as conflictual or consensual but rather as an uneven, complex 'commodified' experience, whose regulation escapes the strategies of control attempted by both producers and consumers.

THE CYCLE OF YOUTH APPROPRIATION
AND INDUSTRY INCORPORATION

The first intellectual task the CCCS collective set themselves, in *Resistance Through Rituals*, was to reject the generic and consensus-oriented notion of 'youth culture' in favour of a:

> detailed picture of how youth groups fed off and appropriated things provided by the market, and, in turn, how the market tried to expropriate and incorporate things produced by the sub-cultures: in other words, the dialectic between youth and the youth market industry (Clarke et al. 1976: 16).

Arguably, this extract provides the essential ingredients of the CCCS account of subculture, framed within a conceptualization of the cyclical conflict between youth 'appropriation' and industry 'incorporation'. This conflict between subcultural youth and the youth industries is described as a dialectic: it is out of this conflicted interaction that resistant styles are produced.

We can usefully set out the contours of the CCCS model and the distinctive concepts employed by the school to chart the cycle of youth appropriation and industry incorporation (see fig. 5.1) as follows. To begin with the youth market is viewed as an agent of capitalist integration and as a promoter of capitalist ideology: the 'classless teenager'. Its role is to integrate youth leisure into capitalist reproduction through the promotion of teen

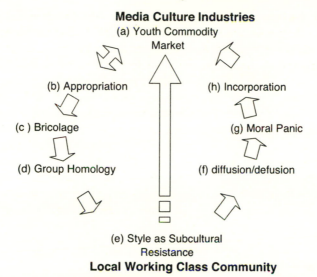

Media Culture Industries
(a) Youth Commodity
Market

(b) Appropriation

(h) Incorporation

(c) Bricolage

(g) Moral Panic

(d) Group Homology

(f) diffusion/defusion

(e) Style as Subcultural
Resistance
Local Working Class Community

Figure 5.1 CCCS circuit of style construction and incorporation.

consumerism. This is why the first act of defiance of would be subculturalists is to refuse this youth market by seeking to appropriate goods for
their own uses. Stamping a group identity upon these conventional objects
is achieved through the act of bricolage—the re-arrangement of a set of
objects in such a way that their original meanings and uses are transformed
into something different and unconventional (Clarke 1976b: 175–92). It is
this act of semiotic transformation that distinguishes the subcultural use
of commodities from that of the conventional teenage consumer who is, in
contemporary parlance, a 'fashion victim' or dupe of the system. The re-
imagining of the uses of bought commodities in the construction of a group
look is therefore an act of stylistic defiance against the commodity system
and capitalist power (Clarke et al. 1976: 55–6). It is motivated, according
to the CCCS, by a desire to reassert a class identity and to embody this
identity in the realisation of the resulting subcultural style.

When there is effectively a stylistic fusion between re-arranged objects
and a group identity, such as were to be found in teddy boys, mods and
skins, a homology was said to be expressed: the objects became the group
and the group the objects (Clarke 1976b: 179). It is at this high point of the
cycle, when a distinctive youth style has been constructed away from the
logic and designs of the youth market, that the forces of capitalist power,
ideology and commerce re-enter the picture, seeking to re-incorporate
the renegade youth ensemble back into the commercial system. However,
this victory can only be achieved, once the subculture which has claimed
ownership of it has been tamed and the class coding of the style has been
watered down.

It is this inevitable process the CCCS term *diffusion/defusion* (Clarke 1976b: 185–89). Essentially, subculturalists are victims of their own success, since the style has such a stamp of authenticity that it is almost immediately subject to mimicry and begins to spread beyond its original context. At this point entrepreneurs, eager to market a version of the emergent trend, enter the picture, allowing the visible markers of the style to further spread. Ironically, it is this greater visibility that provokes a response from control agencies and which leads to media reportage (Clarke 1976b: 186), culminating in bouts of youth moral panic in the national media (Hebdige 1979: 93). All of this eventually exhausts the style (it has been *de-fused*) and it is at this point that it is made safe for media and commercial incorporation (or re-integration) (Hebdige 1979: 92–99). Not long after, it re-emerges on the high street as a safe 'mass' youth fashion ensemble.

Resisting the legacy: Rethinking the subcultural cycle

In this section I want to rethink the highlighted elements of the CCCS model and how they work to produce the cycle of subcultural resistance and incorporation claimed. Central to my criticism is the denial in the CCCS account of the capacity of some youth commodities to carry meanings and ideas that promote particular, distinctive uses, and thereby allow particular kinds of subcultural distinctions to spring up around them.

Youth commodity market

Because the CCCS theorize subculture as an aspect of the wider struggle of the subordinate against the institutions of the dominant, they view the teen consumer industry as agent of capitalist integration and of class hegemony. Yet historical evidence suggests the new teen commercial culture was itself perceived as a threat to dominant values, rather than a legitimation of them (Hebdige 1988; Campbell 1995: 98; Osgerby 1998). One reason for this is that the raw materials of this popular culture, commodified and mass produced by such industries, are the values, practices and entertainments of the subordinate classes as well as the bowdlerization of high culture. A more consistent hegemony theory would view the commercial mainstream as a contradictory site of contestation of value systems, governed by the interplay of logics of production and popular consumption. Surprisingly absent from the CCCS model is a wider media culture that surrounds the production and consumption of teen commodities, seeking to stimulate demand and confer meaning on objects and their possible uses (Thornton 1995; du Gay 1997).

Appropriation

The use of this term suggests that acquiring 'the gear' is an expression of hostility against property relations or a decisive act of insubordination, somehow carried out against the wishes of the sellers (Wai-Teng Lung 1992: 36).[3] What this terminology obscures is actually quite important: the activity of buying the subcultural commodities themselves. As McRobbie notes, there is an absence in subcultural theory of descriptions of shopping as a subcultural activity (1989, 1994: 137), which requires knowledge or judgement of the relative cost and options available and the shops within which purchases can be made. The ways in which subculturalists select and purchase items that go on to form the basis of their subsequent activities clearly ought to fall within the scope of the model.

In addition, the idea of appropriation assumes that youth commodities do not, in themselves, have properties of creativity or if they do such uses are commercially circumscribed by their producers. It is my contention that those commodities that find favour with *would-be* subculturalists, do so because they are able to mediate the commercial space between producers and consumers, allowing extended and meaningful investment by youth groups. That is, a commodified experience is made possible by the uses to which youth-oriented commodities are put by subcultural consumers. These 'uses' (of meaning, engagement, pleasure, etc.) are equally produced by the range of uses suggested by manufacturers as those actually realized by consumers. Both are agents in the shaping process and what it eventually produces.

One way to explore this is to focus on the (would be) subcultural commodity, in terms of the circumstances of production, the relations of production and consumption involved in its sale and purchase and the regimes of value it moves within, throughout its short or extended life (Thompson 1979; Appadurai 1986; Kopytoff 1986). McRobbie (1989, 1994) makes a useful contribution to this debate through her conception of subcultural markets, operating at the 'tat' end of the commercial spectrum, where networks of small-scale entrepreneurs revalorize out-of-fashion items and remarket 'looks' based on reconfiguring past and present haberdashery. But rather than being confined to these arenas, subcultural markets also emerge out of the layers of media and commerce that commodify and recommodify the objects of youth consumption. Commodification by producers leads to recommodification by consumers, comprising a 'circuit of culture' (du Gay 1997)[4] which shapes and redefines the subcultural commodity so that it becomes *more* not less subcultural.

Hodkinson's (2002) account of the development of the goth subculture is illustrative of this process. The origins of goth style arise from the production and consumption of a number of initially unrelated elements which were given a sense of coherence by their aesthetic articulation within certain post-punk records, band pronouncements and music journalism (2002: 35, 111). It was this 'cultural circuit' of music-media and related commerce that made possible the early exposure and success of the goth bands and out of this process a stylistic sensibility emerged which allowed subcultural identification. The further commodification of the goth subculture which followed did not lead to its 'watering down' but on the contrary a greater sense of stylistic coherence and differentiation from other youth styles.

What has sustained the subculture, beyond the commercial decline of the music, has been the development of a network of commercial and subcultural producers who supply the products and services (recording facilities, venues and event locations, records and clothes manufacture, distribution and retail outlets etc.) that allow the culture to reproduce itself (Hodkinson 2002). What determines the exchange value of these items (and therefore subcultural demand for them) is their ability to 'carry' subcultural values, which are multiplied by their social uses in sustaining subcultural experience. It is important to emphasize that the subcultural experience is a commodified experience: the objects of the subculture come to mean that experience because they both carry it symbolically and facilitate it as material practice.

Bricolage

It follows that the act of bricolage is not an exclusive activity of a minority of youth ('originals') nor does it always involve a dramatic departure from the meanings already contained in bought commodities, since such meanings articulate the potential 'social' and 'symbolic' uses of such commodities. A typical ensemble of commodities involved in a youth stylization will probably combine subcultural and non-subcultural items (that is items marketed as already subcultural and other less-specific goods in different combinations) (Hodkinson 2002: 133–35).

Homology

Subcultural homologies may arise from the 'discovery' of a valued cultural commodity or may be stimulated by commodities directed at a subcultural market. Whatever is the case it is likely that once there is a demand for a particular style then that demand will be met with the supply of such commodities. It is only when this has occurred that a recognizable 'style', uniform or practice can become widespread enough for a stylistic fusion to be communicated to 'outsiders' (Clarke 1981: 92). It is debatable what such a style 'ensemble' is actually communicating beyond a generalized sense of youth 'exclusivity'. While youth styles may carry symbols and markers of bourgeois offence and outrage (typically to do with the taboo or the profane) these may be perceived in a range of ways, both within and outside the subculture. What tends to matter, as I show later, is the sense of identity definition that arrives from differentiating oneself from a perceived main-stream or mediocrity of 'others'. Thus, subcultural distinctions are being made and sustained *within* the category of youth rather than between youth and a dominant culture that supposedly oppresses it from without.

Diffusion/defusion

Despite largely ignoring the buying and selling of subcultural products, Clarke's (1976b) account of the 'diffusion of styles from the subcultures to the fashion market' does identify the emergence of a 'network or infra-structure of new kinds of commercial and economic institutions', 'young entrepreneurs, in touch with their markets', 'small-scale record shops, recording companies' and 'boutiques and one or two-woman manufactur-ing companies' anticipating trends and markets (1976b: 187). But we are asked to believe such commercial activities are so many 'levels' of exploita-tion of 'grass roots' style:

> The whole mid-1960's explosion of 'Swinging London' was based on the massive commercial diffusion of what were originally essentially Mod styles, mediated through such networks, and finally into a 'mass' cultural and commercial phenomenon... what was in origin a sub-cultural style became transformed, through increasing commercial organisation and fashionable expropriation, into a pure 'market' or 'consumer' style (Clarke 1976b: 187).

Why is this not, on the contrary, a complexifying and enriching process? For clearly the diffusion/defusion process involves different types of media and levels of interaction between macro and micro forms of representation, local, regional and national networks, semi-independent and large scale commodity manufacture and distribution. Without these 'intermediary' processes, surely no post-war subcultural styles could have gained suffi-cient commercial circulation to render them visible to the CCCS theorists or anyone else? If we take the trajectory of punk style as an example, the so-called authentic stage is actually achieved after the style becomes com-mercialized and copied: it is only at this point that a sufficient volume of young people are involved for the style to be 'street visible' (Clarke 1981: 92). It is at this point we can see evidence of consumer creativity in mixing and matching elements to create a recognisable 'punk look'. The reason for this was not necessarily the pursuit of a DIY aesthetic but because the cost of 'proper gear' was prohibitive (Cartledge 1999; Shedden 2002: 18).

Moral panic

Episodes of macro-media moral panic do not signal the end point of a style or its influence but on the contrary a high profile point of definition involving attempts to name and characterize it (typically involving lists and descriptions). Such coverage may be used as a point of reference (Hodkinson 2002: 159) or stamp of authenticity by youth groups so named (Thornton 1995: 132). Clearly other layers of media are involved in this process of naming and defining scenes, styles and symbolic locations, favoured commodities and styles of consumption (Brown 2003a: 5).

Incorporation

Youth styles cannot be said to be incorporated into either a commercial or hegemonic culture, since the commodities from which styles are constructed and the meanings with which they are associated, are the product of a cultural and commercial interaction, involving youth and various media culture industries. This is not to deny that subcultures frequently exhaust themselves or expire, but to resist the assumption that such an eventuality is coterminous with incorporation into a commercialized mainstream.

It follows that dramatic acts of product transformation are less likely than acts of consumer loyalty to the purchase of particular products because of their symbolic value in signifying membership of subculture and allowing access to the social relations that make it a youth activity. Therefore, the relationship between subcultures and the commodities of the youth market do not depend upon resistance through symbolic acts of commercial refusal or semiotic transformation, but collective acts of consumption, which valorize certain commodities as subculturally meaningful, so that their possession and consumption both signifies and embodies subcultural membership.

THE HEAVY METAL T-SHIRT: AN AUTHENTIC COMMODITY?

In 2003 classic heavy metal t-shirts such as Iron Maiden and Motörhead were available in UK high street chain stores. In September 2003, *Heat Magazine* devoted its regular 'Star Style' feature to location shots of celebrities, such as Drew Barrymore, Geri Halliwell and Robbie Williams, sporting Judas Priest, Iron Maiden and AC/DC t-shirts (*Heat* 2003). In the same month, upmarket *Elle* declared: 'Fashion's going mental about metal' (*Elle* 2003: 25), while in May 2004, *The Guardian* offered the ultimate coffee-table tribute: 'Confessions of a teenage heavy metal freak' (Hunter 2004), including a cover photo of a typical male metaller, circa 1980s: shoulder length hair, jean jacket emblazoned with patches and 'pins', band t-shirt and dirty denims covered in DIY band logos.

All of this, not to mention the emergence of The Darkness as a sort of postmodern pastiche of '80s lite or 'big hair' metal,[5] would seem to confirm Hebdige's claim that a subculture has to be emptied of its 'message' before it can be recommodified for the catwalk and the coffee table. Yet this sort of interpretation is unable to explain why Hebdige denied heavy metal sub-cultural status in the first place (1979: 155, n. 12; Brown 2003b: 211). The problem of heavy metal for subcultural theory was that it was popular, among large groups of the working- and lower-middle classes and its style iconography was one derived from album covers, band looks and logos. In other words, it was clearly based around a manufactured and marketed commodity experience.

Yet, I would argue, the relationship of heavy metal fans and bands was a symbiotic one: a closed circle of taste culture that could claim a size-able portion of the U.K. and U.S. billboards charts, in the 1970s and 80s, and yet be deeply disliked by almost everyone who was not an aficionado (Walser 1993a: x–xi). Although heavy metal has been subject to commer-cial decline and genre fragmentation into the 1990s, up to the present this taste-polarisation continues to characterize its youth appeal (Weinstein 1991: 282–86; Harris 2000; Baulch 2003). It is this central characteristic, that subcultural distinctions can be maintained and strengthened by the process of commodification, which my research attempts to investigate.

The 'Metal T-Shirt Project' was designed to explore the role that the band t-shirt played in constituting the heavy metal youth experience as a commodified experience. While recorded music and live performance are clearly central to metal culture, it is the band t-shirt that announces one's participation to others. While I am equally concerned with the production and distribution of the metal t-shirt, it is the experience of consumption that I report on here. The following discussion is based on six in-depth, taped interviews with three males and three female respondents, aged between 18 and 26, who were (or had been) active 'metal' or 'rock/alternative' fans.[6] As a means of comparison I also recorded focus group discussions with non-metal undergraduate students.

GETTING IT ON YOUR CHEST: T-SHIRT CULTURE(S), FROM WOODSTOCK TO DESIGNER SHOP

The central feature of the t-shirt, as a feature of youth fashion, is its capac-ity to carry a symbol, picture or slogan, usually placed across the chest area of the garment (and sometimes, in addition, on the back). Despite the availability of shops which offer to 'print your slogan or design' the vast majority of t-shirts are bought with their design preprinted. While slogans and images can range from the comic to the pseudo profound, the ironic to the postmodernist conceit (Cullum-Swan and Manning 1994), the heavy metal t-shirt exhibits none of these qualities. This does not mean that you cannot wear a heavy metal t-shirt ironically or with postmodern motives, but it does mean that the wearing of such a shirt will be viewed as in some way claiming an allegiance or connection to the meanings of the heavy metal community.

Despite the fact that they rarely exhibit a home-made design, the wearing of metal t-shirts tends to be viewed as an authentic means of making a statement about allegiance to a music style or particular group. For many of my non-metal respondents, heavy metal designs and band t-shirts were viewed as deliberately setting out to exclude, alienate or cause offence. From their point of view, the category of metal existed as a kind of pariah or category of youth 'other'. Its t-shirts were seen as heavily masculinized and 'exclusionary'in a way that other t-shirts were not. For outsiders, then, the metal t-shirt tended to be regarded as a badge of deliberate obscurantism—a request to be 'left alone' among a group who liked each other's company and who, in the opinion of some, took their music and other issues, like Satanism and the occult, far too seriously.

METAL T-SHIRT CULTURE(S):
'STICKING OUT' TO 'FIT IN'?

I think metal is the one subculture where wearing a t-shirt is very important, a kind of status symbol (Richard 14.01.05).

Heavy metal is internally divided into a number of distinct subgenre defined 'scenes', some of which have an antagonistic relationship to the idea of 'heavy metal' as an 'institutionalized' mainstream (Harris 2000). Yet to outsiders, nearly all members of the various subyouth groups can appear as a homogenous entity, characterized by long hair, denims, leather jackets and black t-shirts. The t-shirt plays a key role both in defining the borders of the youth culture to those on the outside and as a means of signalling important differentiations within it to insiders. It is able to do this because its purpose is to carry the logo of particular bands as a sort of 'advertisement'. In metal culture, musical taste is the arbiter of all other characteristics, from hairstyles to dress, 'dance' and demeanour. So, choice of t-shirt is never arbitrary: it is taken as a means of intentional communication of taste and allegiance, announcing differentiation from other youths and peer-identification with a particular subscene.

While such symbolic understandings clearly pre-existed their 'discovery' by my respondents, each of them negotiated their relationship to them through their selection, purchase and consumption of particular subcultural commodities, most important of which was the band t-shirt. While these items were commercially produced, their relative 'exchange value', that is their subcultural worth, was not in any way diminished by this. Rather subcultural value seemed to rise and fall in relation to the direct interaction between youth and their music (band tours and releases) and in response to niche metal media coverage. Crucially, it was the way peer groups interacted with and responded to media-cycles of promotion and exposure of bands and merchandise which determined what was valued

Figure 5.2   Metal t-shirt (photograph A. Brown).

and what was ignored or devalued. Ultimately, this pattern of participation therefore reflected neither fully 'individualism' (Miles 1995; Muggleton 2000) nor 'subcultural conformity' (Hodkinson 2002: 40) but the combination of a sense of active choice *and* a wish to be part of a perceived socially distinctive 'taste' group.

   One of the things that emerged from the outset of my investigation, was that almost all my respondents rejected the term heavy metal as a self-designation because the term implied a music and style that belonged to their dads; or because it conjured up a clichéd [1980s] image of spandex and guitar solos: 'Just a lot of heavy guitars and drums and screaming down the microphone' as one (Kayleigh) put it. Dave took a similar view:

Dave: 'I think heavy metal is a genre... like Iron Maiden and... 'Judas
         Priest and Def Leppard, n' Saxon and Motörhead. But—I don't
         think any of the stuff I listen to is anything like heavy metal'
ARB: 'So, would you call it metal, at all?'
Dave: 'Yea.... I'd say it was metal—but not heavy metal'

Despite this semantic differentiation almost everyone described their musical allegiance as 'metal' or rock/alternative, such as: death metal, grindcore, hardcore, black metal, industrial metal, nu-metal or rock/alternative. The significance of these self-chosen categories is that they related to particular bands and a sound that was unique to their ongoing experience of records, live events and peer groups. It may be that respondents weren't willing to concede a connection to wider heavy metal youth culture because this would have diminished their 'personal' sense of choice and autonomy or because such a culture seemed too much like a clichéd or inauthentic mainstream they wished to distance themselves from. In either case, it was primarily through the purchase of carefully chosen subcultural commodities that respondents communicated their affinities—both to the general category of metal and to particular subgenres within it.

ACQUIRING THE LOOK: YOUTH SUBCULTURAL SHOPPING

When discussing the details of their initial discovery of 'metal' style, nearly everyone suggested that their desire to 'get hold of' items of dress coincided with 'discovering' the music and acted as a crucial means of announcing their taste to others and as a source of self-identity. Growing your hair and wearing a band t-shirt was an absolute necessity: Without these 'signifiers' there was no sense of actually being a 'death metaller' or 'black metaller'. Buying t-shirts often was a group activity, typically involving a collective trip 'down town' or into 'the city'; sometimes to visit particular shops or record stores, where shirts could be bought. Awareness of where to go to get their gear was regarded as 'common knowledge' that was passed on within the peer group. This underlines the point that although metal t-shirts are manufactured commodities they are not generally available on the high street or if they are (via chain record stores) it is only the most well-known and popular ones that are stocked. To obtain a wider range of bands and subgenre shirts, mail-order distributors were required, some of which were advertised in the metal magazine press. In some cases local record stores offered an order service, via catalogues kept on the counter. Some of my respondents also spoke of punk/alternative type shops that carried second-hand (retro) clothes and items, such as t-shirts and posters; or extreme sports/surf type shops that carried some metal-oriented items.

A value hierarchy informed t-shirt choices and this was partly but not entirely related to peer opinions. I had expected, given the unique commercial relationship that existed between bands and fans, that official band merchandise would be highly valued. I also expected, following Weinstein (1991: 127–28), that vintage shirts, personally modified (sleeves ripped-off), and old tour shirts would be considered more 'cool' and credible than other kinds. Although most respondents considered 'very old, faded' shirts to have a quality of credibility this did not necessarily extend to the purchase of tour shirts ('too big', 'too expensive' 'preferred particular designs') and definitely not to modified shirts. A real issue was counterfeit shirts, not usually because of the source of purchase (most felt it was okay to buy wherever you could) but because the shirt didn't look correctly manufactured: 'naff' or 'it just looks wrong, dun it' were comments offered. While it was okay to modify jeans or other items (school bags, leather jackets), often with favoured band names, it was not okay to do the same to shirts. This suggests that the source of authenticity lay in the relationship (publicly expressed allegiance) to the band being 'advertised' via the wearing of the t-shirt design, rather than any reworking of the item itself. The latter was not deemed necessary because the t-shirt and its lack of favour with most youth achieved the display of authentic allegiance despite its visible commodity status.

THE MEANING(S) OF METAL T-SHIRT CULTURES: GROUP CONFORMITY OR THE PURSUIT OF DIFFERENCE?

Two issues emerged that were common to the experience of wearing particular shirts. One was the approval of other metallers and how this might lead to conversations with complete strangers: 'If I see someone wearing a band t-shirt that I like, I generally will go up and talk to them' (Richard). This sense of shared taste and acknowledgement by others, based on the recognition or approval of the band t-shirt you might be wearing, was mentioned by all my respondents as an important source of social approval and sense of belonging to an 'exclusive' youth culture. Metallers could always be picked out of a crowd by their long hair or t-shirts. Getting a nod of approval or smile of recognition for the shirt you were wearing provoked a feeling of inclusion and 'social honour' (Weber). This social approval from within the extended community of metal fans could be contrasted with the look of disapproval or incomprehension shown by those outside it.

This raises the pivotal question of what sorts of meanings were being conveyed by metal t-shirts and to whom were these meanings being communicated? A good illustration of the fallacy of intentional communication to be found in claims for the 'semiotic guerrilla warfare' (Eco cited in Hebdige 1979: 105) being waged by subculturalists, is the following account of Dave, a death metaller, about reactions provoked by his t-shirts:

Dave: ...I used to quite like wearing offensive t-shirts, really.
ARB: Can you tell me a bit about that? Did you want to be different to other people?
Dave: Yea, I did, you know, did want to be different. It's sort of a little bit of shock value, in it? When people look at it and they're a bit surprised. [Yea] 'cos when you listen to it it's not really that shocking, is it? The music isn't shocking—you know they don't mean it or anything.... But when other people, look at it. Um,

I've sort of always thought they were a bit simple, quite a lot of people who look at it and are shocked by that.

ARB: So, in a way, you look down on the way they are reacting?

Dave: I do— I look down on their, er, taste in music as well. And the whole image thing sort of goes with it.

There is a clear assertion of cultural superiority in Dave's comments. On the one hand he is expecting 'ordinary' non-metal aficionados to be offended and shocked by the graphics and style of his band t-shirts. At the same time he feels superior to their ignorance in not comprehending that 'they don't really mean it'. This raises the oft asserted criticism of heavy metal youth culture that, despite its cultivation of the extreme and grotesque in its subject matter, it remains apolitical or even conservative in its basic values. This judgement is often derived from a comparison with the intentional political communication of other youth subcultures, such as punk or hardcore. Yet it remains a fundamental problem of the methodology of 'reading' in the CCCS account that ordinary subcultural bearers of antihegemonic meanings were never asked to provide confirmation or refutation of such interpretations themselves.

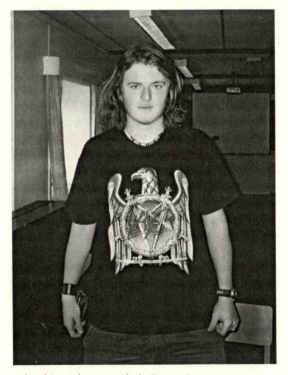

Figure 5.3   Metal t-shirt (photograph A. Brown).

In the well-known discussion of the use of the swastika in punk style, Hebdige (1979: 116–17) stretches credulity to breaking point in arguing that the rage it provoked was confirmation of the way that punk 'laid-bare' the operation of the dominant signifying system, refusing any 'content' to the re-use of the symbol. But in fact provocative slogans and images carried on punk t-shirts were not a product of grass-roots subcultural activity, but the creation of 'intermediary' idea-entrepreneurs and creative-workers, who produced and distributed the items themselves or via arrangement with record companies or larger manufacturers. This would apply, for example, to 'I woke up this morning', the 'Cow-boys', 'Cambridge Rapist', 'Anarchy in the UK' and 'handwritten porno' t-shirts, designed and manufactured by Maclaren and Westwood (and Rhodes) (Colegrave and Sullivan 2001: 145–49) and to the mass-distribution of Jamie Read designs promoting the Sex Pistols (Savage 1992).

A parallel can be found in metal youth culture's use of provocative symbolism, arising out of similar creative and promotional activity. For example, Cradle of Filth's 'Jesus Was a Cunt' t-shirt, which achieved a great deal of notoriety for the band and led, in one publicized incident to a fan being prosecuted for obscenity, for wearing it. Another example is the Slayer fan club t-shirt, which above a grinning-skull wearing a fire helmet is carried the phrase: 'Slatanic Wehrmacht' (Slatanic German Armed Forces) (Roccor 2000: 86–87). As Roccor argues, this symbolism could be interpreted by right wing fans as declaring sympathy for the Nazi period and by left leaning ones as a provocation aimed at the bourgeois suppression of that period. Yet Slayer's published comments on such issues suggest that what they know or comprehend about National Socialism could be written on 'a single sheet of paper' (2000: 87).

It just so happens that one of my respondents wore this particular t-shirt to his interview and when questioned about it was surprised to learn its 'meaning'. When asked whether such knowledge might affect him wearing the t-shirt in the future, he was unmoved. Discovering the origins of the symbolism actually confirmed its power to disturb and shock (it was 'dark' and 'powerful') and thereby his original liking for it. Such symbolism was considered highly appropriate to the band because of their extreme style of music. Wearing such imagery was a public display of allegiance to the band rather than to any historical meanings carried in the symbols, which were neither endorsed nor rejected by such an action.

CONCLUSION

It is clear from this qualitative study that participation in metal youth culture is socially facilitated but also *experienced* via the consumption of commercially produced commodities, such as the band t-shirt. Far from such consumption signalling conformity to a youth mainstream media system, the meanings that such commodities carry and the uses to which they are put allow significant means of differentiation within the space of youth and between different kinds of youth commodities. If it is allowed that the values communicated in metal music culture are in some senses sub-cultural then it is also clear that such values are carried within the com-mercially produced products that form the material basis of such a culture. Such products are not only the market outcome of a process of interaction between metal youth and the culture industries but so is their consump-tion. This quality of fold-back or interaction, is no more clearly evident than in the dual feature of the metal t-shirt: as standardized commercial sponsorship for band logos and album covers and a means of signalling, via the prominence of such images and design, youth taste divisions clearly invoked by reference to the values embedded in the various subgenre styles and culture(s) of metal music.

NOTES

1. I would like to thank Wolfgang Deicke and Paul Hodkinson for their helpful comments and suggestions on an earlier version of this chapter.
2. The overall winner was the Iron Maiden 'Live After Death' design.
3. It literally means 'take for your own use without permission' but the deriva-tion of the usage is from Marx's political economy where, along with expro-priation, it is used in the context of capital acquiring land, property, profit, surplus value and predictions about the outcome of class struggles, when the 'expropriators themselves will be expropriated'!
4. The concept of 'circulating culture' is employed by Du Gay, Nixon and others to explain contemporary 'niche consumerism' within the context of capital regimes, governed by 'flexible specialization', where the key role is played by cultural intermediaries within the culture industries. However, such approaches do not examine the complex web of 'small-scale' commercial entrepreneurs who exist between the global players and the consumer.
5. Lite or big hair metal was so characterized because of the absence of the heavy bass sound characteristic of heavy metal and because of the elaborate, 'poodle-perms' of performers, such as David Coverdale of Whitesnake.
6. Interviews typically lasted between 30 and 45 minutes. The respondents were recruited from undergraduates at Bath Spa University, U.K., on the basis of t-shirts worn and thereafter by 'snowballing'.

6 Resistance or incorporation?
Youth policy making and hip hop culture

Rupa Huq

From the standpoint of the twenty-first century, hip hop is no stranger to academia. The booming market of rap scholarship spans a number of different approaches encompassing *inter alia* Afrocentricism, commercialism postmodernism, post-colonialism and pedagogy in hip hop culture. This chapter takes a different tack and explores how hip hop culture, often regarded as an authentic and resistant form of expression for marginalized young people, has broadened in scope from its original remit and is now utilized in numerous ways in public policy contexts spanning education and the youth services. It draws on fieldwork conducted in Strasbourg (France) and Manchester (England) where hip hop has been deployed by local authorities in projects aimed at channelling youthful exuberance in urban neighbourhoods known for youth crime with the aim of keeping youth on the 'straight and narrow'. The chapter investigates the ways in which these initiatives have been received and how young people have responded to the attempts to co-opt 'street' culture into social policy to argue that our usual associations with the terms *resistance* and *incorporation* have tended to limit themselves to looking at commercial co-optation

RESISTANCE VS. INCORPORATION: A RUNNING DEBATE

The notion of a binary divide positing youth cultural resistance in opposition to incorporation by external forces, has been a long-running subplot in the history of post-war youth culture. Hitherto considerations of incorporation have featured most often in the academic literature in commercial terms. The academic literature on this subject dates back some years. While Mark Abrams (1959) first identified the emergence of the 'teenage consumer' as a distinct sector of the purchasing public, anxieties about commercialisation and an attendant loss of authenticity in popular music date further back to Adorno (1941) and the inter-war era Frankfurt school. There has long been almost a resignation that market forces inevitably deliver a commercialized and subculturally neutered version of youth culture as evidenced in Rutherford's assertion that 'the global market place has transformed youth cultures and their signs of revolt and rebellion into commodities, and an aesthetic of "youth"' (1997: 114). This can be seen in successive waves of pop history and hip hop is littered with examples of once-underground artists who have risen to prominence on major record labels. However, as Andy Brown has pointed out in the previous chapter, it may be a mistake to assume that such movements are necessarily devoid of commercialism to begin with.

Authenticity is regarded as of key significance in youth culture and academic objectifications of it. Sarah Thornton (1995) identifies 'the authentic versus the phoney' and 'the "hip" versus the mainstream' as two crucial cultural hierarchies in pop. As she points out there has traditionally been a greater value attached to 'live' music rather than recorded sounds. Hip hop upsets some of the traditional music divides in a similar way to the dance music sounds which are the focus of her study and hence are subject to the following observation:

> Club cultures celebrate technologies that have rendered some traditional kinds of musicianship obsolete and have led to the formation of new aesthetics and judgements of value. Producers, sound engineers, remixers and DJs—not song-writing guitarists—are the creative heroes of dance genres (Thornton 1995: 4).

The importance of authenticity in hip hop's self-image is evidenced in the expression 'old school' referring to pioneering original rap styles and the principle of 'keeping it real' to connote remaining authentic. Conversely 'selling out'— to lose touch with one's original ideals—usually provoked by material success, is viewed with disdain. Originality, sincerity and uniqueness are all intertwined in notions of authenticity. Hip hop is seen as emanating from the street or ghetto as an authentically produced bottom-up popular musical form. Of course rap has steadily become a commercial going concern, widely available via multinational record companies. Negus (1999: 96), for example, talks about the rap industry as positioned 'between the street and the executive suite'. Importantly, however, there are also other ways in which the anti-establishment tendencies in pop music have become intertwined with the organs of the establishment aside from simply commerce. Rather than examining the economics of youth culture, this chapter focuses on the ways in which hip hop in both France and the United Kingdom has been subject to forms of incorporation associated with public policy.

Popular music has been embroiled with public policy, officialdom and political campaigns for some time now. Its symbolic utilisation by national leaders includes the U.K. Labour Prime Minister Harold Wilson granting the Beatles MBEs, French President Jacques Chirac awarding ageing rocker Johnny Halliday the *Legion d'honneur* and Ricky Martin playing at George Bush's inauguration celebration. The rhetoric of 'Cool Britannia' invoked by guitar playing British premier Tony Blair, who entertained Noel Gallagher at 10 Downing Street, went further in espousing the economic potential of the creative and cultural industries. In Summer 2005, the Live8 concerts illustrated how pop at large was being used as a campaigning tool in the fight for debt cancellation. In 1985, the original Live Aid concerts had only featured one rap act: Run DMC. In 2005, hip hop diversity was manifested in the inclusion of Black Eyed Peas, Snoop Dogg, Kanye West and Ms Dynamite all on the bill. The U.S. concert was hosted by one-time rapper Will Smith. Hip hop and rap, then, are now gaining an acceptance within broader pop music as well as on their own terms.

Hip hop is often considered as a U.S.-centric 'born in the USA' culture as is its musical style, rap. The main body of this chapter, however, is concerned with hip hop in two European settings. My examples of hip hop policy and practice in Strasbourg and Manchester between them highlight how there is more to hip hop than just U.S. versions of it. Although it has long been perceived as an urban menace in the eyes of respectable society, hip hop has undergone intellectualisation by academics, absorption by music industry multinationals, and, most crucially for the purposes of this chapter, officialdom in its use by local government and the educational system in Britain and France.

INCORPORATION 1: U.K. YOUTH WORK

The development of British government policy regarding young people has spanned different government departments including health, education and home affairs, and initiatives have been subject to different party political programmes. The overlap between 'youth' and 'culture' in public policy terms has only been slight with both arenas developing in fairly separate and distinct fashion. As outlined by Hebdige below, there has been a tendency to adopt problem-solving approaches to questions of youth:

> In our society, youth is present only when its presence is a problem or is regarded as a problem... going 'out of bounds' by resisting through rituals, dressing strangely, striking bizarre attitudes, breaking rules, breaking bottles, windows, heads, issuing rhetorical challenges to the law. They get arrested, harassed, admonished, disciplined, incarcerated, applauded, vilified, listened to (Hebdige 1988: 17–18).

The U.K. youth service has struggled to escape a reputation of being run in a top-down fashion and of being somewhat unresponsive to young people's needs. The nineteen page document 'Learning to Listen: Action Plan for Children and Young People 2003/04' issued by the Office of the Deputy Prime Minister contains little mention of culture. Instead are proposals on neighbourhood renewal, housing and newspeak structures such as 'Local Public Service Agreements' and 'Local Strategic Partnerships'.

Yet under New Labour there has been something of a cultural turn in governmental circles. Tony Blair's vision of 'New Britain' placed emphasis on the U.K. as a 'young country' (Rutherford 1997). While official attitudes to the arts have historically tended to concentrate on high rather than popular culture, pronouncements made by the Labour-created Department of Culture, Media and Sport have lauded the role of the creative and cultural industries in the new mixed economy. Other themes propounded by the administration include combating social exclusion, antisocial behaviour and ensuring community cohesion. The combination of elements of all of these aspects of policy along with 'inner city deprivation'— a phrase already in use under the last Conservative administrations—all coincided in the establishment of twenty Music Action Zones in the U.K. in December 2000 up in areas of social and economic need.[1] My first case study, the Cultural Fusion music training project, was set in the Greater Manchester Music Action Zone (GMMAZ). The initiative was also cofinanced by the National Foundation for Youth Music, the North West Arts Board and the A6 Partnership, aimed at regenerating the locale known as the Stockport Road corridor.

Youth Music was established in December 2000. Among its objectives is to 'create a sustainable legacy of music-making for young people throughout the UK'—a phrase later to be echoed in a sporting context in London's successful 2012 Olympic bid. The target population for Youth Music are 'young people living in areas of social and economic need who might otherwise lack opportunity'. Furthermore it 'predominantly supports activities which are held outside school hours'. The 2006 budget alone was £2.7 million. Cultural Fusion was one such project, based in Longsight, inner-south Manchester, and focused upon offering teenage participants the chance to work towards an NVQ (National Vocational Qualification) level 2 music technology certificate for composing, recording and performing live music. Most participants opted to do this through hip hop. The project highlights the entanglement of hip hop style with public sector sponsorship, informal and formal education, as well as its use as a medium to keep youth on the 'straight and narrow' path away from 'the street' with all its negative associations. These issues were highlighted by participants in the teenage rap collective HD when I interviewed them in 2003. The eight-piece band had been in operation for two years; members assumed identities reflected in their pseudonyms, fitting in their hours on the project around other educational commitments in keeping with Youth Music guidelines. Seventeen-year-old rapper and producer Mathew Jay was undertaking a BTEC national diploma in music technology at college. Ravelle Leacock, also a rapper and producer aged seventeen, was doing A-levels in physics, art and environmental science with a view to a career in architecture. Marc Leacock, Ravelle's cousin aged twenty, was studying multimedia while Hamza

Mbeju, seventeen, was a business student. Finally Rosie Garvey, fourteen and still at school was the group's only female, who firmly denied that there was any issue about her as a rapper being a female in a male world, although this may be in part be due to the focus-group dynamic of the interview. All lived with a least one parent. As those who had opted for the NVQ route, my interviewees were by definition 'good respondents'. Intriguingly enough the initials HD stand for 'Helletic Domains'. Mathew explained: 'I came up with it. It means evil territory; like gang life and so on... [it comes] with the habitat'. At once we can see linguistic innovation and reinvention here in this neologism derived from the word *hell*.

NVQs entail no examinations but project requirements are observed by examiners and moderators. Participants undertake a minimum of thirty hours of music production and performance. However, tutor Owen Thomas attested that some participants would put in forty or even fifty hours, explaining, 'Once they come here I can't get them out of the building'. Some Cultural Fusion candidates are former young offenders. Longsight borders Manchester's university district to the south of the city centre. This geographical profile fits Banks et al.'s (2000) description of city fringe cultural quarters, which are frequently in what they call 'the "alternative" (i.e. cheap) workspaces in and around the city centre centre'. Not long before I carried out my interviews Manchester had played host to the Commonwealth games, promoting an image of multicultural tolerance and respect. Longsight meanwhile is an ethnically mixed neighbourhood notorious for gun crime and gang violence.[2] Music as a positive outlet militating against the locale's negative associations was voiced repeatedly:

RH: Longsight's got a bit of a reputation isn't it?

MJ: That's why Cultural Fusion's a good way of getting us away from that. I think music's made a huge impact on my life. It's what I live for. Music's my saviour at the end of the day... being able to come here and trying to achieve my dreams... it keeps me focused and keeps me out of trouble.

RH: What do you make of that whole media label of Manchester as Gunchester?

ML: When I was young I used to get mixed up in that shit then I was seeing a social worker and I'm here now. It's kept me off the streets so I think it's a good thing.

It is important to bear in mind that interviewees may have provided the answers that they thought I wanted to hear, especially if they felt I might have been evaluating the Programme. Nevertheless, their comments are comparable to those made by the research subjects of Fornäs et al. (1995), Finnegan (1989) and Sara Cohen (1991). The latter study, focused on Liverpool, found that music offered: 'a social life, a sense of purpose, and dreams and aspirations outside any responsibilities of work, family or home... an important source of collective and individual identity' (Cohen 1991: 31). The particular enthusiasm of *HD* also serves as an example of the increasing confidence of British hip hop which was long regarded as inferior to its U.S. equivalents. British 'urban' music and its hip hop derived subgenres have risen to increasing prominence in recent years with award-winning artists like Dizzee Rascal and the Streets.[3]

Among the objectives of Youth Music are training and development to provide 'structured music-making activities which are planned to advance children and young people's music skills.' HD members Ravelle and Mathew had at the time I interviewed them already gone further than this in undertaking to tutor younger children in CuBase technology through Cultural Fusion, which they were remunerated for under the government's Connexions youth training scheme. Our discussion covered the possibilities of rap as an occupation:

RH: Could it even turn into a career for you?

ML: I'd like to use it as a career but I'm not good enough. I need to be better.

RG: I'm not in it for the money right now because I'm young. I just do it because I like it but [eventually] I see it as a career, definitely.

RH: Would you need to go through some more training?

RG: My school's trying to get me work experience in a studio for sound engineering and they recommended that I go to Salford Music College after I finish.

Beck's (1992) influential theory of risk society hinges on the new unpredictability of life-paths where trajectories are much less linear than before. Mathew asserted that he had taken up his college course to qualify himself in studio management to insulate himself against the possible outcome of not succeeding in signing a recording contract. If a deal was not forthcoming he could run a studio as an alternative. This shows a rationalized response to the risk of rejection. This new type of risky career structure is alluded to by McRobbie (1999). Banks et al. (2000) make the point that given their market volatility, informal cultural networks and Beck's (1992) notion of 'risk management' are essential in the operating of the cultural industries. However, although it is argued that risk society entails a breakdown of old structures such as the nuclear family, social class, religion and trade unions (Beck 1992), the Cultural Fusion project is goal-oriented with the NVQ outcome within the educational qualifications framework as its outcome. Furthermore as the HD members testify, there are now college courses which are responding to the demands of the new economy where goals are not necessary profit-driven but instead equate with 'remaining cutting-edge' (Banks et al. 2000: 457). In this way hip hop then is being appropriated as a means of risk minimisation.

Paul Willis's (1977) classic text *Learning to Labour,* with its telling sub-title, 'How Working Class Kids Get Working Class Jobs', identifies another type of absorption. The social reproduction model outlined indicates that rebellious youth are ultimately swallowed up by the workforce to become model employees in manual occupations. The rebellion effected by Willis's lads was ultimately futile, as 'resistance' had obstructed their education which could have offered an escape route from their circumstances. The HD members have to a degree opted to follow a conformist path, with the promise of rewards at the end. In some ways the personal trajectories of the members of HD as a direct result of public policy suggest a breaking out of the old preset self-perpetuating circles that Willis's lads were doomed to be stuck in. Beck (1992:131) talks of 'reflexive biographies' whereby people 'can or must choose between different lifestyles, subcultures, social ties and identities'. In the future envisaged by HD, the domains of work and leisure become fused to provide career paths. Furthermore the jobs of old are no more given the decline of Britain's manufacturing base since the period when Willis was conducting his *Learning to Labour* fieldwork. The Cre-ative Industries Mapping Document of 2001 (DCMS 2001) claimed that 1.3 million people were employed in the cultural industries. Four decades ago, Colin MacInnes (1967) wrote: 'Singers, actors, models, dress design-ers, photographers, all in their teens and early twenties, have earned more foreign currency for Britain recently than hundreds of adult grumblers who lament their style, and earn us absolutely nothing'. The idea-generated, flexible, entrepreneurial, risk-taking economy is set to grow. The economic potential of this sector is not to be ignored either. It used to be joked how Sweden's biggest export was Abba. The difference of pop to Britain's bal-ance of payments has been reiterated in government circles more than once (FCO 1999).[4]

INCORPORATION 2: YOUTH WORK À LA FRANÇAISE

Urban imagery also features prominently in home-grown French hip hop culture. Its main sites of production are French *banlieues*—peripheral neighbourhoods perceived as 'problem' areas of unemployment, low skill and immigrant concentration.[5] French writer Calio (1998: 56) equates the term with 'ghetto' while English language commentators stress how the negative connotations associated with banlieue imply the very oppo-site of British 'suburban' imagery of domestic security (Hargreaves and McKinney 1997; Thoday 1995). Following disturbances in some of its ban-lieues in 1995, the city of Strasbourg mounted a large-scale youth initiative to restore the public image of the base of both the Council of Europe and European Parliament.

A sprawling municipal housing estate in a suburb of Strasbourg, Summer 1996. In the middle of the heat wave, youth in baseball caps are creating colourful hip hop style murals on the walls of this drab concrete jungle's functional blocks (see fig. 6.1). A local authority vehicle appears on the scene and some youth workers get out. However, rather than attempting to stop the protagonists, the council officials provide them with fresh spray cans, positively encouraging the graffiti creation. Such activity took part in the context of the 'Université du Hip Hop': Strasbourg's socialist local government sponsored a week long festival designed to entertain youth during the school holidays where an entire HLM (Municipal Housing Estate) in the neighbourhood of Illkirch had been sanctioned as a graffiti-permitted zone for the week. Daily morning debates (e.g.,'Hip-Hop and Institutions'), afternoon workshops (on graffiti, rap and fanzine writing) and nightly free concerts were all encompassed in an event that ran counter to the rebellion function of hip hop.

This lavish event is best understood in the context of the French statist tradition of arts sponsorship at both local and national levels. Unlike Britain, the arts has long been beneficiary of a dedicated government department in France. The first French minister of culture, André Malraux, instituted a national network of local youth centres [maisons de la jeunesse et de la culture] in the 1950s. France's annual National Music Day [Fête de la Musique], when thousands of street concerts take place in every town, was one of the more popular legacies of the Mitterand regime. The municipality of the north Parisian district Saint Denis, labelled the geographic cradle of rap in France (Mayol, 1997: 204), was running hip hop events some five years earlier, backed by a Ministry of Culture initiative FAIR (Fonds

Figure 6.1 Université du Hip Hop, 1996 (photograph R. Huq).

d'Action et d'Initiative pour le Rock). This history then situates the Hip Hop University as a pop festival within defined parameters or limitations rather than a more sinister social democratic engineering project. The official organisation of rap, also practised in Paris (Bureau 1999), is contrary to the subcultural valorisation of the concept of 'underground'. Yet the fact that rap was the musical style chosen to anchor the event is testimony to the music's outreach capability and arguably achieves a repositioning away from the underground. In France both local and national government have employed rap to exploit its potential integrative functions.

Although some readings might label the municipality of Strasbourg as a benign regime, a containment function can be seen in the objective of its youth arts and cultural service (Été Jeune) in the programming of the Université du Hip Hop to channel youthful exuberance and fondness for hip hop into a municipal framework, thus avoiding any risk of it spilling over into unwanted antisocial behaviour. With the pathology of rap and youth already presumed, the Hip Hop University's function to provide youth with a supposedly 'constructive' summer leisure activity comes across as a patronising attempt to pacify them. The use of the banlieue of Illkirch as a site for the graffiti display, for example, is questionable because its far flung location means that none of the people who 'matter' in Strasbourg, such as ambassadors, European parliamentarians and Council of Europe dignitaries would have seen it. Other noteworthy aspects of the festival included a bus donated by the local transport authority for use for graffiti, although this has not been seen in circulation. Such obviously artificial attempts to manage and control the culture seem to sit somewhat incongruously with the dispossessed-protest/rebel aspect of hip hop (Bethune 1999).

An interview I carried out later with local hip hop artist Mr E, highlighted suspicion towards the event and tensions at its heart. He told me:

> I didn't want to be part of it. The Université of Hip Hop is done from a point of view that leads people to see hip hop in a way that it's not. Été Jeune who programmed it get money from the state to help kids. The debates were nothing to do with Hip Hop. Precise subjects would include 'Breakdance: Why Is It Dropping as Part of the Culture and How to Bring It Back', or 'The Indulgence of the DJ'. Instead they had stupid things like 'the police and hip hop', 'girls and hip hop'. The Université du Hip Hop don't give a fuck. They do that to get a lot of money.

He also talked of state intervention here almost as a form of lifestyle policing:

> France is a police state. It's centralized, everything is controlled: the administration, the papers[6], everything is had. Pirate radio gets very quickly fucked up by the state, for example.

There is also a sense of officialdom having got in on hip hop too late:

Hip Hop's been on the French scene since the early eighties but the media didn't believe it or push it. Regular people couldn't get to it. In 1996 it's getting popular, so they want everything under control.

Critiques of the incorporation of hip hop for ends that contradict its ethos were recognized within the administration by Leo, a Strasbourg based commercial hip hop promoter, brought in to the Hip Hop University organising team, interviewed during the proceedings. Interestingly, at a time when the arts community in Britain clamours for increased funding, her complaints were of too much support given to rap from officialdom to the extent that it is being neutralized:

This town is run by the socialists. They've done a lot for social provision but there's a whole policy of 'assistata' [spoon-feeding], it's pretty bad for helping youth manage for themselves. There's a lot of problems in the quartiers here—fights, racism. The political powers just throw money at it. They'll put an assistant [youth worker] on the ground but it'll be someone who doesn't know the terrain, doesn't understand.

The comments of Mr E on the way that state control exercises itself covertly via funding mechanisms could be similarly made of arts programming in the U.K. and that has been discussed in a British context elsewhere (Huq 2005). Mr E here is situating himself as a rebel. However, he is not overtly rebelling against the incorporation of hip hop by capitalism and commodification in the way that previous writers on youth cultural authenticity have advanced arguments, but rather rebelling against a left-wing progressive statist agenda. This locates him still as a 'street' performer through his breakdancing and other activities. By contrast the Cultural Fusion participants, although using a 'rebel' music as their outlet, were conversely conformist youth to some extent, by opting to take the NVQ certificate of their training programme—an optional element thus potentially straitjacketing their creative expression. The fact that I as interviewer, despite trying to stress my independent credentials, was perceived as evaluator/accreditor/assessor—i.e., another agent of officialdom, is worthy of reiteration here. To an extent it demonstrates the acceptance by HD members of hip hop institutionalisation. Crucially, even if we restrict its application to simply policy terms then, incorporation can take multiple forms.

Hip hop is commonly seen as rooted in lived urban expression, having emanated from the U.S. ghetto. Clearly hip hop's appeal has spread from its humble beginnings to reach a position of mass market appeal in contemporary France. As the Hip Hop University demonstrates, it is undergoing incorporation by wider forces than simply the youth culture marketing machine. Bureau (1999: 8) claims that French rap is now more professionalized and feminized than before and thus moving to city centres. Interestingly, when I interviewed Mbegane of the Paris-based group Djoloff, he pointed out that the punitive prices of CDs now puts them out of reach of many banlieuesards, who will nevertheless manage to get hold of such music through illegal copying, distribution and exchange—something which does not show up on any statistics. With the growth of person to person computing, file-sharing and MP3 downloads this unofficial spread of hip hop is likely to rise.

INCORPORATION 3: FRENCH RAP IN THE CLASSROOM

In keeping with French statism, French rap has benefited from protectionist national linguistic policies such as the 1995 introduction of a quota to ensure that 40 per cent of local radio output is constituted of French language songs. However, many aspects of hip hop demonstrate more subtle forms of rebellion than outright mutiny, such as its use of language. Commerce, public policy and culture coincide in the existence of the French Music Bureau—a running campaign to export French music worldwide funded by a consortium of French record labels in conjunction with the French government. The FMB has been at the forefront of rap-led campaigns to export French popular music worldwide via its branches in London and New York.

At the same time, French rap has been utilised in the teaching of the French language, notwithstanding its breaking with linguistic convention. Much analysis of popular music tends to concentrate largely on lyrics, treating them as a written text. Francophone rap is performed in an unwritten, unofficial version of the French language with new inflections utilising its own linguistic codes. Its lexicon is a streetspeak version of French, incorporating African, Arab, and gypsy American (Ball 1990; Verdelhan-Bourgade 1990) and viewed with disapproval by traditionalists for its disregard for traditional syntax and rules of grammar and its liberal use of neologisms. Bocquet and Pierre-Adolphe's (1997) compiled volume of rap lyrics is published in a series of poetry anthologies under the Mille et une nuits imprint echoing Lapassade's (1996: 5) labelling of rap as 'la nouvelle poesie orale des metropoles' [the new urban oral poetry]. Nonetheless there are tensions between its diverse source material and attempts to safeguard 'pure' French. The perception of English as a cultural pollutant can be seen in the 1993 Loi Toubon (legislation proposed by the French culture minister Jacques Toubon), which attempted a wholesale obliteration of English words from French and replacing them with French terms. This was later struck down as unconstitutional. French rap is then being used to export the French language overseas whilst traditionalists attempt to safeguard 'pure' French. Pierre-Adolphe et al. (1995: 3) celebrate banlieue-speak as a language which crystallizes the social and cultural identity of an excluded and uprooted population for whom the official French of school and the exterior is incapable of capturing everyday life.

Recognition of the educational potential of rap by the French Music Bureau is evidenced in the compilation CD series 'Génération Française' issued to French teachers worldwide with accompanying book (livret pédagogique) containing full lyrics and abilty-related range of suggested classroom activities for students. Baker (1993:62) notes how in the United States rap has been broadcast on the children's television programme *Sesame Street* to teach children the alphabet. In 2000 and 2001 the London French Embassy's French Music Bureau organized U.K. tours by French rappers Sïan Supa Crew and Djolof, tied in with French language workshops delivered by the groups to French classes in local schools. Children were given tuition on how to rhyme in French and deliver the resulting lyrics in a rap style. As a result of coverage on Channel 4 television's Planet Pop programme, the *Face* magazine and the *Times Educational Supplement*, the London French Music Bureau (housed in the U.K. French Embassy) was besieged with calls from other schools clamouring for rap bands to come to their language lessons. The deconstruction of rap texts in a classroom context in this way is much more acceptable to pupils than traditional grammar exercises, and there is an argument to be made for it also highlighting how language cannot be divorced from culture. After all French hip hop arguably says more about contemporary French society than many outdated textbooks relied on by schools that still propagate images of moustached men in berets or other outmoded stereotypes.

A body of sociolinguistic literature on 'Le Français branché' (cutting edge French) has grown up to explain this. As with the dissemination of any fashion or music of any youth culture, words are discarded by the pioneers once they become widespread. Perhaps only when these new words enter the *Robert* or *Petit Larousse* (standard dictionaries) will we be able to state that le Français branché has found a place at centre of the French language rather than languishing on its margins. To categorize slang in specialised French dictionaries (Andreini 1985; Oblak et al. 1984; Merle 1999; Pierre-Adolophe et al. 1995), rather than acknowledging its place in the contemporary social fabric of France, will only have the effect of isolating it as something crazy and hip for kids. This attitude can also be seen to apply to local authority involvement in rap culture.

Looking at broader trends, the long-held French defensiveness and fear of being appropriated by what is perceived as 'Anglo-Saxon' culture has characterized much governmental cultural policy in recent years. The opt-out over GATT agreements and cinema demonstrates protectionism in action. French rap has at times been an unexpected beneficiary of this policy position, as, for example, in the case of radio quotas. French hip hop then is as much an agent of political mobilisation—seen in its use in antiracist/anti-immigration law campaigning—as it is a contested terrain of culture in the service of social control, with its aesthetics up for grabs to be interpreted by 'tolerant' leftist patronising patronage (Université du Hip Hop) and far right attacks (censorship via demonisation as antisocial urban malaise). Nonetheless, French rap can be used to exercise resistance to both the centralising and integrationalist French nation-state and fears of being engulfed by U.S. culture that often fuel negative associations attached to notions of globalisation with their built in perceptions of the Americanisation of arts and culture.

'Integration à la Française'—assimilationalist practice regarding ethnic communities, mainly of former French Africa, offers another meaning of the term *incorporation*. This is not one-way traffic, however; managing the twenty-first century multicultural settlement is more about dealing with a process of complex cultural flows. It is not only an incorporation of French culture by the formerly colonized that is taking place in twenty-first century France. Aspects of minority culture have become appropriated into mainstream French life, such as the entry of Arab expressions and food into everyday use. Contradictory though many aspects of it are, contemporary French rap is a multifaceted phenomenon. Rap's academicisation in scholarly texts (Bazin 1995; Calio 1998; Lapassade 1996) and market dominance point to it becoming a French institution in itself. This should not be seen as a necessarily negative thing.

CONCLUSION

Youth culture in the twenty-first century is no longer something freakish and marginal. It is ripe for incorporation both by big business and by local and central government initiatives. There are parallels between the case studies in this paper but significant differences too. The French youth work example is resource intensive but without long-term outcomes, whereas the British one has less resources but has an educational attainment because its deliverable objective is in keeping with the government's emphasis on skills. In Britain traditionally the arts have been a loss-making brief. In the new 'knowledge' economy of the twenty-first century, where the cultural and creative industries thrive, the role of youth culture in urban regeneration is also of key importance. Future understandings of youth cultural policy should take the lead of projects such as Cultural Fusion in genuinely fusing initiatives on 'youth' and 'culture'. Importantly, in illustrating the incorporation of what was once an American form of cultural expression by young people in urban settings from Strasbourg to Manchester, the case studies above demonstrate how rap is not just about one-way cultural domination exercised by the United States.

Hip hop is multifaceted in nature, raising questions of urban relations, public arts provision, commercialisation, artistic control and censorship. Even if public policy may not be the most obvious mode of study for rap it is a key prism through which twenty-first century rap operates. Youth cultural creativity should be nurtured in this climate. Public subsidies for more traditionally 'high' cultures arguably fund elitist leisure habits from the public purse. As Heartfield (2005) points out 'if opera and classical music had mass audiences, they would not need public support'. Obviously a balance must be struck between the two. Future studies of hip hop would do well to investigate this further rather than simply replough old furrows of postmodernism, commercial interests or diaspora. To paraphrase Richard Hoggart, the 'uses of rap' are multiple and shifting; it can be seen as rebel music (evidenced in the utterances of hip hop stars at Live8) as much as commercial machine or as educational tool, instrument for language learning, and now, anchor for youth-work projects. Seeing hip hop as simply about sales and positioning young people outside the dominant order is only part of the story.

Perhaps those in academia would do well to throw off the shackles of authenticity in their analyses if it only operates to constrain. It is clear from interview data from the young people in both the case studies discussed here that they themselves are not as strait-jacketed by this as it would appear theorists of youth culture have sometimes been. To draw a binary of commercial/official (incorporated) = bad, subculturally pure (unincorporated) = good creates a false dichotomy. As we have seen, incorporation can take several forms. Its meaning varies from time to time and place to place. Commercial incorporation is assumed to be the same the world over yet political incorporation takes different forms depending on national political cultures and traditions. No doubt as we progress further into the twenty-first century we will see further applications of it unfold, defying prediction and once again leaving academia struggling to keep up in its wake.

NOTES

1. http://www.youthmusic.org.uk/about_us.jsp
2. Longsight was featured on the BBC national news the week of 5 May 2003 on an item about Manchester police's firearms amnesty and local gangs.
3. Dizzee Rascal was winner of the 2003 Mercury Music Prize. The Streets, music project of British rapper-songwriter Mike Skinner won him Best British male at the 2005 Brit Awards.
4. Whilst Culture Secretary, Chris Smith boasted that pop music was earning Britain more than car building. With the collapse of MG Rover in 2005 this position is likely to grow.
5. Although in some of Britain's cities the eighties saw a process of gentrification that contradicted this to some degree, e.g., cultural industry-led regeneration in postindustrial Manchester's Northern Quarter where former warehouses have been converted into domestic dwellings popular with artists
6. The 'papers' referred to is the generic term for state-issued identity cards/Residence cards [carte d'identité/carte de séjour]. The demand 'Vos papiers s'il vous plait' [papers please] is a significant threat reminding all immigrants of the state's power.

7 Resistance and commercialisation in 'distasteful movements'

Right-wing politics and youth culture in East Germany

Wolfgang Deicke

The relationship between youth, culture and politics is one of the most problematic—and, as a consequence, increasingly under-researched—areas of youth research. Traditionally, Johan Fornäs has argued, young people have served as a canvas on which society projects its hopes and fears (1995: 1). If the conservative 'sociology of youth' saw youth-specific patterns of behaviour as a threat to the social fabric, left-wing theorists such as Marcuse directly pinned their hopes for social change on the (predominantly) youthful counter-cultures that emerged in the 1960s (Marcuse 1967). In a model that very much echoed the social preoccupations of 1970s Britain, the Centre for Contemporary Cultural Studies (CCCS) at Birmingham regarded the emergence of youth-cultural groupings as continuations of the class struggle by other means (see Hodkinson, this volume).

If youth was at that time seen as rebellious, more recently, the pendulum appears to have swung the other way. Well-founded concerns over flagging youth participation in representative politics (party membership, voting) are frequently used as an excuse to caricature young people as lazy, self-interested and politically apathetic, the moniker of 'Thatcher's children' serving as the shorthand of this view (see Bennett, this volume). Such generalizations, as Fornäs reminds us, are dangerous oversimplifications: young people are far too diverse in their views, preferences and practices to be treated as a single homogenous entity (1995: 1–2).

Taken seriously, Fornäs's injunctions have some implications for the ways in which youth researchers should think about and approach politics in their work. Firstly, with respect to the tradition of the CCCS, it should be pointed out that young people and youth culture are not—qua 'youth' or 'class'—necessarily emancipatory or 'progressive' in a political sense. If the CCCS's interest in subcultures lay explicitly in their subversive political potential, captured in the notion of 'resistance', they broadly ignored or dismissed 'mainstream' youth cultures because of their commercialized, commodified and thus 'inauthentic' nature. In this reading, 'politics' becomes equated with emancipatory politics, with resistance to capitalist society. Moreover, narrowly defined as 'resistance', politics becomes something that happens chiefly between subcultures and the institutions that represent mainstream, bourgeois society. This is a very limiting interpreta-tion of 'politics'. Young people's political activity, their 'resistance', is not necessarily directed towards 'authority', but can just as well be directed against other social groups.

Secondly, in the CCCS model, the subversive (political) edge of sub-cultural creativity is permanently threatened with 'defusion' and 'incor-poration' through media reporting and the transformation of formerly 'authentic' youth styles into consumer commodities (see Brown, this vol-ume). Commerce and politics, in this perspective, are seen to be mutu-ally exclusive. A number of authors have since highlighted the crucial role subcultural entrepreneurs and markets play in creating and maintaining subcultures and subcultural identities (Hodkinson 2002; McRobbie 1989), arguing that it is only through a degree of media exposure and commercial-isation that subcultures obtain 'critical mass' beyond a very limited locale (Brown 2003b; this volume). Yet crucially, it ought not to be assumed that commercialized styles cannot carry political meanings, or that the groups with which they are associated are somehow politically neutral. Indeed, while the commercially driven 'diffusion' of subcultural styles may threaten the exclusive aspects of their identity, commodified styles may be an ideal vehicle for the diffusion of political symbols and values, allowing young people literally to 'buy into' politics at minimal intellectual cost and effort. In this chapter I am going to use the emergence of a hegemonic right-wing youth culture in large parts of East Germany as a case study to illustrate this point.

RIGHT-WING EXTREMISM IN GERMANY AFTER 1990: NEW DIMENSIONS OF AN OLD PROBLEM

Right-wing extremism in Germany is, of course, not a new phenomenon, but one that can trace its political heritage back to the late nineteenth century and whose present-day politics are still shaped and influenced by the legacy of Nazi rule, the Second World War and the Holocaust (Backer 2000; Childs 1995; Husbands 1991, 1995; McGowan 2002). For most of the post-war period to date, however, developments in Germany followed what Scheuch and Klingemann called the 'normal pathology of Western industrial soci-eties' (Scheuch and Klingemann 1967: 12): right-wing parties would from time to time—in the West German case in the early 1950s, the late 1960s and the late 1980s—be able to attract the support of 5 to 10 per cent of the electorate before internal fragmentation and the response of the mainstream parties would lead to stagnation and eventual decline. This would be fol-lowed by periods of increased militancy by radicalized and frustrated activ-ists convinced that direct action was the quicker path to political success than the ill-fated parliamentary route (Stöss 1991; Wagner 2002).

However, the developments following German unification in 1990 marked a distinct departure from this pattern in four important respects. Firstly, the extent of right-wing activity became significantly greater and more permanent. The official statistics on recorded right-wing offences compiled by the interior secret service, the Verfassungsschutz (VS) offer a first reflection (Table 7.1). These figures are neither accurate nor comprehensive: they do not cover the many legal facets (rallies, marches, concerts) of right-wing activity and include only incidents that were reported, recorded and considered to have a right-wing or racially motivated background by the recording authorities. A look at the casualty figures illustrates the problem: while the official statistics count a total of 44 deaths with suspected/known extreme right background for 1990 to 2004, alternative sources arrive at 116 right-wing murders over the same period (Dokumentation der Opfer Rechter Gewalt 2004). Also missing here is the shocking qualitative context against which some of these incidents occurred: while the large-scale public support for the pogrom-style riots in Hoyerswerda (17–19 September 1991) and Rostock (22–26 August 1992) caused international outrage, less spectacular events—such as those in the village of Dolgenbrodt, where in 1992 five 'respectable' members of the village paid a right-wing sympathizer to set fire to a newly constructed refugee hostel—received far less attention.

The second distinct feature lies in the emergence of new forms of right-wing organisations and, related to this, the geographical distribution of right-wing activity. The Verfassungsschutz's estimates of the overall membership of right-wing organisations (Tables 7.2a & b) clearly indicate a radicalisation of the right-wing camp between 1990 and 2004. The membership of the three main electoral—and thus at least nominally more 'moderate'—far Right parties, the National Democrats (NPD), German People's Union (DVU) and Republikaner (REP) appears highly volatile and in overall decline. At the same time, the openly and avowedly neo-Nazi scene has almost doubled in size—a development somewhat offset by a trend towards increasing organisational fragmentation (from 43 to 87 known organisations). The most striking feature, however, lies in the 'emergence' and growth of what the VS groups under the umbrella term of 'subculture-oriented and other violent right-wing extremists' (marked as 'Violent RWE' in Table 7.2). 'Subculture-oriented' here refers to youth cliques and young individuals affiliated to the skinhead or hooligan scene, which in turn are linked to, but not under the control of the neo-Nazi scene and the electoral far right. The authorities' reference to subcultural, rather than political, affiliation here is significant in two ways. On one hand, it indicates that the political convictions of these subculturalists—qua their youth and greater interest in music and leisure activities than political theory—are not taken entirely seriously; that their extremism, like their subcultural uniforms, is something they will eventually grow out of. On the other hand, it is precisely this 'subcultural' segment of the far right that is deemed to be the driving force behind the rapid growth in right-wing violence since uni-

Table 7.1 Incidents with right-wing/racist background, by nature of offence 1986–89, 1992–2002

Acts of violence	1986	1987	1988	1989	1992	1993	1996	1997	1998	1999	2000	2001	2002	2003	2004
Murder	0	0	0	1	16	23	1	0	0	1	2	0	0	0	0
Attempted murder	N/A	N/A	N/A	N/A	N/A	N/A	12	13	16	13	15	9	8	7	6
Bodily harm	41	38	36	52	758	899	507	677	595	630	874	626	646	637	640
Arson	5	8	12	12	699	311	33	237	39	35	41	16	26	24	37
Bombings					14	3	0	2	3	2	7	1	1	0	2
Breach of the peace/public order	N/A	N/A	N/A	N/A	N/A	93	71	61	55	65	59	34	32	28	25
Others (from 2001)				*(these include: abduction, wrongful imprisonment, robbery, blackmail, obstruction)*								23	59	61	60
Total (violent)	71 *(includes damage to property)*	76 *(includes damage to property)*	73 *(includes damage to property)*	102 *(includes damage to property)*	2,639 *(includes damage to property)*	2,232 *(includes damage to property)*	**624**	**790**	**708**	**746**	**998**	**709**	**772**	**759**	**776**

Other types of offences														
Damage to property	25 (included above)	30 (included above)	25 (included above)	38 (included above)	1.152 (included above)	903 (included above)	157	301	516	373	704	251	178	225	243
Threatening behaviour	134	115	83	102	1.354	1.699	364	371	276	220	320	190	115	93	97
Display or distribution of banned symbols	695	1.055	1.222	1.483	3.125	3.874	5.635	7.888	6.958	6.719	10.435	6.336	7.294	7.551	8.337
Other offences, including incitement	381	201	229	165	566	2.756	3.160	2.369	2.591	1.979	3.494	2.568	2.543	26	20
Total (non-violent)	*1.210*	*1.371*	*1.543*	*1.750*	*5.045*	*8.329*	*8.106*	*10.929*	*10.341*	*9.291*	*14.953*	*9.345*	*10.130*	*10.033*	*11.275*
All types of offence	*1.281*	*1.447*	*1.607*	*1.853*	*7684*	*10.561*	*8.730*	*11.719*	*11.049*	*10.037*	*15.951*	*10.054*	*10.902*	*10.792*	*12.051*

Source: Figures for 1986–89 from David Childs: 'The far right in Germany since 1945', in: Cheles et al. (eds.) (1995), based on VS reports 1987–89; figures for 1992–93 from Chris Husbands: 'Militant Neo-Nazism in Germany' in: Cheles et al. (eds.) (1995); figures for 1996 onwards from Verfassungsschutzberichte 1996–2004

Table 7.2a **Membership in right-wing and neo-Nazi groups 1990–93**

	1990		1991		1992		1993	
	Groups	*Members*	*Groups*	*Members*	*Groups*	*Members*	*Groups*	*Members*
Militant RWEs	N/A	N/A	N/A	4.200	N/A	6.400	N/A	5.400
Neo-Nazis	27	1.400	30	2.100	33	1.400	27	1.500
Other RWE organisations	34	2.900	38	3.950	41	4.000	38	4.100
Total	*61*	*4.300*	*68*	*10.250*	*74*	*11.800*	*65*	*11.000*

Source: Chris Husbands (1995): 'Militant Neo-Nazism in Germany', in Cheles et al. (1995), based on VS-report for 1993;
  Note: unlike Table 7.2b, these figures do *not* include members of 'electoral' parties.

fication (Verfassungsschutz 2005). The continual growth of this segment, in both absolute and relative terms, suggests that 'culture' and 'symbols' have great appeal, and that subcultural affiliation, styles and activities are a highly effective catalyst for extreme political actions.

The third distinctive feature of contemporary right-wing extremism lies in its youth appeal. The age-profile of known right-wing offenders suggests that militant right-wing activists are getting younger. Husbands calculates that the average age of known right-wing offenders dropped from around 27 years in 1985 to 19.5 years by 1993 (Table 7.3; cf. Husbands 1995: 343). Since then, this youth appeal of militant right-wing extremism has also translated into electoral politics. Up until the 1990s, the under-30-year-olds have been under-represented amongst the members and supporters of the electoral far right (Kühnl et al. 1969: 223, 237; also Stöss 2004: 69f). By contrast, the first electoral successes of the DVU and NPD in the East in the late 1990s were largely due to their ability to mobilize first-time and former non-voters: while the DVU gained 12.9 per cent in the state elections of Saxony-Anhalt in 1998, it polled 28 per cent amongst the 18- to 24-year-olds, thus becoming the party with the largest support base in this age group, with the NPD's result in Saxony in 2004 broadly confirming this trend (Infratest-Dimap 1998; Forschungsgruppe Wahlen 2004).

Finally, according to the authorities, a disproportionate share (40+ per cent) of these youthful militant right-wing extremists is based in the East (which only accounts for 20 per cent of the overall German population). While it should be noted that the large majority of violent right-wing offences occur in the West (482 of 776 in 2004), the fact that almost 38 per cent of such incidents occur in the East means that the per-capita rate of such incidents in the more sparsely populated East is still two to three times as high as that in the Western Länder (Verfassungsschutz, 2005: 36).

MISREADING THE PROBLEM: RIGHT-WING EXTREMISM AS A 'YOUTH' PROBLEM?

This 'rejuvenation' of the extreme right has generated some predictable responses. The relative youth of right-wing voters and offenders has

Table 7.2b Membership in right-wing groups and parties 1995–2000

	1995 Groups	1995 Members	1996 Groups	1996 Members	1997 Groups	1997 Members	1998 Groups	1998 Members	1999 Groups	1999 Members
Violent RWEs	3	6.200	5	6.400	3	7.600	5	8.200	5	9.000
Neo-Nazis	43	1.980	48	2.420	40	2.400	41	2.400	49	2.200
Parties	4	35.900	3	33.500	3	34.800	3	39.000	3	37.000
of which NPD		16.000		15.000		15.500		6.000		6.000
of which DVU		15.000		15.000		15.000		18.000		17.000
of which Rep		4.000		3.500		4.300		15.000		14.000
Other RWE organisations	46	2.660	52	3.700	63	4.300	65	4.500	77	4.200
Total	*96*	*46.740*	*108*	*46.020*	*109*	*49.100*	*114*	*54.100*	*134*	*52.400*
After deduction of multiple membership		46.100		45.300		48.400		53.600		51.400

	2000 Groups	2000 Members	2001 Groups	2001 Members	2002 Groups	2002 Members	2003 Groups	2003 Members	2004 Groups	2004 Members
Violent RWEs	2	9.700	1	10.400	1	10.700	2	10.000	2	10.000
Neo-Nazis	60	2.200	65	2.800	72	2.600	95	3.000	87	3.800
Parties	3	36.500	3	33.000	3	28.100	3	24.500	3	23.800
of which NPD		13.000		11.500		9.000		8.000		7.500
of which DVU		17.000		15.000		13.000		11.500		11.000
of which Rep		6.500		6.500		6.100		5.000		5.300
Other RWE organisations	78	4.200	72	4.300	70	4.400	69	4.600	76	4.300
Total	*143*	*52.600*	*141*	*50.500*	*146*	*45.800*	*169*	*42.100*	*168*	*41.900*
After deduction of multiple membership		50.900		49.700		45.000		41.500		40.700

Source: Verfassungsschutzberichte 1996–2005, Bonn/Berlin, Ministerium des Inneren

Table 7.3 **The age profiles of known right-wing offenders (per cent)**

	1977–85	1981–83, 1985	1/1991–4/1992	5/1992–12/1993
Under 15			3.3%	4.9%
15–17	39%	48%	32.9%	26.4%
18–20			39.1%	29.9%
21–24	32%	30%	16.3%	18%
25–29			3.6%	6.9%
30–45		31–40 = 9%	3.4%	8%
46–60	29%	41–50 = 7%	0.7%	3.7%
60+		51+ = 7%	0.6%	2.1%

Sources: 1977–85=Richard Stöss (1991); 1981–83, 1985=Chris Husbands (1991); 1991–93 = Helmut Willems/Stefanie Würtz/Roland Eckert (1994)

prompted observers to dismiss the seriousness of these developments as 'adolescent protest', a phase that will pass by once the youths in question have successful been tied into the stability and commitments of relationships, work, mortgages and parenthood. There has been a tendency amongst some commentators to dismiss or play down the specific and political nature of these developments by subsuming 'right-wing violence' under the much broader problem of 'youth and violence'. Peter Merkl's comments best exemplify this position. He argues that the adoption of Nazi symbols and slogans by young Germans has less to do with ideological commitment than the shock value of such symbols, ideal to shock teachers 'who [are] likely to belong to the New Leftish 1968 generation' (1997: 23). He concludes that 'unlike the politicized interwar period when fascists and Nazis were actually struggling for power, much of the violent right-wing 'happenings' of today are not very political' (1997: 40). Similarly, the social psychologist Ulrich Oevermann observed of his adolescent respondents that some of them could barely articulate a coherent thought, never mind a political position (Oevermann 1998: 90).

Such analyses— apart from being deeply patronising to the youths in question—fail to recognize the significance of these developments in a number of ways. Firstly, they underestimate the political potential and long-term socialising effects of 'style-based' subcultures. While youngsters may grow out of 'spectacular' or 'heroic' violent activism, they may well retain part of their subcultural and political identities in later life (see Bennett in this volume). The increasing youth support for right-wing parties since the late 1990s may be a first indicator of such developments Secondly, these approaches artificially raise the conceptual yardstick for 'ideological coherence' and restrict the notion of the 'true struggle for power' to the ultimate prize—government control at the national level. In doing so, they fail to capture the impact right-wing politics can have at a local and 'street' level. While the electoral far right may still be far from seizing government, the so-called 'subculture-oriented' far right has become the dominant force in many East and some West German towns and villages

(Schröder 1997; Pfahl-Traughber 2002). Thirdly, as we shall see below, interpretations such as Merkl's arguably misjudge the relationship between 'mainstream' and right-wing 'sub/youth culture'. While 'spectacular' and 'shocking' in appearance and behaviour, the core norms and values of the skinhead movement are not a million miles away from what the CCCS called their 'parent' culture (Clarke 1976a). This, to me, appears crucial: while right-wing youth may symbolically protest against the chimera of a culturally dominant and homogenous 'generation of 1968' (read: left-wing 'political correctness') and physically attack every minority that does not fit their template of 'normality', survey results show that they do so with the tacit (if not explicit) approval of substantial parts of the population (Stöss and Niedermayer 1998, 2005).

Having argued earlier that youth cultural studies has lost sight of the 'political', it strikes me here that 'straight' social and political analysis could benefit from giving 'culture' and the socialising potential of collective youth cultural experiences more serious consideration. At the risk of sounding old-fashioned, I would argue that some of the concepts developed by the CCCS and adapted by more recent theorists remain useful tools in understanding how a subculture with musical roots in Jamaican ska and reggae and 1960s working-class Britain could become the primary vehicle for peddling ideas of white racial supremacy in Germany in the 1990s.

STAGE 1: THE ADAPTATION OF 'SKINHEAD CULTURE' IN GERMANY IN THE 1980S

Contrary to the implications of the Verfassungschutz-data (Tables 7.2a & b), the emergence of the 'subculture oriented' militant right does not date back to some point in the early 1990s at which 4.200 right-wing individuals decided to shave their heads, or 4.200 previously apolitical skinheads took a shine to Nazism. Rather, it has to be understood as the result of a drawn out process of subcultural transformation and adaptation stretching from the late 1970s into the early 1990s.

Skinhead culture, as a style- and music-based spectacular subculture, first emerged in 1960s Britain as John Clarke put it, as an attempt to 're-create through the "mob" the traditional working-class community, as a substitution for the real decline of the latter' (1976a: 99). This notion of 'community' was based around heavily romanticized notions of masculinity (violence; honour; territoriality; heterosexual chauvinism; excessive alcohol consumption), class (group solidarity; expressiveness; work hard, party hard attitudes) and patriotism (Hebdige 1982; Knight 1982; Farin and Seidel 2002). Their emphasis on 'class', 'pride' and 'authenticity', however, had little to do with 'class consciousness' and emancipatory class struggle, and even the apparently 'rebellious' elements such as their disrespect for institutional authority or 'bosses' were counterbalanced by an admiration of personal authority (expressed through physical prowess), their celebration of 'work' as the core of their identity and their active dislike for 'politics', the left and the emerging 'counter-' and 'drop-out' culture. Originally an ethnically 'open' style inspired by the stylized cool of black 'rude boys' and musically rooted in ska, rock-steady and reggae, skinhead pastimes included attacks on ethnic and sexual minorities. It was this ambiguity which made the skinhead and related football culture susceptible to wooing by the organized far right—notably the National Front and the British Movement—in the 1970s (Hebdige 1982; Lowles and Silver 2001).

When the arrival of punk breathed new life into British youth subculture, the skinheads, too experienced a revival: while parts of the 'second generation' revived the culture's roots by following ska bands such as the The Specials, Bad Manners and The Selecter, and retaining parts of the smarter aspects of the rude-boy style (Ferguson 1982), others who had found their way into the skinhead culture via punk or football hooliganism began to develop their own cultural form in 'streetpunk'—later packaged as 'Oi!' by the enterprising *Sounds* journalist Garry Bushell—a punk-inspired faster and harder form of rock à la Cocksparrer, Sham 69 and Cockney Rejects that pitched non-political white working-class 'authenticity' against the politicized 'fakeness' of middle-class art-school punks such as The Clash. Their attempts to stay 'above politics' backfired in July 1981 when, following provocations by British Movement supporters earlier in the day, pitched battles broke out between Asian youths and the audience of an Oi! concert in the Hamborough Tavern in Southall, a London borough with a large Asian population and far away from established skinhead stomping grounds (Lowles and Silver 2001: 24). Inevitably, the media blamed the skins. Like all good moral panics, the subsequent demonization of Oi! and the skins as 'the ugly face of racism' (Hebdige 1982: 33) backfired too; it gave the culture mass exposure and created a powerful popular image of the skins as ugly, brutal and violent, with a subcultural subtext of an 'apolitical' subculture being wilfully misunderstood and misrepresented (Hebdige 1982: 30).

In the wider frame of things, it was this image of 'skinhead-culture' (Mark II) that—along with the 'English disease' of football hooliganism—was transported to and, like punk before it, eagerly adopted in West Germany in the early 1980s and behind the Wall in the East a couple of years later. The majority of first-generation German skinheads had started their subcultural career as punks and switched uniform and allegiance in response to the increasing (left-wing) politicisation of punk, alienation by the increasing prevalence of harder drugs or simply in search for a 'harder' image. Here, contrary to Merkl's assumptions, it seems that a degree of conformism rather than the desire to provoke might have played a role in the new choice of image. Stephan Weidner, bass player of Germany's most notorious former skin-band Böhse Onkelz explained his move out of punk in 1987:

With skins it's like this: most of them were punks in their teens, when they were still in school. Then they realized: now we've got to go and earn some money. And you can't just run around like that [punk], it's just not on, so the skin movement came along at just the right time (in: Eberwein and Drexler 2002: 19).

While the version of skin-culture that was shipped to Germany had already largely divested itself of its black roots, the transposition of 'class' into the German context proved equally difficult, since—courtesy of Hitler, Nazism and the post-war welfare consensus—a vocal, conscious and confident working class no longer existed. However, without class consciousness and class struggle, the ritual invocation of 'the ordinary working man' and 'traditional working-class values' in skinhead lyrics and fanzines effectively became the uncritical hyper-affirmation of the petit-bourgeois values and prejudices of the 'parent' culture: work, patriotism, football, beer, violence (against 'outsiders') and sex (heterosexual, of course) (Büsser 2001: 74–77). Another of Eberwein and Drexler's first-generation respondents also hints at the conservative sentiments that underpin the nostalgia for an English sense of 'classness' never experienced:

'Skinhead' is something romantic, a sentimental feeling for something that never existed in Germany: a class-conscious youth-subculture that did not just rebel against the adults [...]In England they had this sense of solidarity with their own class [...], their parents: if I grew up in Brixton, my father was a miner and my grand-dad was a miner, I would be a miner, too (Michelin X, 1987 in Eberwein and Drexler 2002: 110–1).

In the absence of strong traditions of 'class', such longings for solidarity and intergenerational harmony—being a subcultural hero without offending one's parents—had to find another outlet; this might go some way to explain the fascination of young skinheads with that other 'misunderstood tragic hero' of German history, the ordinary German soldier of World War II. Crucially, removed from its original sociohistorical context and already branded 'right-wing' by the media, 'skinhead' as a subcultural form in 1980s Germany had few internal mechanisms to protect it from the eventual take-over by the far Right.

STAGE 2: ORGANISATIONAL CROSSOVER–FROM STYLE-SUBCULTURE TO MOVEMENT-CULTURE

For this incorporation to occur, however, a shift in the traditional far right's attitude towards consumption-based youth cultures had to take place. Up until the 1970s, the far right's youth policy remained firmly oriented towards the past. The youth of the nation (and the survival of the 'master race') was to be saved from the corrosive effects of vodka-cola imperialism, that is: the dangerous anti-authoritarian influences of the left as well as American consumer culture. The best way to achieve this was through rigorous education in 'German' values such as obedience, endurance, and discipline in paramilitary organisations more or less openly modelled on the Hitler Youth. From the late 1970s onwards, neo-Nazis around Michael Kühnen (born 1955, died 1991) sought to emulate the work of groups like the Young National Front and the British Movement undertook with skinheads and football fans in Britain. Initially, the relationship remained fairly instrumental. While Kühnen's dreams of harnessing the destructive energies of skinheads and hooligans by turning them into disciplined 'shock troops' of the movement failed to materialize, by the mid-1980s a considerable amount of cultural cross-over had taken place: neo-Nazis adopted elements of the skinhead look while the skinhead scene became saturated with right-wing symbols and paraphernalia that were not part of the original 'skinhead style'—i.e., military caps, fatigues and Nazi insignia—and the attraction of previously 'mainstream' football fans to the right-wing image of the skinhead-culture tipped the balance (Farin and Seidel 2002: 101). If Kühnen and his peers had been outsiders who had little time for or understanding of the subcultural aspects of skinhead life, the blurring of boundaries between 'skinheads', 'hooligans' and 'politicos' in small neo-Nazi organisations such as the Freiheitliche Arbeiterpartei (FAP) or the Nationalistische Front (NF) meant that the next generation of right-wing activists had a good understanding of and commitment to both subculture and right-wing politics and were able to move and mobilize in both camps as 'authentic' insiders.

The biography of Thorsten Heise (born 1969) provides a useful illustration of this blurring of boundaries. Heise began his political career as a skinhead in Northeim in the early 1980s where he was—together with large swathes of the local skinhead scene—recruited into the FAP by the exile Austrian Karl Polacek (born 1934) in the late 1980s. Feared and respected for his violent temper, Heise rapidly rose through the ranks of the party and used his street credibility in the skinhead scene to combine political with subcultural activity by organising skinhead parties and concerts, the largest of which—despite being banned by the authorities—attracted up to a 1.000 people in 1995. Shortly after being appointed as acting chairman of the FAP in Lower Saxony in 1990, Heise fled to the then still independent GDR to escape charges of attempted murder (for which he later received a suspended two-year sentence). In 1992, he succeeded Polacek as chairman of the FAP in Lower Saxony, a role he held until the party was banned by the authorities in 1995. Since then, Heise has been a key figure in facilitating closer co-operation between the militant skinhead and neo-Nazi scene and the NPD, a role which became formalized with Heise's co-optation into the NPD's party executive in 2004. At the subcultural level, too, Heise remains a key player: in 2000, his mail-order business for music, books and militaria was raided and 26,000 DM worth of banned CDs were confiscated; in 2004, Heise, alongside Jens Pühse, was tipped to be one of the figures behind right-wing plans to distribute 50,000 free CDs with right-wing music and propaganda in school playgrounds in the East; in 2006 he faced trial for illegally importing 3,000 CDs by the outlawed Nazi-band Sturm 18 into Germany (cf. Grumke and Wagner 2002: 262–64; HNA 7 February 2006).

While the FAP was the main catalyst at the street level of politics, the Nationalistische Front (NF) was instrumental in recognising the political and economic potential of subcultural style and music. A small cadre party, whose main aim was to recruit and train (ideologically and physically) youngsters to become the future leaders of the extreme right, the party was one of the first to specifically target the youth market with fanzines and a successful music- and militaria-based mail-order business (Antifaschistisches Autorenkollektiv 1996: 84). By the mid-1990s, a whole generation of right-wing subcultural entrepreneurs was in place, and even the NPD as Germany's oldest far right party incorporated the mail-order business of Jens Pühse (born 1972) in its mainstream publishing and distribution company, making the former skinhead its director (Grumke and Wagner 2002: 296–97).

Beyond such individual crossover between the diffusely right-wing (patriotic, xenophobic, chauvinistic) skinhead subculture and the organized structures of the extreme right, the early 1990s also saw the emergence—again inspired by earlier developments in the United States and Britain—of the first genuinely subculturally dominated right-wing organisations in the Blood & Honour network and the Hammerskins in Germany, marking a further departure from the subculture's roots (cf. Lowles and Silver 2001; Pötsch 2002; Silver 2001). As Farin and Seidel, two never-tiring defenders of 'genuine' skin-culture note:

> The music changed, too: dozens of new bands had emerged since the mid-1980s, but one sounded much like the other and all sounded much like the early *Onkelz*, like *Skrewdriver* or *No Remorse*. But simply much worse. Instead of noisy Oi! dull, hammering marching music in a heavy-metal rock disguise (2002: 107).

Importantly, this shift in musical genre made right-wing music more accessible to larger audiences with more mainstream tastes. The career of the Böhse Onkelz, one of Germany's first right-wing skin-bands illustrates this. Founded as a punk band in 1980, the band soon drifted via Oi! into the right-wing skinhead scene; its first LP 'Der Nette Mann' (1984) for the independent Rock-O-Rama label appeared in a limited edition of 4.000 copies. Apart from the staple diet of football, sex and violence, the album also contained songs like 'Stolz', a song about skinhead 'pride', and

'Deutschland', as the band's web-page has it: 'the first time since the second World War that a German band uses the line 'we're proud to be Germans' (Böhse Onkelz website, accessed June 2006), which became cult hits with the band's skinhead following. The band—by then the poster boys of the far right— gained national notoriety when 'Der Nette Man' was censored by the authorities for its sexist and extremely violent lyrics in 1986. Following financial disputes with Rock-O-Rama and boycotts by music venues due to the riotous nature of Onkelz gigs, the band switched labels and style: subsequently, their heavy-metal-influenced records sold between 15.000 and 30.000 copies with minimal promotional backing. Whilst publicly complaining about being unjustly persecuted by the media, the Onkelz continued to do well out of their controversial image: in 1992, their seventh album sold over 100.000 copies and the Onkelz entered the charts for the first time. Against the background of the events in Hoyerswerda and Rostock and a growing interest in right-wing music, the Onkelz received massive adverse publicity despite expressing lukewarm regrets over their skinhead past. Although cold-shouldered by parts of the music industry, their commercial rewards remained handsome: their eighth album 'Heilige Lieder' (1992) sold 250.000 copies; they were signed by Virgin in 1994 and in 1998 their thirteenth album 'Viva los tioz' entered the charts straight at No. 1, shifting over 300.000 copies within the first 48 hours after its release. In 2004, with approximately three million sold records to their name, the band announced its retirement.

STAGE 3: THE CONQUEST OF THE EAST— RIGHT-WING EXTREMISM GOES MAINSTREAM

The development of style-based youth cultures in East Germany in the 1980s—then still the German Democratic Republic (GDR)—roughly followed that in the West, with the important difference that opportunities for the development of subcultural niche industries (access to practice rooms, venues, printing presses and personal transport, etc.) were severely limited. In the larger cities—especially in East Berlin—contacts with Western skinheads existed, and it was thus largely the German, right-wing adaptation of 'skin-culture' (Mark III) that provided the template for East German developments. While the authorities regarded all subcultures as expressions of Western-influenced negative decadence, they did not differentiate between the left- and right-wing tendencies that became more and more apparent from 1983. Following an attack by around thirty right-wing skinheads on a punk concert in an East Berlin church in October 1987, the existence of neo-fascist tendencies in the self-proclaimed 'anti-fascist' GDR became harder to ignore and deny (Siegler 1991; Waibel 1996). By 1989, the East German authorities estimated the hard core of militant right-wing extremists to number 1000, with a wider potential of sympathizers in the region of 15. 000 individuals (Wagner 2002: 19), with other sources estimating the number of Nazi skinheads in these groups to be around 1.000 to 2.000 (Siegler 1991: 73).

Following the fall of the Wall, the organized militant right from the West was quick to move into the East and to exploit the political vacuum that existed in the months prior to the GDR's incorporation into the Federal Republic of Germany in October 1990. Larger cities in the East saw the emergence of right-wing squats and housing projects (Farin and Seidel 2002: 71–79); the closure of many formerly state-run 'socialist' youth clubs provided right-wing activists with ample opportunities to promote themselves as the advocates of youth interest in many smaller towns and villages; at the level of subcultural activity, the passivity of the East German police, combined with the absence of organized anti-fascist groups make the East an ideal touring ground for right-wing bands from all over Europe and the United States. Western neo-Nazis and subcultural entrepreneurs supplied the organisational know-how, finance, infrastructure and international contacts, their East German comrades provided the muscle, the 'enthusiasm' and the paying customers.

However, in order for the right-wing youth culture to become a mass phenomenon and in parts of the East a hegemonic force, an external stimulus was needed. This came in the form of media reporting about right-wing violence in the early 1990s, with 'skinhead' becoming the lazy journalistic shorthand for 'right-wing violence'. When it did, the far right was ready to cash in: musically, the culture had moved closer to mainstream tastes; a network of increasingly professional subcultural entrepreneurs, labels and mail-order companies was in place, the Internet revolution and online shopping just around the corner. Within the more traditional far right, former subculturalists were beginning to penetrate the hierarchies of the electoral parties. Lastly— since violence has always been a feature in the 'opening up' of new markets to capitalism—a volunteer army of thugs was at the ready to physically conquer the town squares, youth clubs, pubs and bus shelters of East Germany, as Schröder's reportage on the rise of the right in five East German towns graphically illustrates (Schröder 1997).

The growth in the number of right-wing labels and distribution companies in Germany reflects this success: in 1990 there was only one German company, the now defunct and notorious Rock-O-Rama label, that would produce and distribute German and international right-wing bands; a decade later, the market is big enough to sustain between 30 to 60 such enterprises (Dornbusch and Raabe 2004: 71; Verfassungsschutz 2005: 48), augmented by a network of thirty-plus shops owned by or aimed at members of the right-wing scene. Michael Weiss estimates that, between 1991 and 2001, around 100 German right-wing bands produced in the region of 500 CDs, with print runs between a couple of hundred to over 15.000 copies each; assuming an average print run of 3.000, he arrives at a figure of 1.5 million sold copies (2001: 67).

The growth of the market for unashamedly right-wing music has led to tensions and a dual strategy: some market leaders —for example, Thorsten Lemmer's (boru 1970) RockNord commercial fanzine, label and mail-order company—try to ensure that none of their products (lyrics, covers, symbols) contravene German law. This has inevitably attracted accusations of abusing the political loyalties of the scene to get rich. Others, such as Heise and Pühse, continue to deal with illegal and indicted materials, often using their political contacts for clandestine 'under-the-counter' distribution (Pötsch 2002: 119). Much of this 'debate' must be seen as the political posturing of commercial rivals: from a critical outsider's perspective, what matters more than the sellers' motives is the fact that they are peddling right-wing music. Overall, the increasing dominance of politically inspired entrepreneurs, including Lemmer, over the production and distribution process is reflected in the bands that make it into the online catalogues of RockNord, Nord Versand, the Schwarze Sonne Versand or the End[z]eit Versand. Ostensibly non-political 'fun' or Oi! bands, once a mainstay of the skinhead subculture, are now few and far between, whereas neo-Nazi balladeers, hardrock, hatecore, dark wave and black metal bands abound (cf. Büsser 2001; Speit 2002).

Whilst musical and stylistic boundaries are thus becoming increasingly blurred in the right-wing scene, the political line most definitely is not. Thanks to the obvious imagery and reliance on lyrics, it does not require musicological training to 'decode' the ideology transported by these bands: legal offerings usually glorify the deeds of the Wehrmacht, bemoan the effects of immigration and multiculturalism, and praise 'German' or 'Nordic' virtues in men and women. Indicted products, usually produced overseas, are openly anti-Semitic and prone to incite violence against the far right's political or racial enemies. The banned CD 'Der ewige Jude' ('the eternal Jew') by the band Volkszorn, for example, includes a title called 'Brennende Kohle' ('Burning coals'), a reference to burning black people to death (Verfassungsschutz 2005: 47). For intellectually minded customers, most of the distributors offer a range of books on the same topics: biographies of Wehrmacht and Nazi heroes, revisionist histories of the Second World War ('Dresden', 'Vertreibung') alongside band biographies, books on 'race' and German/Nordic mythology.

Further evidence for the entrepreneurial skills and increasing adaptability of the far right can be seen in the development of its own code of 'ethical', or rather: 'racially conscious', shopping. Whereas right-wing mail-order companies would previously sell brands of clothing traditionally associated with the skinhead (Lonsdale, Fred Perry, Ben Sherman) and hooligan (Pit Bull, Troublemaker) scenes, since the late 1990s they have been promoting authentically 'nationalist' designer brands such as 'CoNSDAPle', 'Thor Steinar' or 'Masterrace'. Rather than give money to companies that promote multiculturalism, sponsor antiracist events or employ 'foreign' workers, the logic goes, the true nationalist should shop consciously and look after his own. The products of these brands are partly aimed at the traditional subcultural market (Harrington-style jackets, polo shirts and hooded tops adorned with none too subtle imagery), but in part clearly designed with broader fashion-conscious consumer groups in mind; here, as in their musical offerings, the far right clearly seeks to cash in on the increasing 'hybridity' of youth and consumer culture (Dornbusch and Speit 2004).

CONCLUSION: RIGHT-WING EXTREMISM AS COMMODIFIED LIFE-STYLE POLITICS?

It would be giving the far right too much credit to assume that these developments are the result of a long-term game plan to develop 'National befreite Zonen' ('nationalist-controlled liberated areas'), as proposed by the numerically insignificant NPD's student organisation in 1991. Rather, as I have sought to demonstrate above, they are the outcome of complex interactions and adaptations between subcultures (skinheads and hooligans), the far right (neo-Nazi groups and electoral parties), the media and the mainstream. Whether intended or not, there can be little doubt that the far right has successfully transformed the youth-cultural landscape in post-unification Germany: whilst technically still denying the existence of such no-go areas, the Verfassungsschutz's chief analyst for right-wing extremism, Armin Pfahl-Traughber, concedes that the extreme right scene now dominates the cultural everyday life in many East German communities (Pfahl-Traughber 2002: 35–36).

It is important to understand that the growth and maintenance of the emergent right-wing youth culture by now follows its own, self-perpetuating dynamic. Young people buy into right-wing culture and symbolism to varying degrees and for any number of reasons: some to demonstrate their already formed political views, others to be 'cool' or gain access to a particular peer group, others simply to conform in order to be left alone. Alongside political stickers and graffiti used to mark territory, openly displayed styles and musical tastes demarcate the boundaries between 'insiders' and 'outsider' and draw the lines along which youth culture polices itself. Subcultural purists like Farin and Seidel will, of course, complain that the right-wing youth culture in Germany circa 2005 have little to do with the English original circa 1969; indeed, as Dornbusch and Speit observe:

> ...in some communities, the classical Nazi-skinhead has all but disappeared from the scene. New brands of clothing and style arrived. But despite the superficial variety [in styles], the new signs and brands also create clarity, if in a more subtle way (2004: 135).

Such invocations of 'authenticity', however, miss the point that it is not academics and subcultural theorists who define what goes and what doesn't, but the media, and ultimately the youths themselves in their roles as consumers and participants (Willis et al. 1990). If there is a lesson to be drawn for other subcultures, it is perhaps that 'politics' is ignored at a price and the attempt to stay 'above politics' in highly politicized climes is bound to fail. Instead of putting up a conservative defence of bogus 'authenticity', researchers with subcultural sympathies might be better advised to look for and critically engage with the less savoury aspects of their subcultures. From a cultural point of view, the commodification of subcultural styles may strain the exclusivity of their identities; the diffusion and hybridisation of styles, however, does not necessarily involve their political defusion. In fact, for those with actual political interests, diffusion must be a necessary step towards gaining cultural hegemony. While the die-hard Nazi-skin of old may grumble about the lack of stylistic courage and commitment amongst 'mainstream' right-wing youths, Heise and his Nazi colleagues are laughing all the way to the bank. Not only does their Kulturkampf by subcultural means pay off financially, but their ideology has penetrated deep into the music collections of 'mainstream' German youth culture.

8   Gender, status and subcultural capital in the goth scene

Dunja Brill

Given that subcultures have often been regarded as a vehicle through which young people resist dominant norms and structures, one might expect that such groups would have raised significant challenges to the boundaries of gender. However, there exists a long-standing connection between subcultures and dominant ideologies of masculinity. Girls have traditionally occupied a marginal position in the terrain of youth culture and academic studies about it. McRobbie (1980) deplores an exclusion of female presence from subcultures on two levels; firstly, the male domination of subcultures and their leisure spaces, and secondly, the masculinist bias of early subcultural studies. The second factor, she argues, is rooted in academic sociology and its tradition of researching male-defined issues centring on public spaces and delinquency, which led to an exclusion of girls from youth cultural theory. The first presents itself as a typical feature of the classic postwar subcultures (e.g. rockers, mods, skins), which McRobbie dismisses as offering no attractions to girls.

The male domination of the subcultural terrain can still be felt to the present day, as authors like Macdonald (2001) and Leblanc (1999, 2002) have shown in their feminist analyses of graffiti and punk, respectively. In the course of the 1990s, however, incisive developments took place on the youth cultural front. There emerged new, more gender-balanced subcultures like goth (see Hodkinson 2002) and rave (see Pini 2001), which— despite their focus on public spaces like clubs or music festivals— attract a strong female following. One crucial question subcultural studies have to tackle now is to what extent such gender-balanced subcultures actually advance progressive renegotiations of the traditional gender binary.

This chapter approaches the question by analysing the style practices of the goth subculture through the lens of gender. It focuses on *male androgyny* and *female hyperfemininity* in the self-representation practices of goths, and especially on their relative value in terms of subcultural capital. Drawing on field data gathered in Internet forums and ethnographic interviews, it demonstrates that despite the 'ideology of genderlessness' pervading goth, the (sub)cultural values attached to the typical dress styles of male and female goths differ markedly and privilege maleness.

THE NOTION OF SUBCULTURAL CAPITAL

An interpretation of subcultural practices solely in terms of 'resistance' toward hegemonic powers ignores what Sarah Thornton (1995: 163) calls the "microstructures of power" at play within all forms of social groups. Thornton sees contemporary culture as a 'multi-dimensional social space' structured by intricate patterns of inclusion and exclusion. With reference to Bourdieu's (1984) notion of 'cultural capital', she introduces the concept of subcultural capital, a mark of distinction which can be objectified (e.g., in 'hip' clothes and well-assembled record collections) or embodied (e.g., in subcultural knowledge and 'cool' demeanour) and 'confers status on its owner in the eyes of the relevant beholder' (Thornton 1995: 11). A closely related concept is that of subcultural ideology, a particular way of envisioning social worlds, discriminating between social groups and measuring cultural worth. Behind the overt rhetoric of egalitarianism and inclusiveness which typically accompany subcultural ideologies, Thornton maintains, lurks a thinly veiled elitism which serves to reaffirm binary oppositions between 'alternative' and 'straight', 'radical' and 'conformist', and most importantly between 'mainstream' and 'subculture'.

The notion of subcultural capital presents a useful means of conceptualising the division of youth culture into different sets of values, ideologies, and ways of achieving status. Hence it is well suited to examine the hidden hierarchies of cultural worth stratifying youth culture and its various subcultural niches. Crucially, subcultural capital as a resource of 'power brokering' within youth culture is 'a currency which correlates with and legitimizes unequal statuses' (104), the axes of social difference along which it is most systematically aligned being age and gender. Subcultural capital is fraught with a strong masculine bias, and the gendered stratification of subcultures often all but mirrors the marginal status of femininity in dominant hierarchies of cultural worth. This bias is expressed most clearly in a femininisation of the denigrated 'mainstream' of pop culture against which subcultures define themselves. Thornton cites the derogatory label 'handbag house', coined by hardcore clubbers in the early 1990s to distance themselves from melodious techno music perceived as 'sell-out', as an example.

If (postmodern) culture is defined as a multi-dimensional social space rather than a monolithic system of hegemony, and it is further assumed that the idea of any collectivity—including subcultures—is grounded in discourse, which 'by definition has the effect of excluding, annihilating and delegitimizing certain views and positions, while including others' (van Zoonen 1994: 40), this points to the necessity of critically analysing even seemingly counterhegemonic cultural practices. In addition to tracing the relation of subcultural practices to hegemonic cultural norms, it is crucial to analyse the interior logic of such practices within their subcultural context. The following case study of gendered subcultural capital in goth presents just such an analysis.

GOTH AND THE IDEOLOGY OF GENDERLESSNESS

The goth subculture emerged in Britain in the early 1980s, in the wake of a musical genre originally labelled post-punk (Gunn 1999). The presentation of this music—whose protagonists included bands like Bauhaus and Siouxie and the Banshees—involved elements of theatrical performance, most notably black eye make-up on pale grounding, black clothes with conspicuous cuts and fabrics, elaborate big hairdos, and melodramatic gestures. Adopted and further developed by the fans of the genre, these performative features came to constitute the mainstays of goth style.

In contrast to more traditional, overtly masculinist subcultures, goth and existing academic studies about it (e.g., Hodkinson 2002; Gunn in press; Williamson 2001) tend to highlight femininity rather than masculinity. Feminine styling is very prominent in this subculture, as make-up, jewellery, long hair and traditionally female modes of attire like skirts and tight fishnet tops have long been staples of goth style for males and females. More recently, aspects of the fetish scene like PVC and rubber clothes have also been embraced by goths of both genders. Hodkinson and Gunn stress the strong theme of androgyny—more precisely, the veneration of a particular, dark and mystical version of femininity for both sexes—running through the subculture. Goths themselves frequently portray their scene as a space where a 'genderless' aesthetic is realized as in the following example:

> The aesthetic of gothicism isn't really affected by gender. (Lady Lazarus, www.slashgoth.org, 28/02/02)

The rhetoric of the goth scene in relation to gendered style is based on an ideology of genderlessness, which members of the scene commonly refer to as androgyny. This ideology emphasizes the values of equality and self-expression. Its attendant rhetoric is also used to mark out the subculture against what its members perceive as the ignorant mainstream. The following statement illustrates this mechanism by juxtaposing the goth scene as a tolerant, enlightened space for unbridled gender-experimentation and self-expression against an 'ignorant' and intolerant mainstream of 'townies':

> Androgyny is commonplace and IMHO [in my humble opinion] is to be encouraged. The goth scene is one place where everyone can be themselves without ridicule—THAT is left for the ignorant townies. (Taoist, slashgoth.org, 11/11/02)

Both male and female goths frequently stress that gender is not very important, or even completely irrelevant, for their assessment of and relationships with other people, especially with other goths. This rhetoric of genderlessness is not unique to goth, but can also be found in other subcultures[1] and even in some sections of so-called mainstream culture. However, the goth scene differs in two important respects from most other sections of society entertaining this fantasy. Firstly, in goth the ideology of genderlessness is not only expressed verbally as a form of rhetoric, but also directly translated into subcultural style codes. Secondly and connectedly, goth style and the rhetoric surrounding it do not really promote a 'genderless' aesthetic, where masculine and feminine elements are toned down to such an extent that they practically merge—as in the early Rave movement with its stress on comfortable, loose-fitting clothes (Pini 1997b)—but rather a strongly feminized one for both sexes.

MALE ANDROGYNY AND FEMALE HYPERFEMININITY

Although goths typically argue that being prescriptive with regard to style and appearance would run counter to the ideal of free self-expression at the heart of the subculture's ideology, the personal preferences individual goths state regarding male and female style are striking for their conformity, in that they almost univocally mention long hair, make-up, a feminine dress

Figure 8.1 'Femininity' in goth style (photograph S.L. Hodkinson).

style and fine facial features as desirable on both men and women. The ideal of androgyny is frequently invoked in such statements:

> I like androgynous males 'cause I like the imagery. And so any male who has put on make-up, who wears a corset and stockings, but without trying to hide that they're male—we're not talking about being a transvestite for that's something totally different—is a lovely image to see. (...) In terms of females I have to confess just like the vast majority of other males, seeing a pretty female in tight clothing, curvacious, hugging her body as she dances is celebratory, it's wonderful, yes. (Veeg, m, 40, Edinburgh)

> I suppose I like feminine men. I don't like them being all like big tough blokes and all man and 'I'm male', I just like it a bit more androgynous, that's it. (...) I like women to be more feminine, basically that's what I like. Because some women are just dressing in trousers and like in... it just doesn't look nice. (Nin, f, 27, Brighton)

As these quotes indicate, however, the idealization of androgyny in style and general appearance is strictly reserved to goth men. Male androgyny as an ideal is valued highly in the goth scene; by contrast, its ideal female style amounts to an excessively feminine look, a hyperfemininity diametrically opposed to female androgyny. Consequently, what the rhetoric of the goth scene calls 'androgyny' can more precisely be described as a cult of femininity for both sexes. Furthermore, the implications of this cult of femininity in goth style are very different for male and female goths. If sported by a man, such an effeminate look is in direct opposition to traditionally gendered stereotypes of style and appearance. Sported by a woman, however, such a look assumes different connotations, as it is far more commensurable with the common cultural norms of femininity.

As goth style for both sexes idealizes femininity, gender-bending as a source of subcultural capital and veneration works only for male goths. This is particularly significant as the ideal of hyperfemininity the subculture espouses for women means that female androgyny is strongly discouraged. As Nin's above statement already indicates, goths generally agree that a lack of feminine styling—or worse even, a conscious adoption of an androgynous look—on the part of women is highly undesirable:

> S: I think androgynous is good, it's a good look for guys. I think it's a look that I prefer on guys than girls.
> Me: Really, why?
> S: Because I like girls to look as feminine as possible. I like them, you know, to look like strong personalities who are, you know, really expressing themselves, but also very feminine, and obviously if they look sexy then that's a good thing. Whereas if a girl looks androgy-

nous—which is kind of by definition sexually ambiguous—then it's not as attractive as a girl who looks really feminine, do you see what I mean? Whereas for a guy to look androgynous is a good thing because, I mean, you're accepting a lot of aspects of how to look that are usually sort of taboo for a man, 'cause you're not going for the sort of short hair, no make-up macho sort of thing, and I think you can look more beautiful and more refined and also more artistic, more like a sort of work of art, more expressive. And also you're kind of neutralising certain preconceptions that people usually have about what it is to be a man in normal Western modern society.

(Synara, m, 33, Brighton)

Synara's statement performs a variety of rhetorical functions by drawing on different and sometimes competing discourses. Firstly, he stresses that while he likes women to look 'very feminine' and 'sexy', they also should be 'strong' and 'really expressing themselves'—an obvious reference to the ideal of free self-expression which forms an important part of goth ideology. But most importantly, his statement juxtaposes a purely aesthetic judgement of female androgynous style against an assessment of male androgynous style which is mainly based on its perceived social and cultural functions. Female androgyny is simply regarded as unattractive, but male androgyny is accorded a certain sociopolitical relevance; namely, the potential to neutralize common preconceptions about masculinity and disrupt social norms.

The status of androgyny as a predominantly male privilege can be traced back to the very origins of the term in Greek mythology. Writing about the roots of the beauty ideal of androgyny in ancient Greek statues of double-sexed beings, Weil (1992: 3) points out that in these statues, 'the feminine element served only to soften and complement the masculine, not to challenge its privilege of representing Man'. O'Flaherty (1980: 331), discussing the figure of the *androgyne*—a creature combining male and female physical attributes—in the myths of various cultures, also points to 'the non-equality, the primary maleness, of the androgyne'. Although androgynes are popularly supposed to stand for equality and balance between the sexes, male androgynes by far outnumber female ones and are usually regarded as positive, while female androgynes tend to have negative connotations.

Masculinist overtones in the construction of androgyny also run through various subcultures preceding or coexisting with goth.[2] Regarding the alleged valorisation of a 'feminine principle' in the hippie movement of the 1960s, for example, Weil (1992) argues that the expansion of gender boundaries practised by male hippies was counterbalanced by the fact that it kept women strictly tied to their conventional identification with nature and sensuality. Weil (1992: 1) sees the same mechanism operating in contemporary popular culture with its trend towards androgyny in pop music, film and other media representations; androgyny here largely consists in 'a relaxing of gender stereotypes for men, allowing them to stretch the boundaries of masculinity by appropriating the best of "woman"', without offering any significantly new role models or aesthetic codes for women.

From this perspective, gendered goth style codes could simply be regarded as one specific incarnation of a pervasive, historically grounded tradition of a feminine/effeminate but still strictly masculinist ideal of androgyny. However, this interpretation is complicated by the fact that fashion historians generally agree that in our current cultural climate, androgyny in ordinary people's dress mainly consists in the one-sided appropriation of traditionally male clothing by women. Steele (1989) cites the so-called 'unisex' look (e.g., suits for work, jeans and t-shirts for leisure) adopted by many women from the 1980s onwards as a prominent example of an exclusively female androgynous style, and Paoletti and Kidwell (1989: 158) conclude that "the closest we have ever come to androgyny is for women to dress like men". Consequently, goths rightly argue that their version of androgyny presents a challenge to the everyday styles commonly worn by men and women. In the goth scene, men are enabled to share in the freedom of choice in dress which women are already enjoying to a much larger extent in our society, so the argument goes.

The conundrum is that on the one hand, goth style codes can be seen as perpetuating a masculinist ideal of androgyny, while on the other hand presenting a challenge to the ordinary dress codes predominating in current 'mainstream' culture. This apparent contradiction can be solved, however, if the competing conceptions of androgyny underlying it are examined more closely. In modern Western societies, the female version of androgyny Steele (1989) and Paoletti and Kidwell (1989) refer to is firmly rooted in the everyday practices of ordinary people, and hence of a casual, inconspicuous character. By contrast, the masculinist ideal of androgyny Weil (1992) and O'Flaherty (1980) describe in relation to ancient myths, and also to the 'modern myths' of our culture (i.e., pop music, film and other media representations), is an ideal far removed from the mundane sphere of the everyday. The androgyny of mythical creatures—and this rule just as well applies to pop stars and other media figures whose image partly relies on a self-styled 'mystery'—crucially depends on a transcendence or transgression of the common and mundane for its effect. The notion of transgressing common social norms and style codes is one of the core ideals of a conspicuous subculture like goth, and hence closely linked to the attainment of subcultural capital for its members.

FEMALE ATTRACTIVENESS VERSUS MALE REBELLION

I have already pointed out that while the socio-political relevance of male androgyny is generally acknowledged and valued by goths, female goth style is judged primarily on aesthetic grounds. Bearing in mind the ideal of hyperfemininity the subculture espouses for women, this means that female style tends to be assessed according to fairly traditional criteria of feminine attractiveness and sexiness—even if with a dark edge—by goths of both genders. Contrary to what the subcultural ideology of genderlessness would have us believe, goth style and its valuation by members of the subculture are based on a gender-specific dichotomy of *female attractiveness* versus *male rebellion against social norms*. Certainly this dichotomy is not mutually exclusive, as aesthetic criteria also play a significant role in the evaluation of goth men's style. However, their style is not viewed primarily through the lens of beauty and attractiveness, and especially they themselves often interpret their style-related practices in quite different terms, as the following statements by male goths regarding their motivations for wearing make-up show:

> (...) I'll put on some eyeliner and whatnot if the spirit moves me. I do think it can be attractive, regardless of gender, if done correctly. Part of me likes to spit in the face of social norms by wearing it. (Seth Warren, slashgoth.org, 01/08/02)

> For me, it's as much about repelling trendies—no I don't want to discuss what happened on pop idol, East Enders or blind date, so f@ck off!! (morbidbloke, slashgoth.org, 06/08/02)

In the first quote, the ideology of genderlessness is invoked by stressing that make-up can be attractive 'regardless of gender'. Yet the statement following this rhetorical affirmation of that ideology shifts the focus from issues of attractiveness to the arena of social norms, and draws heavily on the above-mentioned tradition of transgressive male androgyny. According to Seth, make-up cannot only look good on a man, but more importantly can be employed to signal rebellion against and transgression of common social norms. The strong language used in the second quote ('f@ck off'), and the fact that morbidbloke sees make-up as a tactic for 'repelling' rather than attracting people—at least those 'trendies' outside the subcultural sphere—furthermore suggests that for male goths, putting on make-up can be quite a defiant act. In the eyes of many goth men, their make-up signals the style-based transgressiveness and rebellion typical of conspicuous subcultures rather than any form of conventional attractiveness. In the case of females, by contrast, far more conventional motivations for and attitudes towards wearing make-up predominate, as the following fairly typical statements by female goths indicate:

> (...) although i tend to wear make-up a lot of the time, i usually only do coz im an ugly cow, and it makes me look better! (DarkFaerie, slashgoth.org, 04/08/02)

My younger cousin is more of a traditional goth, but I'm afraid to ask her for help [with make-up]. We've always been kind of competitive and I don't want her to hold it over me. At the same time I don't want to run into her at clubs with a flaky face and boring eye make-up. (The Empress of Nothin', slashgoth.org, 19/08/02)

For goth women, make-up does not primarily work as a signifier of subcultural transgression, despite it being a specific subcultural style of make-up whose use of strong dark lines and effects suggests a certain excess and hence transgression of conventional codes of female appearance akin to a 'feminine masquerade' (Doane 1982). It rather tends to be employed in a traditionally feminine vain, namely as a way of enhancing the woman's attractiveness. While male goths can partly escape the pressures and limitations of traditional masculinity through their style practices, female goths seem to remain tied to fairly conventional norms of feminine beauty and attractiveness in their style-related practices and self-perceptions. Make-up is a requisite matter of course in female goth style creation, not a luxury one employs for special effect as in the case of goth men. Consequently, being caught out with 'boring' or badly done make-up can be humiliating, and—as is the case for women in general in our beauty-fixated society—can entail loss of status.

HYPERFEMININITY: SEXINESS AND SELLABILITY

The double standards for judging male versus female style described above seem mainly based on the perceived closeness of female goth style to conventional femininity. Despite their dark edge, subcultural beauty norms for girls (e.g., dresses or skirts, make-up, long hair, sexy outfits) are highly commensurable with current cultural ideals of youthful feminine beauty. In particular, the increasing trend towards fetish wear and extremely revealing clothes among goth women—which has relegated the traditional style of flowing gowns and velvet dresses to a marginal place in female goth fashion over the last decade—parallels a larger trend towards an increased sexualisation in young women's fashion. The following discussion by a couple I interviewed indicates that goths themselves are very aware of this close relation between goth and 'mainstream' norms of female style, and obviously struggle to negotiate the sometimes rather subtle differences between the two sets of norms.

MN: In women I like a good cleavage I have to say—when it's there, when it's exposed that's quite nice; short skirts and tights, sort of a bit slutty, I like that.

> V: I mean, most of it... I mean, it has to be explained, that's what
> most females would wear at traditional straight dance clubs. In goth
> clubs it tends to be darker, with a certain edge or darkness to it.
> MN: Well, short black skirt and fishnet tights.
> V: Yes. And a certain distant attitude.
>   (Mistress Naté, f, 24, Edinburgh/Veeg, m, 40, Edinburgh)

The relative compatibility of subcultural beauty norms for girls with common cultural ideals of femininity is also reflected in the gender-specific reactions goths report getting from other people. As the hyperfeminine style of
female goths is commonly regarded as attractive even by outsiders, they are
perceived as less prone to getting abuse than male goths. Goth men's effeminate style often makes them a target for homophobically tainted abuse.
Both males and females in the subculture generally agree that goth men
take a considerably higher risk of harassment and social censure with their
style, while goth women have it a lot easier because they are still regarded
as sexy and pretty in the conventional sense:

> Anyone noticed that if you're a girl-goth the population goes "phwoar",
> yet if you're a bloke they go "poof/queer/batty boy"? (ChromeNewt,
> slashgoth.org, 29/10/02)

> B: I think it's worse for men, to get away with it; women tend to be
> left alone a little bit more. But if you're a guy I think it's harder because,
> well, I don't know, if you're female I suppose you're prettier, whereas as
> a guy you're gonna have a lot more abuse I suppose.
> Me: What kind of stuff do they get?
> B: 'Freak, get your hair cut', 'you transvestite, don't wear make-up',
> yeah, stuff like that. (Batty, f, 30, Brighton)

Some of my interviewees also mentioned cases which show that in certain situations, female goths are explicitly singled out for abuse by men
from outside the subculture. Yet closer analysis reveals that such instances
of abuse or harassment directed at goth women differ in some significant
respects from the type of negative remarks goth men are typically faced
with. Firstly, female goths tend to be hassled by outsiders not because their
appearance is in discord with the gendered style norms of our culture—as
is the case with male goths—but precisely because their hyperfemininity
makes them sexually attractive to ordinary males. Secondly, this has direct
implications for the kind of abuse or harassment goth women get, which
is often of an explicitly sexual nature. Explicit sexual harassment seems a
specifically female-directed form of abuse levelled at goths, whereas goth
men are typically confronted with quasi-homophobic abuse.
   While both forms of abuse can be disturbing to the individual, on the
collective level the subculture regards the risks and the abuse male goths

have to take for their effeminate style as higher and heavier than the risk of sexually tainted harassment female goths have to deal with. Certainly there is some truth to the argument that males generally face heavier social restrictions regarding flamboyant style. Yet I would argue that goth men are perceived as risking more trouble partly because women are still tacitly expected to be used to sexual harassment. For a straight man, the adoption of effeminacy with its consequent risk of homophobic abuse can be seen as a deliberate—and hence courageous—step toward the marginalized position women and gay men occupy in our society. For a woman, by contrast, at least the milder forms of sexual harassment are a fairly normal experience; they simply come with the territory of the inferior social position women have been assigned in our culture.[3]

To summarize, the highly feminine ideal of beauty goth girls aspire to is commonly held to be sexually attractive in conventional terms despite its dark and theatrical slant; not only by ordinary people, but significantly also by goths themselves. Of course this has certain implications for the perceived co-optability of male versus female goth style by 'mainstream' media and fashion. Female goth style is seen as relatively easy to commercialize, mainly because of its hyperfemininity and sexiness. By contrast, male goth style—because of its very effeminacy—is seen as too much in discord with common heterosexual masculine norms to be co-optable. In terms of subcultural authenticity and status, androgynous male goth style is hence accorded a much higher value in the subculture, whereas the hyperfeminine style of goth women seems almost too close for comfort to the dreaded spectre of the commercial and inauthentic 'mainstream'. For instance, in 2002 *The Sun* printed a fashionable 'goth' style guide geared to conventional women, which was hotly discussed and much deplored in goth Internet forums. The following comment from a thread about that style guide illustrates the postulated gender difference regarding potential co-optation with which goths view their subcultural style:

> (...) the reason that goth will never be fashionable is because you're not going to get your average trendy putting on the make-up before going out (or dressing extravagantly). So only women will be 'dressing goth', which is only half of the sub-culture (...). It's just a femme fatale diversion for mainstream culture, and will be forgotten by next year (or until next time they try to push it into the mainstream) (sheridan, slashgoth.org, 04/10/02)

MALE ANDROGYNY: COURAGE AND TRANSGRESSION

While female goth style is perceived as fairly close to—even if still significantly different from—the 'mainstream' with its negative connotations of inauthenticity and sell-out, androgynous male goth style is regarded as the crucial purveyor of subcultural authenticity and transgressive potential. Goths of both genders frequently link male androgyny with qualities like transgressiveness and courage:

> i must agree with most of the ladies here—men in skirts are tres gothic and super sexy!!! (...) i think they are so sexy and wonderous because other than inherent loveliness in skirts, i appreciate any man who is confident and cool enough to wear a traditionally female article of clothing. The same goes for make-up—endearing, adorable and highly encouraged! (scarlett severine, slashgoth.org, 15/11/02)

> The media seem to have deftly skipped over the issue of male gothic fashion for some reason. I think they just don't get it, or maybe they think that your average girl is more likely to go goth than your average guy. Male goth fashion is, after all, something that takes more "bollocks" to wear than female goth fashion, IMHO. Probably because of its sexuality-challenging androgyny (Taoist, slashgoth.org, 03/10/02).

Male androgynous style is regarded as requiring courage and displaying the confidence of its wearer. The second quote furthermore illustrates the paradoxical nature of the subcultural rhetoric concerning gender norms. On the one hand, the androgynous style of goth men is seen as a challenge to the traditional gender norms of general society; Taoist speaks of its 'sexuality-challenging androgyny'. Yet from the perspective of subcultural norms, androgynous male style here functions as an affirmation of a traditionally masculine status criterion, namely courage. The fact that Taoist uses the word *bollocks* in this context, a word with a highly masculinist charge, is particularly telling.

The qualities attributed to male androgyny—transgression, posing a challenge to common social norms, displaying courage and confidence vis-à-vis outsiders—score highly on the subcultural scale of values, and hence are important sources of subcultural capital. The thought that androgynous male style functions as a major status criterion in goth may at first seem odd, considering the dominant academic opinion on the relationship between cross-sex dress and social status. Theorists of culture and fashion (e.g., Lurie 1992; Paoletti and Kidwell 1989) overwhelmingly agree that because masculinity is valued more highly in our culture than femininity, a feminization of the male generally implies loss of status. Elements of male attire on a woman are socially acceptable as long as she remains identifiably feminine, and (like the female version of the business suit) can sometimes even 'confer touches of masculine status' (Woodhouse 1989: 14). By contrast, apart from closely demarcated areas of socially sanctioned play like the drag act or the fancy-dress party, 'men cannot appear in *any* item of women's clothing without immediate loss of the superior status attached to the male and the full imposition of ridicule and censure' (6).

Paradoxically, in the goth subculture exactly the opposite is true. While female androgyny is discouraged and the adoption of masculine style by a woman would incur a loss of social status within the scene rather than a gain, the adoption of feminine style by men is encouraged and forms an important source of status and subcultural capital. To make sense of this apparent paradox, we have to remember that goth men draw on a well-established tradition of transgressive male androgyny. In this tradition harking back to ancient myths, the transgressive or transcendent powers of androgyny are strictly reserved to the male. In the subcultural sphere, this tradition can be deployed to turn an apparent 'wilful appropriation of subordinate status' (Amico 2001: 373), that is feminine status, by the androgynous male into a form of courageous masculine defiance. The following exchange between a particularly effeminate goth man who has experienced harassment because of his style and a goth woman illuminates this mechanism:

> (...) I've had my fair share of sexist abuse, harassment & "are you looking for business" type comments. But none of that has put me off and I'll continue to cause gender confusion for as long as I feel happy to do it. (Nikki, slashgoth.org, 15/11/02)

> YAY! That's the spirit Nikki! Keep giving us goth girls something to admire :)—and be jealous of :P (Princess Thais, slashgoth.org, 18/11/02)

As I have argued before, the way androgynous male goths open themselves up to quasi-sexist and homophobic abuse through their style can be seen as a deliberate appropriation of the marginalised position assigned to women and gay men in our culture. This deliberate act of self-marginalisation vis-à-vis general society is regarded as courageous and admirable within the subculture. For goth women, by contrast, the marginal position of femininity with its attendant risk of sexual harassment appears natural and hence is not rewarded with special admiration, despite their particular style of femininity as an excess of conventional codes (see Doane 1982) being accorded a certain subcultural value and transgressive potential among goths. While the smiley symbols punctuating Princess Thais's statement indicate a tongue-in-cheek tone, the suggestion that goth girls have reason to envy the perceived transgressive potential of male androgyny—and the subcultural capital linked to it—does have a serious point. Although goth women are always keen to stress that they love androgynously styled men, discussions about male goths wearing female clothes regularly contain 'complaints' by females voicing similar feelings:

I'm so jellous [sic] of blokes, they dont have to try too hard at all to look strikingly good, a man wearing a bit of eyeshadow and a dress makes so much more impact than anything females dream to dress up in! (Lvciani, slashgoth.org, 11/11/02)

Men can wear women's clothes and look instantly stunning, whereas us women spend hours getting ready and just look the same as every other time we go out. It is just so frustrating. (Witchygoth, slashgoth. org, 11/11/02)

Of course these quotes indicate that men in the goth subculture are also judged according to aesthetics to a significant extent; however, there is a downside to this apparent feminisation of male status criteria. Weil (1992) points out that an exaltation of the feminine as an abstract aesthetic or spiritual principle often goes hand in hand with an effacement of women as actual people. She further argues that the fantasy of genderlessness, which she sees as ideologically linked with the transcendent/transgressive tradition of androgyny, in a patriarchal culture where men occupy a dominant position and women a marginal one can easily 'lead to a denial of difference—the assimilation of woman as "the feminine" to a male model' (Weil 1992: 165). In her study of male transvestites, Woodhouse (1989: 87) pursues a similar line of argument; she speaks of 'the transvestite's enjoyment of the best of both worlds by becoming "better than" a mere woman, because he is a "woman" with a penis'. The above quotes by female goths demonstrate that in the goth subculture, androgynous males also tend to be seen as "better than" actual women with regard to feminine style. In the value system of goth, femininity on men is accorded more value than on women.

CONCLUDING REMARKS

Through the style practice of male androgyny, goth men can draw on the transgressive charge of gender-bending as a major source of subcultural capital, from which goth women with their normative hyperfemininity are largely excluded. The ideals of male androgyny versus female hyperfemininity can entail considerable and sometimes contradictory pressures for women in the subculture. For one thing, they cannot join in goth men's pose of rebellious gender-bending in their quest for subcultural capital as female androgyny is valued negatively in goth style codes. Moreover, the hyperfemininity these codes prescribe for women is certainly valued in the subculture, yet primarily on the aesthetic/erotic level traditionally applied to female style and only secondarily in terms of subcultural capital. As I have shown, it is seen as easily co-optable and hence not as subversive as male goth style. It follows that for goth women, the main option to gain acceptance and status through subcultural style is capitalising on feminine beauty and attractiveness in a fairly traditional sense—a practice which at the same time defines them as inferior to goth men in terms of transgressiveness and subcultural capital in the value system of the scene.

Considering the widespread assumption that 'subcultures in some form or other explore and celebrate masculinity' (Brake 1985: 182), which dominated subcultural studies until the late 1980s, a subculture like goth in which both men and women are encouraged to explore and celebrate femininity certainly constitutes a progressive development. As it stands, however, this valorisation of the feminine entails that goth women's potential for gender-related transgression remains largely muted through a one-sided veneration and appropriation of traditionally feminine codes of style and appearance as tropes of male transgression within the scene.

NOTES

1. A prominent example is the Rave scene (see Bradby 1993; Pini 2001; Thornton 1995).
2. Such overtones have frequently been discussed in relation to Glam Rock and Glam Metal in particular (Denski and Sholle 1992; Reynolds and Press 1995; Simpson 1994; Walser 1993a, 1993b).
3. For a discussion of female sexual harassment as a structural factor of society, see Kissling (1991), Kissling and Kramarae (1991), S.E. Martin (1989), Wise and Stanley (1987).

9 Homegirls remember
Discourse and literacy practices among U.S. Latina gang girls

Norma Mendoza-Denton

Ever since the work of the Birmingham School in the 1970s, subcultural studies has been heavily focused on materiality and consumption, the effect of which has been to render language invisible in theoretical attempts to link subcultural formation and 'structures of feeling' (Williams 1977). Commodity fetishism à la Marx and commodity stylization were major features of this theoretical move, an example of which was the do-it-yourself nature of punk rock in the 1970s, where an *objet trouvé* (ou cherché) such as a safety pin could be incorporated into a coherent dress style via homologous signs (Hebdige 1979: 107). More recent writings on the subject (McRobbie 2000; Thornton 1993; Brown 2003b) continue to understand subcultures primarily through artifacts and commodities, though occasionally references to space and place are made as the focus shifts from local to globalized/ing youth subcultures (Nayak 2003). Subcultures and scenes have been identified through larger social moral panics (S. Cohen 1972), through musical tastes, and through consumption and the fashioning thereof, regardless of whether this fashioning takes place on the street, in the bedroom, or at raves and clubs. Conspicuously absent have been the structures of language as the vehicle for all this fashioning (striking U.K. counterexamples include Hewitt 1986; Rampton 1995, 1999; Stuart-Smith et al. (in press); Moore 2004). For CCCS and post-CCCS scholars, oppositional self-fashioning through the acquisition of *material* distinctions and their related impact on *taste* is at the core of the definition of a subculture.

Following G. Clarke (1981), Andy Brown's contribution to this volume observes that subcultures have to reach a certain critical mass before they can exist in any recognizable sense either to themselves or to others and that consumables such as clothes and music comprise symbolic materials central to subcultural structures of feeling. One of the aims of this chapter is to show that language cannot be ignored as a vehicle in the constitution of such structures of feeling. As it happens, the examples in my research come from youth participating in ethnonationalist projects, who have identities that are indexically linked to a minority language (Spanish in the United States in their case). However, the same processes of linguistic differentiation hold for nonminority youth, and have been amply demonstrated in research worldwide (Bucholtz 2002). In contrast to their European counterparts, scholars of youth (sub)cultures in the American tradition have primarily focused attention on language structure as a resource that is used by young people to create and maintain both cohesiveness and division, and as a major source for our understanding of processes of language change (Eckert 1988). A strong focus on the micropatterning of language may be traced back to the work of Labov (1972a), whose linguistic studies of African-American English-speaking children and youth (AAE; 1972b), including the gang-affiliated Cobras and Jets in New York City, served as the starting points for much of modern American sociolinguistics. Indeed, sociolinguistics has been a major player in studies of youth (sub)cultures in the United States for two primary reasons: on the one hand sociolinguistics has always been engaged with educational, social and ethnoracial equity issues, and on the other hand it focuses on language acquisition, socialization, and language use through the lifespan.

The purpose of this chapter is not to review ethnographic studies of language and youth (sub)cultures, for such reviews already exist (Bucholtz 2000). Rather, my purpose is to draw readers' attention to possible avenues for the ethnographic investigation of language-related practices, citing as a case study the work I have conducted among Latina adolescents involved in gangs in Northern California. What can the study of linguistic practices of a youth subculture tell us about the persistence of subaltern identities, about history, about memory, about language, and about our understanding of youth itself?

THE SETTING: A NORTHERN CALIFORNIA
HIGH SCHOOL IN THE MID-1990S

My ethnographic work employs data distilled from sociolinguistic interviews, participant observation, and recordings of naturalistic interactions conducted in and around an urban/suburban Northern California public (government-funded) high school (which I will call Sor Juana High School) over the course of two and a half years of ethnographic fieldwork, from 1993 to 1996, with follow-up visits to participants over the course of the following seven years. In other work (Mendoza-Denton 1996, 1997, 1999, in press), I have traced how expectation-violating gestures; practices such as makeup, fighting, swearing, transgressions of space, of the voice, and the body, combine to create a textured style that distinguishes Latina girls involved in gang activity from other Latina girls in Foxbury, Northern California at the time of this research. Growing into a young gang girl involves growing far beyond the categories with which society is equipped to handle girls in general. Many of the things the gang girls do then are transgressions of normative categories for what is a child, what is a woman, for what to do with one's body as a woman/child, for how to carry out one's will, and how to protect and defend oneself. Still there remain questions of how this knowledge can possibly be preserved.

At the time of the study, Sor Juana High School (SJHS) had approximately 1200 students, of whom 20 per cent were Latina/o and half of those native English speakers. Located in Santa Clara County, which had the fourth largest Hispanic population in the state of California (Camarillo 1985), SJHS had changed in the prior twenty years from a predominantly Euro-American school serving one of the wealthiest communities in the Silicon Valley, to a predominantly (65%) 'minority' school that drew many of its students from nearby neighborhoods, reflecting the deep demographic changes in the area.

A BRIEF OUTLINE OF TWO GANGS:
NORTEÑAS AND SUREÑAS

As in many other schools across the United States (Monti 1994), street gangs played a part in the social networks of all ethnic groups at Sor Juana High School. However, the definition of a 'gang' by the police, by school administrators, and by members themselves became ever more inclusive, sweeping in its wake everything from hard-core incarcerated gang members to 'wannabes'; groups of young people who participated in the symbolic displays associated with gangs (for example, by writing gang slogans or graffiti on their school notebooks, or by wearing baggy clothes) but had little to do with the more committed aspects of gang affiliation.

Among the Latinas/os in Northern California, gang alliances mirrored the larger politics of the Latina/o community in the state (Camarillo 1985; Donovan 1993). The polar extremes of the Latinas[1] in the school consisted of a group of mostly recent immigrants who identified with a Spanish-language-dominant, Mexican identity, called Sureñas (Southerners); and another group of Latinas, usually U.S. born, who identified with an English-language-dominant, bicultural Chicana identity, and called themselves Norteñas (Northerners). Although Sureñas and Norteñas were technically of the same ethnicity (sometimes their parents were even from the same towns in Mexico), they were in deep conflict over the politics of identity in their community, and this conflict was reflected in their language attitudes, discourse patterns, and eventual success (or lack thereof) in the American educational system. Here I want to stress that committed gang participation in the school was low, at less than 10 per cent of the school population, but because members were highly visible and articulated a coherent ideology, other students oriented to them and designated them as noticeable and important in the social landscape. Although the extreme ends of this social/symbolic gang framework were consistent with a binary split between Chicanas and Mexicanas (Norteñas and Sureñas respectively), in for nonminority youth, and have been amply demonstrated in research worldwide (Bucholtz 2002). In contrast to their European counterparts, scholars of youth (sub)cultures in the American tradition have primarily focused attention on language structure as a resource that is used by young people to create and maintain both cohesiveness and division, and as a major source for our understanding of processes of language change (Eckert 1988). A strong focus on the micropatterning of language may be traced back to the work of Labov (1972a), whose linguistic studies of African-American English-speaking children and youth (AAE; 1972b), including the gang-affiliated Cobras and Jets in New York City, served as the starting points for much of modern American sociolinguistics. Indeed, sociolinguistics has been a major player in studies of youth (sub)cultures in the United States for two primary reasons: on the one hand sociolinguistics has always been engaged with educational, social and ethnoracial equity issues, and on the other hand it focuses on language acquisition, socialization, and language use through the lifespan.

The purpose of this chapter is not to review ethnographic studies of language and youth (sub)cultures, for such reviews already exist (Bucholtz 2000). Rather, my purpose is to draw readers' attention to possible avenues for the ethnographic investigation of language-related practices, citing as a case study the work I have conducted among Latina adolescents involved in gangs in Northern California. What can the study of linguistic practices of a youth subculture tell us about the persistence of subaltern identities, about history, about memory, about language, and about our understanding of youth itself?

THE SETTING: A NORTHERN CALIFORNIA
HIGH SCHOOL IN THE MID-1990S

My ethnographic work employs data distilled from sociolinguistic interviews, participant observation, and recordings of naturalistic interactions conducted in and around an urban/suburban Northern California public (government-funded) high school (which I will call Sor Juana High School) over the course of two and a half years of ethnographic fieldwork, from 1993 to 1996, with follow-up visits to participants over the course of the following seven years. In other work (Mendoza-Denton 1996, 1997, 1999, in press), I have traced how expectation-violating gestures; practices such as makeup, fighting, swearing, transgressions of space, of the voice, and the body, combine to create a textured style that distinguishes Latina girls involved in gang activity from other Latina girls in Foxbury, Northern California at the time of this research. Growing into a young gang girl involves growing far beyond the categories with which society is equipped to handle girls in general. Many of the things the gang girls do then are transgressions of normative categories for what is a child, what is a woman, for what to do with one's body as a woman/child, for how to carry out one's will, and how to protect and defend oneself. Still there remain questions of how this knowledge can possibly be preserved.

At the time of the study, Sor Juana High School (SJHS) had approximately 1200 students, of whom 20 per cent were Latina/o and half of those native English speakers. Located in Santa Clara County, which had the fourth largest Hispanic population in the state of California (Camarillo 1985), SJHS had changed in the prior twenty years from a predominantly Euro-American school serving one of the wealthiest communities in the Silicon Valley, to a predominantly (65%) 'minority' school that drew many of its students from nearby neighborhoods, reflecting the deep demographic changes in the area.

A BRIEF OUTLINE OF TWO GANGS: NORTEÑAS AND SUREÑAS

As in many other schools across the United States (Monti 1994), street gangs played a part in the social networks of all ethnic groups at Sor Juana High School. However, the definition of a 'gang' by the police, by school administrators, and by members themselves became ever more inclusive, sweeping in its wake everything from hard-core incarcerated gang members to 'wannabes'; groups of young people who participated in the symbolic displays associated with gangs (for example, by writing gang slogans or graffiti on their school notebooks, or by wearing baggy clothes) but had little to do with the more committed aspects of gang affiliation.

Among the Latinas/os in Northern California, gang alliances mirrored the larger politics of the Latina/o community in the state (Camarillo 1985; Donovan 1993). The polar extremes of the Latinas[1] in the school consisted of a group of mostly recent immigrants who identified with a Spanish-language-dominant, Mexican identity, called Sureñas (Southerners); and another group of Latinas, usually U.S. born, who identified with an English-language-dominant, bicultural Chicana identity, and called themselves Norteñas (Northerners). Although Sureñas and Norteñas were technically of the same ethnicity (sometimes their parents were even from the same towns in Mexico), they were in deep conflict over the politics of identity in their community, and this conflict was reflected in their language attitudes, discourse patterns, and eventual success (or lack thereof) in the American educational system. Here I want to stress that committed gang participation in the school was low, at less than 10 per cent of the school population, but because members were highly visible and articulated a coherent ideology, other students oriented to them and designated them as noticeable and important in the social landscape. Although the extreme ends of this social/symbolic gang framework were consistent with a binary split between Chicanas and Mexicanas (Norteñas and Sureñas respectively), in practice there was continuum, with the rosters filled by rotating groups of young people with varied life experiences. They included native Spanish speakers who had never been to Mexico; Mexico-raised youth who had been born in the United States and claimed against all evidence to speak only English; and circular migrants who spoke excellent English and could translate for their parents but whose allegiance led them to claim monolingual Spanish status (which could result in English as a Second Language placement if claimed loudly enough to teachers). Thus, there were Chicana Sureñas, Mexican-born Norteñas, and different combinations of ethnicity, language, and nationality in both groups. In my interviews with members of the different groups I found that the groups were so fluid that a six-month affiliation benchmark was difficult to establish in many cases.

Nevertheless, there were clear lines of distinction between the two groups in terms of their symbolic repertoires. Table 9.1 illustrates some of these markers:

As illustrated by the table, each gang had adopted a symbolic color, dress, music and makeup practices, which have been explored in Mendoza-Denton (1996, 1999, in press). Because the conflict they were orienting to was ideological and had nationalistic bases, there was an indexical relationship to place as well. Broadly allegorical, concepts of 'North' and 'South' were transferred to space, place and language, with Sureñas claiming to use more Spanish and Norteñas more English. I say 'claim' here because since both groups were by and large bilingual, the differences between them rested on *ideologies of language use*, not on proficiency, course placement, or active language use. Many of the youths, whether Norteñas or Sureñas, spoke Spanish at home with their immigrant parents and grandparents, or in their extended family networks. At school, much of the instruction was in English, so that was the language of the classroom. On the campus, language choice depended on perceived fluency of the interlocutor, on topic of conversation and on overhearers and privacy concerns. The fact that many

Table 9.1 Semiotic correlates of Norteña and Sureña gang participation in So. SF Bay area, ca. 1995

Name	Norteñas	Sureñas
Color	Red, Burgundy	Blue, navy
Indexical place	The North	The South
Language	Varieties of English	Varieties of Spanish
Music	Motown Oldies	Banda music
Hairdo	Feathered hair	Vertical ponytail
Eyeliner	Solid first, then liquid	Solid only
Lipstick	Deep red/burgundy lipstick	Brown lipstick

of the youth spoke fluent Chicano English, however, did not help them in their schoolwork. Young speakers of nonstandard varieties were often classified as LEP (Limited English Proficient); I trace the consequences of these scholastic classifications elsewhere (Mendoza-Denton 1999).

MEMORY AND THE GANG AS AN INSTITUTION

Studies of social memory (Linde 2000, Swidler and Arditi 1998) have taken up the study of how memory functions in specific institutions. Institutions such as a church, a nation-state or a corporation are socially sanctioned institutions and their processes of memorialization might involve setting up a cathedral, an archaeological museum, commissioning history books, or decorating the lobby of the company with original artifacts. Because a gang is an organization that is not sanctioned and operates under persecution, and furthermore is not located in a single place (consider for instance transnational gang membership of Mara Salvatrucha and circular migration between gang members in the United States and El Salvador), gangs operate under different constraints and affordances for memory.

Among the girls, there were many disincentives for memory and memorialization: the danger of police investigation; social constraints against gossip and tattling; speech acts of provocation; and the lack of stable physical premises for the storage of artifacts. The accumulation of material related to being in a gang has been legislated to be evidence of gang involvement, and starting with the presidency of Bill Clinton, this automatically converted the smallest infraction into a felony. Meanwhile, youth in this community had very little privacy, often sharing close quarters with siblings and other live-in relatives. The few things that they might want to keep, like the original bandanna from their induction ceremony, for instance, often got thrown out by unsympathetic parents. Despite this lack of privacy (often even a lack of personal space at all, as was the case when youth ran away from home), there was a distribution network of artifacts and narrative knowledge that could not be archived in one place but instead were copied, passed around, and shared, belonging to no one in particular.

These resources allowed for a powerfully binding memory that reinforced on many levels, and yet unlike a museum or an archive it lacked the quality of having a single storage place. The lack of premises for storage means two things:

(1) there was no 'official' authorized version of any given narrative, and (2) no one person or entity could hold all the pieces to this memory. Every individual had a slightly different collection of personal artifacts, and everyone's version of 'history' varied. This instantiates what I call distributed memory, connecting individual identity to group identity and stabilizing it over time.

Let's begin by looking at the effect on one of the most fundamental vehicles for self-expression, narrative, of constraints on memorialization that are faced when one is member of a gang.

DISCOURSE PRACTICES: TATTLING, 'TALKING SHIT,' AND THE INHERENT UNTRUSTWORTHINESS OF NONPARTICIPANT NARRATIVES

In his work on anti-languages, Halliday (1976) describes an anti-language as equivalent in function to the language proper: both languages and anti-languages have reality-generating properties, but anti-languages are structured to support and maintain the anti-societies from which they spring. Halliday's set of anti-language examples consists of argots, slangs, and occasional creoles tied to groups or identities (prostitutes, vagabonds, criminals, homosexuals, etc.) whose activities are construed as oppositional and subversive by the larger mainstream. *Grypserka*, for instance, was a language created by prisoners in Poland to render their communication obscure to their guards by altering aspects of Polish vocabulary, morphology, etc. (Halliday 1976); more readers will be familiar with cockney rhyming slang, or *polari* (British "gayspeak", a form of pidginized Anglo-Romanian; Hancock 1984), or French *verlan*. 'Backwards speech' is a distinctive ironic speech mode in Smith Island, Maryland (Schilling-Estes 1995). Just as an anti-society, according to Halliday, is a conscious alternative to society proper, an anti-language is a conscious, marked alternative to the mainstream language.

Tattling

Words and ownership of one's words emerge as an element of crucial importance for membership among both the Norteñas and the Sureñas. In this broader illicit community, being quiet has exalted value, while talking too much is associated with being untrustworthy or tattling to the police. One of the ways in which social hierarchy was continually tested and settled is through a speech act that I call 'talking shit', after the terminology that was used by the girls themselves (see also same description by youth described in Morrill et al. (2000: 537). Talking shit is quintessential gossip, except that it has an optional confrontational *dénouement* at the end. It is either a third-person account where the speaker portrays the third party unfavorably, or a narrative where one brags about one's own factual or imaginary victory against an absent one. This type of bragging is intended to aggrandize one's own reputation, but if it should get back to the other party, as it most assuredly will, it can be considered a provocation and grounds for fighting.

Goodwin (1994) describes a very similar speech routine which she terms He-Said-She-Said among a group of young African-American girls in Philadelphia, while Shuman (1986) also documents what she terms 'storytelling rights' in a multi-ethnic high school in Philadelphia. I have augmented Goodwin and Shuman's descriptions with my own below:

A says X about B in the presence of C
C tells B that A said X
Which causes B to confront A (Goodwin 1995; Shuman 1998)
B then says: C said that you said X about me
At which point A can deny it and say that C is a liar
(and then B can tell C that A said that)

OR

A can admit it, lose face with B, and then later confront C.
Alternatively B can choose not to confront and lose face with both A and C.

Consider this example, from an interview with fourteen-year-old Alejandra, a code switching Sureña with a no-good boyfriend, Fernando:

1. The next day me habla una de sus amigas:
   I get a call from one of his friends
2. 'Hey bitch why are you talking shit?'
3. 'What are you talking about?'
4. 'Fernando me dijo that you said that I was a bitch.'
   told me
5. le digo 'Oh yeah?'
   I say
6. le hace 'Sí'
   She goes 'Yeah'
7. le digo 'Ok fine,'
   I say
8. le digo 'I said it,'
   I say
9. le digo, 'Pero tráemelo aquí para que me lo diga en mi cara.'
   I say, 'But bring him here so he can say it to my face.'
10. And since that day nunca lo he visto.
    I haven't seen him again.

Social control here hinges on the assumption that the party being gossiped about won't find out. In this case, Fernando, the errant boyfriend of Alejandra, is caught in a talking-shit triangle and depicted as exiting the situation by not owning up to his own words. The implication here is that Fernando was somehow afraid of facing Alejandra personally, or not brave enough to bear the consequences of his words. Note how this short narrative itself aggrandizes Alejandra by showing that when she talks shit she owns up to it, and that her undeserving boyfriend doesn't.

Let's look at another example. In this instance we are going to hear from Babygirl, a Norteña, describing an instance of bragging gone wrong. As it turned out, the braggart talked shit about Babygirl to her own brother, who didn't claim any gang affiliation and had only recently arrived from Mexico.

1. G: He was sitting in tutorial one day
2. and there's Sureñas you know
3. talking to him you know
4. and you know
5. his sister—I'm a Norteña in the other group right?
6. So you know I come in tutorial you know
7. I just-
8. 'cause every time I come in
9. everybody like
10. turns around and looks at me
11. and says hi you know whatever
12. so I came in you know
13. I like you know
14. like went like this to him
15. like you know whassup you know
16. and walked out.
17. So then this girl right
18. she's a Sureña
19. she's all
20. 'Yeah, you see that ruca right there?
    girl
21. I beat her ass.'
22. NMD: !!!
23. G: 'You know,
24. she was CRYING.
25. you know I beat her ASS
26. you know I made her CRY.'
27. and then um
28. and then my brother goes:
29. 'Oh you DID?'
30. NMD: Heh.
31. G: And then
32. and then she's all
33. 'Yeah, man.
34. You know,
35. they don't—
36. she don't fuck with ME.
37. and she a—
38. (.)
39. and then my brother goes

40. 'oh that's really weird
41. she never told me that'
42. and then she turns around she's all
43. 'what
44. you talk to her?
45. what
46. you a Norteño?'
47. he's all
48. 'No I just got here from Mexico
49. but you know
50. I mean she's my sister.'
51. NMD: Huh-huh.
52. G: And then she's all Hu::hhh
53. and then she's all
54. 'Oh
55. I gotta go to class.'
56. She's all
57. 'Oh you know
58. you believed me huh?
59. I was just playing.'
60. you know
61. and he came and told me
62. and I was just like cracking up you know
63. and like
64. you know it's like
65. You know when you're in a gang
66. it's funny how people could make things up
67. you know it's like
68. um
69. it's like um
70. it's like
71. 'Oh yeah you know what?
72. I got rushed by the scraps you know?'
73. and sometimes they be cutting themselves
74. you know
75. just to make trouble you know.

Exaggerated accounts of one's own exploits are deeply mistrusted among members of both gangs. As Michel de Certau states:

> Storytelling has a pragmatic efficacy. In pretending to recount the real, it manufactures it. It renders believable what it says, and it generates appropriate action.... The voices of narration transform, reorient, and regulate the space of social interaction (Certau, 1986: 200).

We can see in the examples from the girls that *it is precisely their mis-trust of the manufacture of reality that is at stake*. Great weight is placed on personal recollection rather than on citation and recitation, and within that, 1st Person Narrative (where the speaker was present), or 2nd Person Narrative (where the interlocutor was present), rather than 3rd Person Narrative (where neither was present), or Non-Participant-Narratives (where the speaker was not present but narrates as though they have the storytelling right anyway, for instance a police officer (or an anthropologist) telling the history of the gang, even though they were not a participant). We can thus construct an implicational hierarchy of emergent evidentiality:

$$1PN< 2PN< 3PN< NPN$$

First person narratives are by far the most trusted and 'true', while non-participant narratives are assigned lesser value and more instability. This situation not only has the outcome of creating an evidential hierarchy in a language without much evidential marking[2] , but it can further can lead us to understand how, in this particular group, projected consequences and responsibility for them take the form of the constraints against gossip. Why should it be that the circulation of artifacts (drawings, poems, bandannas, etc.) is practiced with great anonymity, while in order to circulate stories young people must make careful attributions? Part of the answer seems to lie in the potential anonymity of circulated material culture, whereas the traceability of stories, their cite-ability and their potential use as evidence, both within the school structure and in the legal system, demands greater standards of evidence.

CODES, CLOWNING AND *ALBUR*

An embodied innovation of the sort that is only acquired through intensive practice is that of word games (also known as secret languages or play languages) that depend both on fluency in the language and on practice in the form of the game. English-speaking readers may have grown up with a word game called Pig Latin, which relies on syllable suffixation as well as segment transposition, and Mexican Spanish-speaking readers will recognize *hablar en su* as a widespread children's code in Mexico. The use of secret word games has been well-documented by linguists and folklorists in argots and young people's speech all around the world, with examples ranging from *verlan* in French (which relies on reversing the order of syllables (l'envers ‡ verlan), to *Kibalele*, a secret creole in Bukabu, Zaire whose contributing languages are Swahili, Lingala, Shi, English, and French (Goyvaerts 1996), and which exhibits syllabic permutation. Here I'd like to use Ingold's (2001a, b) notion of continuous embodied innovation, where participants seek to direct or influence others' engagement with the environment. The Sureña girls, most of them quite fluent in Spanish, were able to convey messages to each other in school through the use of phonological word games, establishing an exclusive practice where mere participation in such games required a high degree of fluency.

For example, one popular game involved the insertion of a dummy syllable before or after each syllable in the base. In the game of *hablar en su* ("speaking in su"), the phonological syllable /su-/ is prefixed before each syllable of the word. The base and the result look like this:

> ¿Como estás? (Trans: *How are you?*)
> Base: /ko mo es tas/
> Result: /su ko su mo su es su tas/

Games of increasing phonological complexity make the original base string much more opaque and difficult to recover in online parsing. For instance, the girls thought that a more difficult recovery involved the prefixation of the syllable /su-/ combined with the suffixation of the syllable /-che/

> /su ko che su mo che su es che su tas che/

Avoidance of CC (consonant-consonant) sequences yields the final result:

> [su ko che su mo che su eø che su taø che]

The most opaque strings are produced through a combination of highly marked affixational segments (suffixes, prefixes, and less frequently infixes) and sheer speed. Skill in production of these secret performative codes is prized, and speakers who dominate them can easily agree on a sophisticated linguistic rule to use *just for one single day*. Thus, they could walk down the hallway, having a secret conversation, completely unperturbed, and shed this complex embodied practice the very next day.

Among youth who were more fluent in English (and less fluent in Spanish) and unable to participate in the *hablar en su* routines, I observed a different kind of practice that was called *clowning*. Also known in the linguistic literature as ritual insults or playing the dozens (Labov 1972), this type of creative joking involves a frame of the following type:

> Your (possession/relation of the interlocutor) is so (unflattering adjective) that (outrageous result).

Here is an example I overheard at the lunch counter reflecting an intercultural jest element (Paredes 1993):

> Your mama is so tiny that she could hang-glide on a Dorito.

The retort to a clown is ideally a better, funnier, more creative and daring clown, created on the spot, riffing on the interlocutor's less-desirable qualities. Clowning battles can go on for a while, and usually end when the last target can no longer think of something to say, or when the mock-insult has finally caused real offence (Labov 1972). Well known in the literature on African-American English, the practice of clowning among English-speaking Chicano youth at first glance points to the interdigitation of the two communities. And yet there is another, less obvious source of influence: vernacular Mexican Spanish boasts another type of verbal art which involves "topping" another person's insult: the *albur*. *Albur* (Gutiér-rez Gonzalez 2005; Cardeña 2003; Moreno-Álvarez 2001) is a type of casually-uttered double entendre that exploits lexical ambiguity or potential rhymes to entrap an unsuspecting interlocutor into a sexually explicit verbal game. Here is an example that was common in the school—also attested in Tepito, Mexico City by Cardeña (2003):

Asked innocently: Te gusta ver gotas y no mojarte?
Trans 1: Do you like to watch [rain]drops without getting wet? (ver gotas)
Trans 2: Do you like huge penises without getting stained? (vergotas)

If the interlocutor suspects that they are being made the potential target of an *albur*, he or she will take an out-of-the-blue utterance like this and reanalyze it on the spot to unscramble possible sexual innuendos (as in translation 2). The trick of an *albur* is of course to '*alburear*' one's target, that is to say, to direct an ambiguous sexual innuendo and have the target reply to the surface meaning without registering the sexual meaning, thus outwitting them and demonstrating both the target's innocence and one's superior cunning and verbal skill. In a group of Spanish-speaking Mexican youth, being the target of an albur is a constant risk, and the very best (most skillful) *albures* are considered to occur when the target does not notice the innuendo (the *albur* in this case does not sound out-of-the-blue), and responds to it earnestly, while the overhearers all 'get it.'

Sometimes sayings can also be albures, as in the following, constantly used to taunt a blond girl at the school:

Güera, Güera, ¿Quién te encuera?
Blondie, Blondie who'll disrobe you?

This rhyme eventually became so popular at the school that Güera considered changing her moniker: just the utterance of her name with a particular intonational contour was enough to recall the albur.

Secret language games, albur in Spanish and clowning in English are practices that are simultaneously on display and secretive, and whose successful oral performance depends in the most crucial way on embodiment: in the repetition and practice, either to acquire the fluency to be able to instantly analyze the syllabic/semantic structure of language in the case of hablar en su and albur, or in the ability to analyze the social situation to think of ritual insults with just the right amount of insult, codeswitching and jest that do not overshoot perceived community norms. Note that the competitive aspects of these games mirror the dynamics of talking shit as well.

SECRET LITERACIES: POETRY NOTEBOOKS

Although some teachers complained about students' literacy skills, it was evident that students were not displaying their full range of literacy capacities under the structured chronometer of school assignments. Earlier I pointed out how often the texture of the community involved the circulation of objects that were neither the property of a single person and that could be added to or modified. One example of these practices are poetry notebooks in Spanish circulated mostly by Sureña girls. Poetry notebooks were simply small notepads where different girls wrote poems, often in a strict quatrain form, of the form ABAB or ABCB, with seven or eight syllables in each line:

> Me gusta la fresa
> *I like strawberries*
> Me gusta el helado
> *I like ice-cream*
> Pero lo que mas me gusta
> *But my favorite thing*
> Es estar a tu lado
> *Is being close to you*

Often the poems would offer commentary on the nature of love and its associated problems, and occasionally they could be racy:

> De aquel lado del cerro
> *On the other side of the hill*
> Hay muchas flores pa' escoger
> *There are many flowers to be chosen*
> Tu no tienes ni pa' cigarros
> *You don't have enough money for cigarettes*
> Y quieres tener una mujer.
> *And you want to have a wife.*

Sometimes the poems were in the form of anagrams, spelling out the name of the beloved or other words:

> En la calle de la A
> *On L street*
> Me encontre a la M
> *I found O*

Y me dijo que la O
Who told me that V
Era amiga de la R
Was friends with E.

Sometimes girls' poems were longer and free form, involving reflections on family, death or growing up. Remarkably the poetry notebooks, as far as I could tell, really did not belong to anyone at all. All the poems were unsigned (though of course participants knew each others' handwriting), some of the poems were written in code, and many of them involved commentary on current friendships or romances that circulation network members already knew about. Thus, if a notebook were intercepted by a teacher (an occasional event and always a risk with class-time distribution), identities were not revealed; and words in this case did not get participants into trouble (a major feature of talking shit, as described above). After school, the notebooks might be taken out and read aloud, their contents memorized and further poems would be composed and added.

Anonymous poetry notebooks circulating among the Sureñas share numerous characteristics with documented popular literatures that emerged in Spain in the seventeenth century. The verse forms, the illustrations, and the tendency for girls to memorize and recite them all recall popular Spanish oral literature, where traveling bards, who were often blind, called out the contents of broadsheets inscribed with news of the day, general advice and religious signatures, and were therefore called *aleluyas* (Martín 2005). Aleluyas were exactly in the verse form that the girls now utilize, also eight syllables, and as with the poetry notebooks, they served as a way to reach broad audiences and inform them of current events. Popular literatures of this sort migrated to Mexico along with the colonists, and were transformed into Mexican poetic forms such as *corridos* folk ballads (Paredes 1993). What is remarkable here for scholars of youth is that illustrated aleluyas served as the earliest vehicles of children's literature, and had a tremendous impact on its subsequent development. Not only did aleluyas allow children and youth to engage the public sphere (albeit as addressees), but the production of poetry notebooks by SJHS Sureñas provides evidence of the continuity of such engagement historically, with new forms of public sphere participation utilizing traditional forms (classical octosyllabic quatrains) and technologies (aleluya-like circulating sheets), yet appropriating agency for their production and modifying technologies in accordance with internal norms (no gossip, no tattling, no talking shit).

Just by being shown the notebooks, I was granted an honorary and short-lived membership into the poetry circulation network. When in the second year of fieldwork I broke up with my then-boyfriend, poems of sympathy and solidarity started appearing in two different notebooks, instructing me on ways to get over heartbreak, or providing humorous descriptions of the former boyfriend's flaws or an enumeration of other fish in the sea. Only then was I able to experience firsthand the social support function that the notebooks also served, and the ways in which they serve as forums for public advice giving and problem solving. Here is a poem that was composed on the spot for me on that occasion:

Cuando veas mi pañuelo
When you see my handkerchief
Acuérdate de mí
Remember me
Para que despues no digas
So that you won't say later
Que por mi culpa te perdí
That through some fault of mine I lost you
Si porque te perdí
If because I lost you
Voy a dejar de amar
I were to stop loving
Pero lo que no sabes
You are not yet aware
Es que me he vuelto a enamorar
That I have found another.

I have briefly alluded to the use of codes in the notebooks and in kids' notes to each other (as has Shuman 1986). Because the girls knew that I was interested in literacy practices, they often passed on to me their code practice sheets. Codes were extremely common in handwritten notes meant to be passed in class, with different codes in simultaneous use, and new codes being invented continuously. Codes, poetry, secret language games, talking shit and clowning all form part of the oral and literate performative linguistic practices that involve high degrees of embodiment. A young gang girl, by virtue of her involvement in the symbolic production of this type of community, becomes more and more adept at the implementation of these underground linguistic skills.

CONCLUSION

This discussion in this chapter has had a twofold purpose: one is to describe how particular anti-linguistic practices (talking shit, clowning, secret word games, and poetry notebooks) come to accompany broader participation in gang-affiliated networks in a community of high school students in Northern California. The second purpose is to argue that despite the greater emphasis given in the United Kingdom and Europe to materiality and media consumption, analysis of youth linguistic practices is crucial in providing a more complete picture in our understanding of youth (sub)cultures. Language-based practices, through their links with embodiment and their reinforcement of material practices, create and extend social memory for youth groups. Norteñas and Sureñas are an extreme example of a broader youth subculture that is literally prevented by parents, teachers and the police from holding onto much of the material culture they generate. Distributed memory in the form of discourse and literacy practices reflects the forging of subaltern youth identities; these forms allow us a glimpse into the history of youth literacy (*aleluyas, albures*) and into the degree of contact with language practices of other youth groups (clowning adopted from African-American youth). Focusing on language as part of youth practices can tell us what material practices sometimes cannot, explaining the emergence of unspoken rules (don't tattle) and how these create solidarity over time.

Ephemeral embodied practices such as language are thus linked to other systems of symbolism that rely on levels of increasing repetition and conventionalization, or ritualization as per Haiman (1998). Young Sureñas and Norteñas combined commercially available resources such T-shirts, cars, oldies music, rap music, and even commercial toys, with locally-meaningful practices such as gang colors, hand signs, makeup, drawings, poetry, and narrative conventions. *That* is how homegirls remember, by combining different semiotic levels, always including language and embodiment as well as commercially available, though often illicit, material culture.

NOTES

1. I will henceforth adopt the feminine gender in Spanish as the generic, both because my study deals primarily with girls and for stylistic simplicity.
2. Linguistic evidentiality refers to language-specific mechanisms for marking how a speaker has come to know what they know, or how much confidence they have in their utterance. English doesn't have a system of morphological evidentials with prefixes or suffixes, though we can optionally mark evidentiality in discourse with markers such as 'apparently', or 'obviously'.

10 Youth culture and ethnicity
Emerging youth interculture in South London

Ben Gidley

Black expressive culture has decisively shaped youth culture, pop culture and the culture of city life in Britain's metropolitan centres. The white working class has danced for forty years to its syncopated rhythms. There is, of course, no contradiction between making use of black culture and loathing real live black people, yet the informal, long-term processes through which different groups have negotiated each other have intermittently created a 'two-tone' sensibility which celebrates its hybrid origins and has provided a significant opposition to 'common-sense' racism (Gilroy 1993b: 35.)

At least since the emergence after World War II of the spectacular figure of the teenager, British youth culture has been a space of encounter and dialogue across lines of ethnicity. These lines of ethnicity have been perhaps less carefully patrolled than in adult culture, and thus youth culture has also been the site onto which adult culture has projected anxieties about 'race' and difference and Britain's 'multicultural drift' (Hall 2001: 231). This story has been the focus of much writing about youth culture since Dick Hebdige's seminal work at the Birmingham Centre for Cultural Studies (1974a, 1974b, 1979, 1982, 1983). In a series of important occasional papers and in *Subculture: The Meaning of Style*, Hebdige explored the subterranean dialogue between black and white young people which took place in the spaces of youth culture, and in particular in skinhead style which was based on a passion for Jamaican and African-American music. Skinhead culture has been defined both by the profound influence of Jamaican ska and rocksteady and by periods of identification with far right and fascist politics.[1]

The story of the ambivalent relationship between skinhead culture and reggae culture vividly illustrates what Les Back (1996) calls the 'metropolitan paradox': that the spaces of the most intense forms of intercultural exchange have also been the spaces of the most intense forms of racialized violence. As Hebdige wrote:

The succession of white subcultural forms can be read as a series of deep-structural forms which symbolically accommodate or expunge the black presence from the host community. It is on the plane of aesthetics: in dress, dance, music, in the whole rhetoric of style that we find the dialogue between black and white most subtly and comprehensively recorded, albeit in code. (Hebdige 1979: 44–45).

While official discourses imagined immigrants from the Caribbean seeking to assimilate and integrate into 'British culture', in the dance halls and street corners of the inner city the reverse was happening; 'British culture' was being re-imagined and re-created under the influence of the postcolonial presence. By the late 1980s, Simon Jones, in his work on reggae culture in Birmingham, could write about the casual, everyday intercultural encounters and dialogues in the spaces of youth culture.

They are visible everywhere in a whole range of cross racial affiliations and shared leisure spaces; on the streets, around the games machines, in the local chip shop, in the playgrounds and parks, the dances and blues, right through the mixed rock and reggae groups for which the area has become renowned... in some areas, the culture and politics of young people exhibits a seamless and organic fusion of black and white sensibilities (Jones 1988: xiv, 232).

Has the post-racial utopian possibility invoked by Jones two decades ago been sustained? Are the spaces of dialogue opened up by youth culture strong enough to carry the burden of forging a new intercultural sensibility between black and white? And what is the fate of a 'two-tone sensibility' as Britain's inner cities become increasingly diverse, beyond the simplicities of 'black' and 'white'?

In this chapter, I will draw out some of the issues raised by young people's interculture, drawing on a series of research projects with which I have been involved in inner South London. These research projects have all been collaborative, so the collection of the data I will present in this chapter—and the process of thinking about that data—has been profoundly collective. The first research project I worked on in this context was the 'Finding the Way Home' project in Deptford, led by Les Back, Phil Cohen and Michael Keith, where I briefly worked on a participatory mapping project (described below) in the late 1990s. Since then, I have been involved in a series of research projects in or near the same area: the 'Evelyn Arches' project on Evelyn estate in Deptford (with Imogen Slater), the 'Hyde Sports Inquiry' on two estates in the borough of Greenwich (with Alison Rooke, Kalbir Shukra and Debbie Humphreys), the 'Positive Futures' case study research project in Battersea and in the area around Elephant and Castle (with Imogen Slater, Jane Tooke and Gavin Bailey), and the 'Pepys Portrait Project' on Pepys estate in Deptford (with Simon Rowe and Francesca Sanlorenzo).[2]

In these projects, we have used a range of qualitative methods to account for the cultural and social life of young people in inner South London, attending carefully to their voices and practices. The social formations this chapter describes, then, are very specific to one part of Britain, but arguably parallel phenomena could have been observed in other urban settings.

'RACE', GLOBALISATION AND 'URBAN CULTURE'

> The branded multinationals may talk diversity, but the visible result of their actions is an army of teen clones marching into the global mall. Despite the embrace of poly-ethnic imagery, market-driven globalization doesn't want diversity; quite the opposite. Its enemies are national habits, local brands and distinctive regional tastes (Naomi Klein 2000:129).

In the mainstream media, young people are routinely represented through a set of signifiers drawn from the hip hop culture that originated among urban African-Americans but which has subsequently been disseminated globally: baseball caps, trainers, hooded tops. This is indeed the dominant mode of dress among the young people I have encountered on the estates of South London in the course of these research projects. In particular, a small number of sportswear brands circulate in and out of fashion.

While radical African-American academics like Tricia Rose (1994) and Michael Eric Dyson (1993) see hip hop culture as politically subversive because of its 'ruthless alterity' (Gilroy 2001: 179), global capital has built a massive industry on the culture and its 'crossover' appeal (Klein 2000: 71–76). Gilroy calls this 'hip-hop's corporate developmental association with the commercially sponsored subcultures that have been shaped around television, advertising, cartoons, and computer games' (2001: 180). Writing about black film-maker Spike Lee's relationship with advertising giant *DDB Needham* to form *Spike/DDB*, Gilroy writes:

> The new company placed a respectable corporate imprimatur on the realization that the American 'urban consumer' (you know who they mean) now fixes *planetary* patterns for selling and using some highly profitable products. This shows that the culture industry is prepared to make substantial investments in blackness providing it yields a user-friendly, house-trained and marketable 'reading' or translation of the stubborn vernacular that can no longer be called a counterculture (242).

Despite Gilroy's 'you know who they mean', 'urban' is not—or at least not exactly—a euphemism for black. As he recognizes, 'the agency is not specifically targeting African-Americans but is pitching its clients' products at the younger, trend-setting, sports- and fashion-conscious consumers who compose the "urban market"' (2001: 243).

The idea of 'urban culture' is complex and interesting. On one level, it can be read as a euphemism for 'race', and thus a form of racialisation. Former So Solid Crew member Lisa Maffia—who emerged from precisely the sort of intercultural spaces this chapter describes in relation to our Positive Futures case study—sees the term as racist because it erases black identity (Kwaku 2004). On another level, though, its erasure of 'race' allows non-black young people to enter into its identity casually.[3]

The story of 'urban culture' can be traced to marketing strategies in the entertainment industry. The term *urban* in the sense being used in this context first emerged as a name for a radio format in North America, originating as early as the 1970s with WBLS in New York, playing music from a range of musical genres to predominantly African-American audiences. In the mid-twentieth century, the markets for North America's recording and broadcasting industries had been segregated along racial lines, in particular around three large blocks: the white mainstream, African Americans, and Southern whites. Records targeted at African Americans were initially labelled as such—as 'race' or 'sepia' records—while records targeted at Southern whites were labelled as 'hillbilly'. In the post-war years, more sophisticated labelling emerged, with these markets reframed in terms of genre: 'pop' (for the white mainstream), 'rhythm and blues' (subsequently 'r&b'), and 'country and western'.[4] On one level, then, 'rhythm and blues' was a coded reference to 'black', a euphemism, a covert form of racialisation. On another level, though, the fact that this was not explicit meant that white consumers in the United States and elsewhere could access the musical forms, particularly through radio transmissions, which could not be segregated.

Focusing on the background to 'urban culture' and the corporate globalisation of culture allows us to see the way in which the global culture industries and their branding strategies facilitate a kind of top-down dissemination of culture, driven by the desire for profits. Nonetheless, I will argue in the next section that this cultural formation is able to facilitate complex intercultural conversations.

SPITTING: LOCAL INFLECTIONS OF THE GLOBAL

So you get the *So Solid Crew* coming in one direction, right, which shows that, you know, the rude boys are back, some of them are girls, some of them are white, they're ruder than ever. Then you get the *The Streets* coming back and you know, he's like the other moment of that equation which links to cultural exchange, a process of exchange (Gilroy 2003: 4).

A simplistic view of the corporate globalisation of 'urban culture' sees 'cultural imperialism': a U.S.-centric aesthetic replicated wholesale, overriding the particularity of 'local' or 'native' cultures outside the United States. This critique—politically radical but culturally conservative—misses the way that the products of the global cultural industries are never consumed in a purely passive way. They are always adapted to local needs and desires. Gilroy talks of the 'possibility that globalization has pushed the hip-hop nation into a *complex intercultural predicament*', citing fascinatingly ambiguous examples:

> Missy 'misdemeanor' Elliot appears in ads for [stereotypically white clothing label] *GAP*; Lord Tariq and Peter Gunz make anthemic, karaoke-style hip-hop out of cannibalized and recycled *Steely Dan* [a stereotypically white band of the 1970s]; and 'No Woman No Cry' is sung-over again by [The Fugees,] Caribbean settlers in New York, belatedly becoming a hit twenty years after Bob Marley's first version' (2001:181–2, emphasis added).

In other words, corporate culture has facilitated complicated global conversations across vast gaps of time and space and across lines of 'race', rather than simply reproducing a single 'dominant' culture on a wider scale.

Further complicating the cultural imperialism thesis is the way hip hop culture has circulated both through corporate channels (sportswear ads, computer gaming, satellite TV) and also more 'underground' DiY channels (pirate radio, home-made mix tapes, specialist record shops, Internet sites).

The sorts of popular music consumed by young people in South London exemplify such complex conversations, previously carried out through underground channels, but increasingly taking place through mass-market corporate channels. Paul Gilroy first took up this history in its subterranean phase in *Ain't No Black in the Union Jack* (1987). In a widely cited section, he analyses 'Cockney Translation', the 1984 hit by Deptford DJ Smiley Culture (194–97). The record features Smiley Culture moving between Cockney English and Jamaican Patois[5] as spoken by Black British youth.

> Cockney say grass. We say outformer man
> Cockney say Old Bill. We say dutty Babylon

Both Cockney and Patois are minor languages,[6] implicitly defined in opposition to "the Queen's" standard English. Gilroy concludes his analysis by noting that

> neither of the two languages available to black Londoners appears adequate for the expression of their complex cultural experience by itself... [The record suggests a new generation of black British citizens] beginning to discover a means to position themselves relative to this society

and to create a sense of belonging which could transcend 'racial', ethnic, local and class-based particularities and redefine England/Britain as a truly plural community (196).

In some senses, though, it was precisely the record's articulation of shared 'local and class-based particularities' shared between black and white working class Londoners that made possible the transcendence of 'racial' and ethnic particularities suggested by the record. Thus, due to the sustained proximity of black and white Londoners, particularly in the spaces of youth culture, it was not just black Britons who were able to enter white cockney language, but also white Londoners who were able to enter the languages of blackness.

Thus, less than a decade after 'Cockney Translation', the U.K. hip hop scene would return to the theme with MC Average and the Lords of Rap's 'This Is How We Talk Down South'.[7] Where Smiley Culture's 'we' spoke Patois, 'we' in this record talks in a South London accent that is the sole possession of neither black nor white. In 'This is how we talk...', the 'we' is not contrasted against white Londoners but against African-Americans. Responding to debates within the U.K. hip hop scene of the time, the record was asserting the possibility of taking up the American idiom of rap and rendering it in a profoundly British—and specifically local—voice in order to express the experiences of life as lived in south London.

The story of popular music and youth culture in Britain, and in London in particular, has been a story of such trans-Atlantic conversations, with idioms developed on one side of the Atlantic passing across and being reconfigured to express a very different lived context, before passing back to be reinvented again. The site for these intercultural dialogues has been black expressive culture and particularly the sound system culture that has built up around the musics of the African diaspora in the age of mechanical reproduction. This culture—centred on participatory collective consumption in spaces such as dance halls and on a bricolage aesthetic which 'versions' or samples favoured snippets of sound over and over again, denying any record the possibility of being definitive—has truly flourished in London.

It is also clearly a feature of sound system culture that it is *sonic* rather than visual. The central place of music in youth culture is foregrounded in the accounts of writers like Hebdige and Jones, and it is the power of black music over white youth that made possible the forms of encounter and dialogue they describe. Les Back has argued for the ethical importance within youth culture of music in particular and sound in general.

It is significant that it is in sound (i.e. musical culture and language use) that the most profound forms of dialogue and transcultural production are to be found. The ontology of race is profoundly visual. In this sense sound is preontological in that it is impossible to read a human being's body from the sounds that they make. [Whereas the] definition of 'racial types' is profoundly linked to fixing the social attributes of human beings in a visual or scopic regime (2002: 443).

In the darkened spaces of London's night-time leisure underworld, visual regimes of colour and skin are less legible; the sonic reconfigures the racial order. Similarly, sound systems' versioning aesthetic, based on repetition and adaptation, and the intense forms of affective identification between audience and performer central to its style of collective consumption, have proved particularly well suited to facilitating intercultural dialogue. And, paradoxically—paradoxical because sound system culture is so deeply rooted in black expressive culture—it has proved especially hospitable to articulating a new, local identity that transcends racial and ethnic difference. Therefore, it has been those musical genres that have most faithfully reproduced sound system culture and its Jamaican-derived drum and bass lines that have been best able to articulate such an identity. Thus, at the beginning of the 1990s, hardcore, happy hardcore and then jungle techno underpinned dance music developed by African Americans in places like Detroit, with Jamaican drum and bass lines and supplemented the beats with words spoken in a defiantly a London vernacular. A couple of years later, U.K. garage or speed garage took a version of house music developed in New York and emphasized Jamaican-derived bass notes and a demotic London voice.

Writing in jungle's heyday, Les Back wrote

> Jungle demonstrates a diaspora sensitivity that renders explicit the Jamaican traces within hip hop culture along with a radical realignment of national images. Black, white and Asian junglists all claim that the music uniquely belongs to Britain, or more specifically that jungle is 'a London somet'ing'. For these citizens, jungle is music to feel at home in... simultaneously local, national and transnational.... This refashioning is part of a profound process in which the politics of race and nation is claimed and redefined by young people, a project that still possesses a vitality and urgency within Britain's cities' (1996: 234).

The local inflection—the London accent—of the spoken words in jungle and U.K. garage is central to this process, and song titles (e.g. 'It's a London Thing') have reflected this. A more recent example is grime music, a promiscuous hybrid of a whole host of global musical forms—r&b, jungle, hip hop and ragga, but also with elements from bhangra, Brazilian baile funk and Bollywood occasionally pulled into the mix, along with a collage of bleeps from computer games, mobile phone ring tones, police sirens and other urban found sounds. Drawing all of this together is a characteristic form of rapping, known as "spitting", in a voice that draws on African-American rapping and Jamaican toasting styles, but takes a new, emphatically British (or, rather, London) form.. This is analogous to the emergence of trip hop in Bristol, discussed by Peter Webb in chapter 12 of this volume, with specifically local patterns of speech—rapping in a West country accent—exemplified a very local articulation of American hip hop.

Interestingly, the visual language of grime (like its name itself) eschews the glamour of the 'ghetto fabulous' American r&b that global corporations use to sell 'urban culture' in favour of a mundane, quotidian realism: high street sportswear as much as high value logos, London buses rather than SUVs, the characteristically British working-class sovereign ring rather than large quantities of 'bling' jewellery, and above all the ubiquitous image of the post-war council estate. For example, white grime singer Lady Sovereign's assumed name invokes both the sovereign ring of British working-class culture and the African diaspora popular culture tradition of taking a royal name. She sings 'me nah have fifty rings, but I've got fifty tings to say, in a cheeky kinda way', a gentle rejection of American export conspicuous consumption.[8] Likewise, The Streets' name similarly implies a refusal of glamour; the cover of their first record 'Original Pirate Material' (2002) is illustrated by a photograph, named 'Towering Inferno', of a tower block by Rut Blees Luxemburg. Similarly, Dizzee Rascal's publicity photos feature the low rise estates of East London.

If the 'metropolitan paradox' means that the most violent forms of racism to coexist with intense proximity and sharing, it is a further paradox of metropolitan culture that young urban dwellers are most intensely subjected to the pull of corporate global culture yet also produce stubbornly local identities, often circumscribed by the most microscopic of geographies. Again, there is a parallel with Bristol's trip hop milieu culture, discussed in chapter 12: emphatically local cultural forms—grime, the 'Bristol sound'—emerge from confrontation with global cultural forms such as US hip hop.

FROM THE SOUTHSIDE: NEIGHBOURHOOD NATIONALISM

> They look as if they own the territory. Somehow, they too, in spite of everything, are centred in place (Hall 1987:44).

A number of research projects have shown that, in this age of global communication, young people in London—especially young working-class men—move through incredibly small parts of the city. Diane Reay and Helen Lucey (2000), for example, found white middle-class boys in Camden travelling vast distances across the city on buses and tubes, while their white working-class peers rarely travelled off their estates. Where the middle-class boys in the study saw all of London as a dark continent for them to explore and conquer, the working-class boys had rich and detailed knowledge of every corner of their estates—and a strong sense of territorial ownership of them. The 'Finding a Way Home' project in Deptford had similar findings. Cartographies of fear and risk kept working-class boys to a fairly narrow patch of South London, while their female classmates, especially black girls, frequently shopped and socialized as far afield as the West End.[9]

More recently, our 'Positive Futures' research project had similar findings: We asked male and female teenagers from an estate near the Elephant and Castle to draw maps of the places where they spend time. Without exception, the maps produced were remarkable both for their detail and for the tiny amount of space they represented. Benches and raised flowerbeds that go beneath the notice of many adult residents clearly had significance for the young people, while the world beyond the edge of the estate was a blurry terra incognita.

The intensely local geography of young urban dwellers, especially young men, has two dimensions. The first is the exclusion—and powerful *sense* of exclusion—from the freedom of the city. For the 'Positive Futures' project, we interviewed young people living in South London within sight of St Paul's Cathedral on the north bank of the Thames who almost never had cause to cross the river. Living in a zone marked above all by its lack of cultural capital—an area seen by others as a cultural wasteland (Collins 2004; Ackroyd 2001: 539–42)—to enter spaces filled with cultural capital, such as the West End or City of London, can be an extremely intimidating act.

The second dimension of this intense localisation is a very strong sense of attachment and belonging to the local. Young people we interviewed for the 'Positive Futures' and 'Pepys Portrait' projects frequently spoke of their loyalty to their neighbourhood and their estate in particular. In the vernacular the young people speak, their 'ends', the locality to which they belong, is charged with a powerful ethical significance. The size of the place to which the young people are attached can vary, from the estate upwards: in Deptford, young people wear clothing branded 'SE8/SE14' to signify their commitment to the area; one small part of Deptford is known amongst young people as 'Ghetto' and attracts a particularly fierce loyalty; while, in several parts of South London, crews of young people give themselves labels like the Southsiders. The symbolic importance of the image of the post-war council estate in grime music, discussed in the previous section, gets some of its resonance from this sort of localism.

This loyalty is closely related to the 'neighbourhood nationalism' and 'our area' discourses Les Back identifies in *New Ethnicities and Urban Cultures* (1996: 49–72, 101–22). These are understandings of place Back found among young people on two Deptford estates which he names 'Riverview' and 'Southgate' respectively, whereby commitment to *place* in some sense transcended skin colour. Racism was ruled 'out of order' in the moral order of the young people; black and white youth were able to negotiate their identities together; but some groups (e.g., Vietnamese young people) were excluded from identification with the new 'community' which emerged, or were allowed to belong only contingently.

Such understandings of belonging persist in today's young Deptford, with attachment to place figuring far more strongly in young people's discourse than attachment to ethnic or 'racial' identity. Thus in the context of South London youth culture, the branding 'SE8/SE14' becomes more visible and more significant than skin colour. Revisiting Back's ethnographic field two decades on, I found extraordinary continuity but also significant differences. Attachment to whiteness has diminished considerably in 'Riverview', making it more like Back's 'Southgate'. But in both areas, demographic change—and a resulting ethnic 'hyperdiversity'—means that there are many more potential identities to be negotiated within the space of the neighbourhood, making it slightly easier for previously excluded groups (e.g., Vietnamese or Somali young people) to belong.[10] All the young people we interviewed from the estate, of a range of ethnicities, expressed sentiments exemplified by this one from a young Nigerian-born man: 'I see myself always representing [Riverview]. I think I always will, no matter where I end up, because it's where I'm from... like if I was a musician I would give a shout to [the estate].'

The negative side of this sort of neighbourhood nationalism is that the proprietary sense that young people, especially young men, have over their ends can often turn violent. In the late 1990s, for example, the road separating Rockingham and Heygate estates near Elephant and Castle, one of our 'Positive Futures' case study areas, was literally a battle line; incursions across it were met with violence. Sometimes this sort of territorialism can be racialized—with Heygate seen by some Rockingham youth then as a 'white' estate while Rockingham was marked by its black and particularly Asian populations (c.f. Alexander 2000).

This sort of territorialism is often 'segmentary' (c.f. Suttles 1968; Southall 1988) in the sense that two areas might be opposed, but unite in relation to a third area. Thus the tension between young people from 'Ghetto' and young people from other parts of Deptford is forgotten in the context of confrontation with young people from Peckham and, to a lesser extent, Woolwich. Here are extracts from interviews with three young people from Pepys estate in Deptford, the first two (Y and C) young men of African origin, the third (A) a young white woman.

Y: I won't go to Woolwich, not by myself and not on public transport or anything like that. Not because—just because of like there's been a long rivalry between people from like Woolwich and people from like Lewisham area, kind of things like gangs and stuff like that, so I don't know, I probably wouldn't venture up there. Maybe Peckham as well, not to say that I wouldn't go there just to say that I'd be a little bit cautious, do you know what I'm sayin', like when I'm going there, like I might not go there late at night or anything like that. Not that I've got like a beef or like with anyone in that area, it's just like you can be at the wrong place at the wrong time and people just ask you where you're from and you say the wrong place and then, anything can happen. I'd just be a little bit cautious about going to those places by myself on public transport or something like that.

C: I think Pepys is respected, so like, but everyone in Deptford gets along with each other, it's only when you start moving up to like Peckham or maybe Woolwich then there's conflict. But within Deptford and New Cross and even Brockley I think, everyone pretty much knows each other and gets along.

A: There's like a hate thing going on between Pepys like Ghetto and Peckham. I was going out with a boy not too long ago and when he came down to see me, they started; they had a fight with him. And I think the boy that started on him and had the fight with him was trying to say how my boyfriend beat him up and I was like, 'no he didn't'. I was like 'he wasn't around the area to beat you up, he was at a football match', and he says 'oh but he's from Peckham so I'm going to beat him up anyway'.... Now that boy I used to go out with can't come down Pepys because they said if he comes down Pepys that they're going to kill him and all that crap. Because he comes from Peckham basically. Like if I was to go down to Peckham like with a top wearing the post-code SE8 or SE14 or whatever I'd get beat up or something because I'm showing I come from Deptford. Well, it's the same as someone coming from Peckham, I don't know what their postmark... they won't come down here, they get beat up straightaway, just from the fact that they [don't] live on the area, but they may not know the people they've got the actual beef with, it's just because they come from that area, they'll get beaten up.... It's like I say if Peckham was to come, people from Peckham was to come down here and start trouble with people in Pepys, you'd have people from Ghetto come down to support Pepys because they're from the same area.

To adults and youth from other areas, the crews which emerge to defend these sorts of territories appear as 'gangs'—young people in Deptford will talk about 'gangs from Peckham'; young people from 'Ghetto' are seen by young people from other parts of Deptford as being organized as a gang; and the 'SE8/SE14' brand is often read by non-members as a gang logo. However, this labelling is more often a projection of adult fears about young people or of young people's fears about leaving the comfort of their familiar territory.

CREOLIZED IDENTITIES

> Different characters, it's the same as the music innit, it's every element.
> The name So Solid says it. It's solid—we don't break, we take. So we
> got Oxide, he's a white guy, we got Neutrino, half-white half-black,
> Sniper and Trigger, they're Cypriots, they're from Ayia Napa. We're a
> mix of everything man but we started off black ghetto hustlin' strug-
> glers from the same estates and we just adopted other people from dif-
> ferent places. (Safe, So Solid Crew, interview in MurderDog[11])

When young people identify so intensely with place, what is opened up is
a very strong possibility of explicitly inhabiting multiple identities. To have
such a strong sense of loyalty to Ghetto or Pepys *and* to Deptford *and* to
South London already means that multiplicity is taken for granted. At the
same time, the demographics of inner London estates means that hyperdiversity and proximity to difference is something that young people have
experienced from birth. Young people we interviewed on the Pepys estate
as part of the Pepys Portrait Project revealed complex family histories that
made multiple identifications inevitable: Nigerian *and* white British *and*
Jamaican; Ghanaian *and* Irish; Bajan (from Barbados) *and* West African.
A frequently expressed theme among these young people was a simple pride
in 'who I am' and 'where I'm from', which is hard, because of this multiplicity, to map on to any absolutist version of ethnic belonging.

Even among white British young people in these areas, the casual het-
erogeneity of their peer groups means that identities that lend themselves to
absolutism and singularity—such as whiteness itself—are weakened. This
extends the phenomenon Back identified in his fieldwork in the same area
in the late 1980s whereby white youths 'evacuated' their whiteness, at least
at particular times and in particular spaces (1996: 341). As with Back's
fieldwork, the cultural space created by this evacuation was entered by a
'whole host of black idioms of speech and vernacular culture' (341). However, today, this is the case not just with white youth, but also with Turkish,
Filipino or West African youth.

The glamour of (African-American) blackness carried by global corporate 'urban culture' certainly helps black idioms enter into this cultural
space. But the dominant voice among London youth today is Jamaican
Patois. Roger Hewitt's book *White Talk, Black Talk* (1986), an analysis
of young people's speech in two South London neighbourhoods, one of
which is the area where most of my research has taken place, describes the
emergence of a generation of black and white young people able to strategi-
cally switch between the 'codes' of Patois, Cockney and standard English.
In Back's ethnography a couple of years later, it was no longer a case of
code-switching, but of 'a process whereby lexical items filter through into
a shared speech community' (1996: 51). Today, this speech community is

open to a wider range of ethnicities— not just white British and African-Caribbean youth, but also African or Cypriot origin youth.

Another shift is that not only does Patois's lexicon make up a significant percentage of youth language, but the very grammar and syntax of youth language is modelled to a great extent on Patois. The Patois-derived Lady Sovereign lyric quoted above—'me nah have fifty rings, but I've got fifty tings to say, in a cheeky kinda way'—exemplifies this. The language—like the identifications of the young people—is irretrievably 'creolized': mixed, impure, to the point where young people are unable to separate out the constituent elements. Just as in sound system culture's versions and samples, it becomes impossible to establish an authentic, definitive original, so with the versioned identities of inner South London youth.[12]

THE BURDEN OF YOUTH

The creolized identity of urban young people, I believe, marks the limits of official multiculturalism as a body of theory and policy. Multiculturalism, as it is practised by youth clubs and schools, assumes a mosaic of authentic, definitive 'cultures'. In youth clubs and schools in South London, it is common to see displays about the customs, celebrations, clothes and foods of different 'cultures'. But the hyperdiversity and chronically impure cultural identifications and belongings of the users of the youth clubs do not fit into the boxes represented by these discrete 'cultures'.

Stuart Hall (2001) contrasts multicultural*ism* to the stubborn fact of multiculture, which he terms *multiculturality* or *multicultural drift*. These words, like *multiculture*, signal that contemporary metropolitan *culture itself* is already multiple, through and through, while multicultural*ism* in its official forms suggests that many singular '*cultures*' encounter each other in urban space.

At the same time as urban multiculture has made multiculturalism less viable, black radicalism as a cultural force has declined. In one of the youth clubs in Deptford where we did some of the interviews with young people quoted above, there is a faded 'Black History Month' display left over from a previous year or decade, with a gallery of (mainly male) African-American and African-Caribbean hero figures, many involved in black radical politics. Alongside the erasure of blackness implied in the words *urban culture*, fashionable forms of black expressive culture consumed by young people today are profoundly de-politicized,[13] making the youth club display seem worthy and dull. Something is lost in this shift—the ethical power of an oppositional black culture. But something is gained too in making intercultural dialogue more open across the carefully policed lines of ethnicity.

This tension, between what is lost and what is gained, as with the tension between corporate globalisation and local articulations, cautions us against too quickly celebrating the hybrid identities of urban young people. As Back writes,

> the verity of multiculture brings no guarantees.... These moments of critical opening cannot be reduced to a political manifesto, or some didactic call to arms of the sort that tenured revolutionaries yearn for. Rather, they point to quiet transformations and fleeting moments in which living with and through difference are realized (2002: 450).

As I have shown in this chapter, the intimate geographies and localized affect that facilitate intercultural dialogue in the inner city also generate forms of territorialized violence. These forms of dialogue are also punctuated by name-calling, including racist name-calling. This chapter is not intended to celebrate youth interculture, nor to make the claim that racism is disappearing from the inner city. Rather, youth interculture opens up the possibility of new forms of identification and belonging, but in contradictory, paradoxical ways.

NOTES

1. See also Gilroy (1987:160–71) and Deicke in this volume.
2. Details of most of these projects can be found at http://www.goldsmiths. ac.uk/cucr/. I would like to register here my profound gratitude to my colleagues for the material presented here, and to the young people who gave us their time and their engagement. The Positive Futures project was part of a larger national study funded by the Home Office (see http://www.positive-futuresresearch.org.uk); my colleagues in the national research team were Tim Crabbe, Tony Blackshaw, Adam Brown, Clare Choak, Gavin Mellor, Bob Muir, Kath O'Connor, Imogen Slater and Donna Woodhouse. The Hyde Sport Inquiry was funded by Hyde Charitable Trust. The Evelyn Arches project was funded by Deptford Youth Forum from the Neighbourhood Renewal Fund. Thanks to all my research partners and participants, and also to Tim Rapley for his helpful comments.
3. The arts project 'What is Urban?' has been exploring this question. See http://www.whatisurban.org.uk/
4. The term *blues and rhythm* was used by the record label RCA Victor in 1948, with *rhythm and blues* coined by Jerry Wexler (later of Atlantic Records) in 1949, to replace the term *race records*. *Billboard* magazine, the music industry journal, had been using the latter term since 1920, along with "Harlem Hit Parade" (Shaw 1980).
5. I am using the word *Patois* to refer to Jamaican Creole language, the everyday language of Jamaica, also spelled *Patwah* or *Patwa*, rather than to the category of languages linguists called *patois*, which can be understood as a derogatory term for Jamaican Patois.
6. This term, taken from Franz Kafka, referring in his diaries to Yiddish, has been taken up by Deleuze and Guattari (1986).
7. Thanks to Joe Davies and Dave Bibby for alerting me to this song, back in the mid-1990s.

8. "Cha ching" *Run the Road* (2005) 679 Recordings.
9. The ways in which the young people did on occasion travel off the estate were structured by ethnicity: many of the white working-class young people went in the summer to family caravans on the Kent and Sussex coasts, while non-white young people often travelled within London to visit fairly dispersed members of the extended family, or travelled with family members to "community" resources further afield—to Brixton to buy Caribbean or African food, for example, or to North London to attend a religious ceremony. See the working papers of the project at http://www.goldsmiths.ac.uk/cucr/
10. Although I have spent less time on "Southgate", it seems that the discourse of "black community" Back identifies is much less available, partly due to ethnic "hyperdiversity" and partly due to broader cultural shifts which have seen politically oppositional concepts of blackness retreat. I will return to this theme later in this chapter.
11. http://www.murderdog.com/archives/solidcrew/sosolidcrew.html   [last accessed 24/06/2006]
12. A further shift is that many of the specific Patois words Hewitt and Back list are no longer used, as they are tainted with an unfashionable association with previous generations.
13. This shift is indexed in how black expressive culture reference points for young people have changed since Back's ethnography—from explicitly political artists like Public Enemy —to artists with very little explicitly political lyrical content.

11 Youth claiming space
The case of Pittsburgh's Mr. Roboto project

Stewart Varner

YOUTH AND SPACE

Scholarship that focuses on youth and subcultures reveals the struggles young people engage in over meaning creation and expression. Social geography is often crucial to this work because the networks of power in which these struggles are located are particularly visible through their spatial orientation. Because the relationships between youth, subcultures and space are richly dynamic, scholars have approached the concerns they raise in a variety of ways.

Some studies suggest that youth in general and some subcultures specifically have no proper place at all and that their mere spatial presence can be oppositional. For example, the key to Hebdige's famous argument in *Subculture: The Meaning of Style* is that punks only became, to use his words, 'noise,' 'interference' and 'disorder' in spaces that were not theirs (1979: 90). Whether this happened in face-to-face confrontations on the public street or through mediated interactions in the mass media, any potential capabilities that punks' oppositional style had could only be exercised in the space of and in relation to its other. Other research focuses on spaces that are appropriated by young people and covers a broad range of activities. For example, Angela McRobbie and Jenny Garber document the appropriation of private spaces like bedrooms in their essay 'Girls and Subcultures' (1977). At the other extreme, William Foote Whyte theorizes the illicit activities on public street corners in his book *Street Corner Society* (1943). In his essay, 'Knowing Their Place: Local Knowledge, Social Prestige, and the Writing Formation in New York City', Joe Austin highlights the empowering quality of such activities. He documents how the practice of graffiti writing 'emerged around and through the appropriation of spaces and places that are designed for other purposes' and allowed the writers to 'claim a place for themselves within a public order that often renders young people, particularly young people of color, as "invisible" at best and as "outsiders" more typically' (1998: 241).

When attention is paid to spaces that explicitly cater to youth, the focus is almost always on spaces that have been created by or are controlled by adults such as shopping centres, dance clubs, youth centres and schools. Myrna Margulies Breitbart's article "'Dana's Mystical Tunnel": Young People's Designs for Survival and Change in the City' about a youth program in Detroit, is a good example of such work. This program originally was aimed at giving underprivileged young people an opportunity 'to exert influence over their neighborhood space' through 'a variety of projects and social programs' (1998: 307–9). Yet, because the space, like most youth centres, is managed by adults, its activities tend to sanitize youth expression even as they encourage it. It is telling, given Austin's work on graffiti writers, that a major component of the program Breitbart studied had the young participants paint murals in selected locations around Detroit.

Given this context, the story of the Mr. Roboto Project, a cooperatively run music venue in Pittsburgh, Pennsylvania, is an interesting addition to the study of youth, subculture and space. The fact that the vast majority of bands that perform at Roboto, as the cooperative is usually called, clearly owe a debt to the subcultural groupings Hebdige studied in the 1970s, shows that, at least in Pittsburgh, they do have a place of their own. Also, because the space has been open in a rented storefront since 1999, with the blessing of local authorities, it can hardly be seen as unofficial, temporary or illicit. Furthermore, the Mr. Roboto Project was conceived of and created by young people and continues to be maintained by young people. Though some of the founding members are now hovering on either side of thirty, the space's website still proudly proclaims, with some degree of

Figure 11.1 The Mr Roboto project (photograph J. Varne).

justification, that the Mr. Roboto Project is run 'for the kids, by the kids' (Mr. Roboto Project 2005).

THE DIY ETHIC IN THE AGE OF BRANDING

DiY, the loosely organized British youth cultures of the 1990s, is the focus of George McKay's collection *DIY Culture: Party and Protest in Nineties Britain* (1998). The essays document the dance parties, music, drugs and political protests that defined this culture. The book pays particular attention to the potential this culture had—and occasionally realized—to create a liberating space for those who took part, and to expand the national political discourse on issues from road construction to capitalism. Though the Mr. Roboto Project's mission statement announces that the goal of the cooperative is to provide, 'a comfortable and open space for people to experience a true DiY (do-it-yourself) community' (Mr. Roboto Project 2005), the DiY community alluded to here is technically unrelated to the music/dance/protest culture that is the focus of McKay's collection. At Roboto, there are no bike powered sound systems, no open air raves, and drugs, including alcohol, are forbidden in the space. Furthermore, while many of the members are activists, direct action political protest is not something associated with the cooperative. In fact, with its permanent home, its business plan and its widely publicized show schedule, Roboto may seem to have more in common with conventional music venues than with the DiY culture described in McKay's book.

However, the differences between Roboto and other venues (and the similarities between Roboto and British DiY culture) become more obvious at the level of discourse. McKay argues that, what defined DiY culture was not a particular aesthetic or even standardized activities but rather two general principles that formed an ethic. First, DiY maintained a dedication to action and creating a positive example, rather than just a negative critique. Second, DiY sustained itself through a collective mutual aid (McKay 1998: 4–27). From its insistence on operating as a democratic, non-profit cooperative to its determination to support independent artists, both DiY ideals identified by McKay are fundamental to the operation of Roboto.

These similarities are not purely coincidental as Roboto shares many common ancestors with British DiY. McKay traces this ancestry back through punk and 1960s hippies to the British skiffle phenomenon of the late 1950s. Furthermore, both Roboto and the British DiY culture can be seen as like-minded reactions to, and products of, the contemporary challenges posed by the perceived commercialization of culture in the era of multinational corporations and neo-liberal globalization. It is easy to exaggerate this point but it should not be totally ignored either. While commerce has always influenced culture, since the 1980s the commercial imperative to create an emotional bond between a corporation, its products and consumers—a process known as branding—has dramatically increased this influence. 'Branding's current state of cultural expansionism is about much more than traditional corporate sponsorships,' writes Naomi Klein in her unapologetically and in every sense of the word popular book *No Logo* (2000: 29). 'The effect, if not always the original intent, of advanced branding' she argues, 'is to nudge the hosting culture into the background and make the brand the star. It is not to sponsor culture but to be culture' (2000: 30).

Such branding strategies often have a distinctly spatial component that blurs the already fuzzy lines between private, public and commercial space and determines the interests these spaces serve. As corporations seek more ways to develop their brand image, and less public support is available for cultural events, cultural spaces like music venues often become part of ambitious marketing campaigns. The skate-punk themed, shoe company sponsored Vans' Warped Tour is a particularly transparent example of this. This touring festival takes dozens of bands across the United States each summer and has attracted some of the largest corporations who pay to have their logos attached to almost every available space. While Vans grew out of the skateboarding culture, it is now unclear whether the culture continues to create the fashion or whether its corporate sponsors are designing the culture. The latter seems most likely given the tightly orchestrated stylistic homogeneity of the tour. 'Captain Dan', the tour's official reporter, wrote on the tour's Monster Energy Drink sponsored blog, "[i]t was as if the Vans Warped Tour people were created by a video game where you can choose how your character looks but they all end up looking the same anyways"('Captain Dan' 2005).

The intimacy of the relationships between commercial interests and cultural production has raised concerns that, as corporations become the primary stakeholders in what are ostensibly public spaces, there will be less room for non-corporate voices. Whereas the people and groups in McKay's book often confronted this head on with direct action protest, Roboto comes at the issue from a different angle by establishing its own space. In doing so it stands as a possible alternative to branded spaces. However, it also runs the risk of becoming just another space in the constantly fragmenting cultural landscape. Drawing on e-mail interviews with people who frequent Roboto, the following sections examine these possibilities and risks.

DIY ORGANIZATION: IDEALISM AND PAYING THE BILLS

As the first section indicated, space and place are important considerations for scholars trying to understand youth culture. Youth spaces—whether they are spectacularly seized, temporarily appropriated, or officially designated—allow for the expression, testing and development of identity for young people at a time when their identity is very much in flux. Yet, this very insecurity makes young people particularly attractive for the kinds of branding strategies discussed above. So, in a space like Roboto, young people theoretically have a rare opportunity to negotiate their identity with a large, though by no means absolute, degree of control.

Whether it was youthful ambition, youthful naiveté, or both, the founding members of Roboto were idealistic when they thought about how to use this control. Founding member Mike Roth remembers that those first few people started with a belief in 'music as community. Music should be open to all... and encourage community' (Roth, Interview: 17 May 2005). Yet, as it seeks to build and support this kind of community, Roboto faces the same practical concerns as any other organization that wants sustain itself independently. Specifically, Roboto has to figure out how to organize its activities and how to generate enough money to maintain itself. How it tries to balance its idealism with these responsibilities is the focus of this section.

Many of the bands that play at Roboto are from Pittsburgh and the bands that play at the venue from out of town are generally unknown outside of the relatively small networks of fans that keep track of genres that are completely unfamiliar to the vast majority of people. For example,

Figure 11.2 'Brain Handle' playing at the Mr Roboto project (photograph: C. Wright).

bands who describe their sound with phrases like 'powerviolence,' 'super sludge,' 'thrashcore,' and 'grind-pop' are common at Roboto. While these bands are invariably passionate, very few of them have been able to, or even seriously want to, play music full time.

Not surprisingly, attendance at shows is usually modest, averaging between 20 and 40 people. Even if the organizers were comfortable with the idea of running the space as a for-profit, commercial venue (which they are not) it is doubtful that such a structure would be viable. So, with inspiration from New York's legendary music and art space ABC No Rio and a local organic food co-op, Roboto was structured as a cooperative. In an article first published in a Pittsburgh zine, *Here Be Dragons*, (and later reprinted in the long-running music magazine *Maximumrocknroll*), Roth explained how this works:

> A Board of Directors is chosen [through election by the members] and these individuals are given a certain amount of control over the cooperative's activities (although they are ultimately accountable to the rank-and-file of the cooperative). The Board is then responsible for the day-to-day operation of the cooperative and also for mobilizing the cooperative members to ensure that other tasks get completed (Roth 2000: 14).

Examples of how this system works abound in the minutes of the monthly meetings which, in the name of transparency, can be found on the Roboto website. From minor issues such as how to recoup expenses for broken equipment to large issues such as the purchase of a new building, everything is discussed at these monthly meetings that are open to all members. While Roboto's organization as a cooperative gives its users more of a direct voice than a typical single-owner business, it is technically less democratic than a collective that makes decisions based on consensus. Defending the structure, Andy Mulkerin, a Roboto member since 2003, says 'I'm a fan of collective decision making as a model, but in some cases that's not a very efficient model' (Mulkerin, Interview: 20 June 2005). Continuing, he says, 'I think a board of directors making decisions with input from the cooperative members is a good way of going about everyday business. It's a comfortable way of keeping the power of the space in the hands of the members of the 'scene' without letting the whole project slip away in disorganization' (Mulkerin, Interview: 20 June 2005). It should be noted that several similar spaces have been run as collectives but very few of them have been run as smoothly and for as long as Roboto.

Board members do their work on a strictly voluntary basis and there are no paid employees at all in the cooperative. However, there are still many financial costs involved in making sure the cooperative can stay open. Money to pay for rent, utilities, maintenance and equipment comes from annual membership dues and from money collected at shows. While both revenue streams may seem fairly straightforward, like the cooperative structure itself, they illustrate how the cooperative strives to balances its idealism with the requirements of staying open.

In 2005, Roboto had approximately two hundred fifty regular members, who each pay $25 initially with a $10 annual renewal fee, and twenty 'lifetime' members who pay a one-time fee of $100. One does not need to be a member of the cooperative to attend shows or to perform. However, only members are allowed to vote on issues regarding the space and run for spots on the board of directors.

Another privilege of membership, and the other source of revenue for the cooperative, is the ability to book shows at Roboto for a fee of $50 or 25 per cent of the money collected at the door (whichever is greater). Because of this, a number of members have joined for the sole purpose of having the opportunity to schedule bands—usually their own. Because there is practically no cash incentive to book shows at Roboto, it is clear that the reason most people get involved is because the cooperative gives them something they want that conventional venues cannot provide. Exactly what that something is can be interpreted idealistically as a space run by creativity and passion rather than profit or, cynically, as a place where whoever is paying gets to do as they wish. Realistically, some combination of the two is probably at work.

Whatever the motivation is, this method of operation allows something unusual to happen: because Roboto is maintained exclusively by volunteers, any money that comes into the cooperative from the shows and from membership dues is kept there to be used for upkeep and improvements to the space. Any money that a band makes, if it makes any money at all, helps the band stay active by going toward equipment, recording or touring. Thus, while the mere mention of membership fees and money changing hands—however small the amount may be—may cause some to question the cooperative's idealistic talk, these methods allow the creative community that orbits around the space the opportunity to sustain itself. In a city like Pittsburgh, with limited artistic infrastructure, this is no small feat.

Furthermore, Roboto has also been an influence outside of the city's music scene. Many people were quick to point out how Roboto has become an example for other groups who want to work in a similar fashion. Member Zach Furness reports that, '*Roboto* was... instrumental in the development of the Free Ride bike program [a bicycle repair cooperative], and the Big Idea infoshop [a politically radical lending library]—both of which got their start in the building adjacent to the venue' (Furness, Interview: 23 May 2005).

DIY SCENE: OWNERSHIP AND COMMUNITY AT ROBOTO

Emma Rehm says she attended her first show at *Roboto* out of 'idle curiosity' in the summer after her first year of college in 2001 (Rehm, Interview:

17 June 2005). She remembers, 'I'd seen a flyer for a night of lady punk bands [at Roboto]. My roommate and I... figured out which bus to take, and busted into the scene' (Rehm, Interview: 17 June 2005). Rehm soon began attending shows regularly and eventually became a member of the cooperative. 'A year or so later, I set up my first ever show, and one of the bands we'd seen that [first] night played my show. Man, I felt like a badass' (Rehm, Interview: 17 June 2005).

While the dedication of the volunteers and the cooperative's commitment to running the space in a more or less professional manner are essential to Roboto's ability to function, the sense of shared ownership and the opportunities for involvement this creates are just as vital to making the space what it is. Members like Rehm are able to play an active role in making the space work and are not necessarily confined to the role of passive consumer. As a result, the space is, in a very material way, the creation of its participants who feel a sense of responsibility towards it. This creates a desire to see it continue and improve. As Rehm puts it:

> the main difference that I see between Roboto and, for example, ModernFormations (a space that is primarily an art gallery and a venue after that) is that there are only two people who run MoFo and I worry about them burning out and running out of steam. Roboto has a big enough core of people working on it at any given time that I don't worry about its sustainability (Rehm, Interview: 17 June 2005).

Mulkerin provides an illustration for Rehm's comments. He says, 'because of the nature of the Roboto Project, I generally feel more of a sense of ownership at shows there. This means I'm more apt to make sure things are cleaned up... and I'm more offended when someone at a show "breaks the rules"' (Mulkerin, Interview: 20 June 2005). Continuing, he says, 'at Roboto, where we're all essentially equals, and [because] it's my friends and myself who make and enforce "the rules," they feel a great deal more like agreements... than "rules" handed down from above' (Mulkerin, Interview: 20 June 2005).

This sense that Roboto is run by a community of equals is one of its most commented on characteristics. Everyone I spoke to touched on this when distinguishing the cooperative from other venues in the city. Kaytee Nolan, a Pittsburgh area high school student said that she had been to shows at several local venues and that the 'biggest difference is that at every other venue I felt like a customer' (Nolan, Interview: 18 May 2005). She said that the 'bouncers were cold, mean, bossy, and treated me like shit. The crowd at most of those venues were also cold and unwelcoming' (Nolan, Interview: 18 May 2005). In her experience, Roboto is remarkably different. Recalling her first visit, she says, 'I felt like I just walked into a family gathering. It was informal, no evil guards, and everyone was very warm and friendly' (Nolan, Interview: 18 May 2005).

Furness, a musician who has played several shows at Roboto also appreciates the way the cooperative operates:

> Roboto is a place where people don't have to deal with greedy club-owners, surly bar crowds, promoters, or oligarchic media corporations. Furthermore, there are a lot of people who don't like dealing with smoky bars or drunk people, and Roboto creates an environment for those people to play and/or enjoy music without having to deal with said factors (Furness, Interview: 23 May 2005).

Furness's comments bring up another aspect of Roboto's personality that distinguishes it from the other venues in the city. The neighborhood of Pittsburgh where Roboto is located does not allow businesses to sell alcohol. While this may discourage some businesses from opening there, it is not a problem for Roboto because the original organizers envisioned the space as a venue where people of all ages would be welcome and safe. To this end, drugs and alcohol are absolutely forbidden at Roboto and smoking is only permitted outside the venue. While such rules may seem odd to some people, they are welcome by many. Rehm explains, 'I never go to shows at bars full of drunkensteins, and I never go to shows at venues that are likely to be really smoky—two things I really love Roboto for NOT being' (Rehm, Interview: 17 June 2005).

Another part of Roboto's effort to maintain a safe environment has been the creation of the 'Acceptable-Performance Policy' which bans homophobic, racist and sexist lyrics in performances. Because only members can book shows, it is their responsibility to preview a potential performer's music to make sure it is suitable for the space. Jeremy Hedges, a Roboto board member explains that,

> In the past, bands have had mics turned off when they started spouting 'fag this' and 'bitch that.' For the most part, we have headed off uncomfortable situations at the pass by not allowing bands with reputations for that sort of thing to play or, if they play and this sort of behavior is present, they are not allowed to play there again (Hedges, Interview: 17 May 2005).

Mulkerin explains the need for these restrictions by saying that, 'political ideals are pretty important at Roboto, and in a lot of cases, policies... and general methods of operating make a point of excluding those who have less tolerant points of view' (Mulkerin, Interview: 20 June 2005).

ROBOTO AND THE POLITICS OF IDENTITY:
COMMUNITY, CLIQUE OR NICHE-MARKET?

Everyone who participated in this research is active in the cooperative and agreed that the restrictions on alcohol and drugs and the 'Acceptable Performance Policy' are necessary in order to insure that the space remains safe and comfortable. Yet this points toward a central paradox in the cooperative. If people who do not agree with the decisions of the board of directors are excluded, banned or simply made to feel unwelcome, who exactly is the space safe and comfortable for besides the relatively small group of people who pay to keep it open? It is clear that Roboto is very different from most music venues but it is not so clear how it is different from a private social club. Because of this perceived exclusivity, Roboto has been charged with elitism in the local music scene from the very beginning. Rehm says, 'the assumption is that "Roboto people" only go to Roboto, and think they are better than the people who run other venues or go to other types of shows' (Rehm, Interview: 17 June 2005). While she denies these charges, she admits, 'I can see how the idea has come about. The people who work on/with/play at Roboto ARE really dedicated to it and spend a lot of time there, and since [only] members can book shows there, the "Roboto kid's" bands play there a lot' (Rehm, Interview: 17 June 2005).

Furness also acknowledges these complaints. He said, 'There have… been problems with people feeling alienated from Roboto because they didn't feel like they were part of the scene there' (Furness, Interview: 23 May 2005). Yet, while he also understands why this happens, he argues that 'one has to recognize the fact that there will always be problems of this nature when groups of people are in social and/or artistic settings' (Furness, Interview: 23 May 2005).

Roboto's experience with charges of elitism may be at least partially understood through the concerns Sarah Thornton raises in relation to the notion of subcultural capital. Writing against work like Hebdige's that tended to foreground the active political character of subcultures, Thornton highlights subcultures' tendency to be hierarchical, cliquey and controlled internally by disciplinary codes. Building on Pierre Bourdieu's concept of cultural capital, she argues that subcultural capital 'confers status on its owner in the eyes of the relevant beholder' (1995: 11). She writes, 'subcultural capital is objectified in the form of fashionable haircuts and carefully assembled record collections' (1995: 11). The overwhelming majority of shows at Roboto are some variation of punk or metal, which indicates that some kind of code is at work, whether it is explicitly stated or not.

At the same time the subcultural codes Thornton describes confer relative status within the group, they also form the boundaries of the subculture that separate it from the larger culture. This is markedly different from Hebdige's early conception of subcultures as engaged in spectacular semiotic struggles with 'the dominant culture'. The picture Thornton presents is one where subcultures are willfully *disengaged* and where their styles offer little more than colorful analogs of 'adult economies' with much the same concern for status. The eagerness of large corporations to latch onto these styles further calls into question their ability to be oppositional. The result is a weakening of the subculture's ability to be political as the participants segregate themselves into groups defined by taste.

Stephen Duncombe identified this de facto segregation in his work on networks of zine writers. He argues that, while interactions between groups is not unheard of, 'there is also a tendency to move in the opposite direction: hunkering down in your microcommunity, surrounded by only your reality' (1998: 448). While this can offer comfort, particularly if 'your reality' is a particularly marginalized one, the problem, as Duncombe points out, is that 'there's no need to integrate' (1998: 448). The stunning diversity of the contemporary marketplace is more often characterized by distinctions between groups and defensive insularity than by mutual respect and cooperation. Though it was not the intent of the organizers, *Roboto* can be seen as just another insular outpost in the contemporary landscape of consumerism.

Just how harmful this tendency toward insularity can be became apparent in the Fall of 2005. The *Pittsburgh City Paper*, a local entertainment weekly, reported that Jasiri X, the minister at the Wilkinsburg Nation of Islam mosque, along with neighborhood residents and students from the University of Pittsburgh approached the board of directors at Roboto about a flier for a show at the space. The paper described the flier, advertising a performance by the band *1913 Massacre*, as 'bearing images of black minstrel characters with dark skin and puffy lips...bracketed by [racially provocative] text from the Unabomber Manifesto written by Ted Kaczynski' (Mock: 2005). A meeting was scheduled to discuss the matter and, while the show's promoter did not attend (though he was repeatedly invited to do so), the board of directors apologized for the flier and explained that all show promotions are handled by individual promoters and not the board.

Paradise Gray, one of the people who approached the board, explained to the newspaper that the people from Roboto he met with were 'to their credit very receptive and understanding.' However, Gray added '[progressive white people] are blinded to the fact that racism is alive and well in America and sometimes they take lightly the issues that are sensitive to us' (Mock: 2005). 'You look around,' he said to the reporter, 'and see no venues for African-American artists anywhere but it's so amazing how the young white kids have this great outlet in a *black* community where we don't have anything' (Mock: 2005).

This comment reveals the heart of the problem for Roboto. There is absolutely no formal structure keeping African-American youth from becoming members and performing. Furthermore, barring the insensitivity of the *1913 Massacre* fliers, which was an extremely isolated event, there is no indication that greater diversity of performances would be discouraged. However, as the cooperative has worked hard to carve out its own space, it has failed to engage with the broader community in which it is located. Its not that the cooperative's actions are profit driven or that it is inherently racist, but rather that, in a society that is continuously encouraged by advertisers to divide itself into groups defined by consumer habits—and not, as is often feared, simply homogenizing—people have learned to see and judge others (and themselves) in terms of more or less distinct groups and not necessarily as citizens of diverse communities, with all the rights and responsibilities that entails. This segregation has made it hard for people to relate to one another across the boundary lines that separate them making integration almost unimaginable.

This segregation and the problems it creates are, almost ironically, the result of social, political and economic processes that were supposed to be personally and politically empowering. Writing about the rise of what she calls a consumer's republic in post- World War Two America, historian Lizabeth Cohen argues that the marketplace of mass consumption was presented to Americans as supremely democratic and that their participation in it was to be both pleasurable and patriotic. She writes, 'Americans merged their aspirations for an adequate material provision and a legitimate place in the polity, expecting the two to go hand in hand or for the former to encompass the latter' (2003: 408). The resulting tendency to confuse personal consumption with political engagement seems to be the source of Roboto's failure to be a truly diverse space, despite its stated to desire to be just that.

Perhaps all of this is why the people I interviewed, who were generally straightforward and helpful throughout the process, became guarded and, occasionally, suspicious when I asked about Roboto's role in the Pittsburgh scene or DiY subculture. It is also the only line of questioning that resulted in conflicting answers—even between longtime members. For example, Deanna Hitchcock, a founding member, said, 'I think that punk is a subculture and Roboto is a part of punk so, hmm, I guess it's a subculture within a subculture' (Hitchcock, Interview: 2005). Yet Roth, also a founding member, said, 'I'm not sure [if Roboto is part of a subculture]. I don't know whether I would consider any of the communities/scenes involved in Roboto to be true subcultures' (Roth, Interview: 17 May 2005). Relative new-comer Nolan, struck a kind of balance between the two saying, 'I would consider the Roboto Project as part of, not just the 'Punk' subculture, but the underground music scene in general' (Nolan, Interview: 18 May 2005).

Others agreed to the term *subculture* but defined it in terms so broad that the category ceased to have a usefully specific meaning. For example, Furness answered the question about *Roboto*'s subcultural status by saying,

> It is definitely part of the subculture here in town, and I would define that subculture as one based upon a DIY (Do it Yourself) ethic... whether one is booking their own shows, making their own music,

hosting events for out of town bands, or creating artistic and/or activist projects that are independent of corporate money/influence. (Furness, Interview: 23 May 2005).

Mulkerin's answer to the question began concretely enough with the simple statement, 'I would call Roboto part of a subculture' (Mulkerin, Interview: 20 June 2005). Yet, his answer went on to provide numerous qualifications and exceptions. He said, 'while there are sub-subcultures within that subculture, I suppose, I would say that the overall subculture is characterized by (generally but definitely not necessarily): progressive-to-radical political thought, youth, a concern for loud music' (Mulkerin, Interview: 20 June 2005). Sensing that perhaps the question did not really make sense from his perspective, he concluded saying that, 'it's hard to characterize the culture that surrounds a place like Roboto because the different general characteristics that the people involved show aren't necessarily enforced ideals but are definitely encouraged by default' (Mulkerin, Interview: 20 June 2005).

The variety of answers and their occasionally convoluted nature could simply reveal different understandings of what a subculture actually is. However, it could also highlight a general uneasiness with any attempt to locate the Mr. Roboto Project within a specific social context. Everyone seemed to agree that what made the cooperative special to them is that it creates so much potential for anyone who wants to put forth the effort to do something that simply would not be possible in a commercial context. Trying to capture that potential within the too-close quarters of a defined subculture or a specific scene would ignore that very quality. Besides, given the now painfully obvious problem of insularity, narrowing down what *Roboto* is seems unnecessary compared to the task of realizing all that *Roboto* could be.

CONCLUSION

Against a backdrop of a culture that is increasingly only possible through corporate sponsorship, the Mr. Roboto Project can easily be seen as a positive and empowering organization. Because youth culture in America is typically only of interest to the adult world when it can be commodified, packaged and sold back to the youth, the cooperative represents a kind of safe space for the people who use it. Because the members control the space and because profit is never a question, a great deal of trust has developed between the cooperative and those who use it. The people I spoke with genuinely appreciate the opportunities this provides. The cooperative's relative longevity and continued popularity are testaments to this appreciation. However, in constructing this safe place, the cooperative has effectively—if only by default—cut itself off from other groups. It is no doubt true that individual participants exist in many worlds. As students, employees and neighbors, they interact with a wider community. However, Roboto stands apart from these communities. It is a welcoming and much needed refuge for those who identify with it, but is alienating or illegible—if not invisible—to those who don't. This story is not specific to The Mr. Roboto Project. Insofar as youth cultures define themselves in opposition to the wider culture, while making little effort to constructively engage with it, they will remain something that one is expected to grow out of eventually. Whether or not Roboto specifically, and youth cultures in general, choose to accept this fate will, as always, be up to the people who create them.

12 Hip hop's musicians and audiences in the local musical 'milieu'

Peter Webb

This chapter investigates the changing relationship of young people to place and space through the study of the intersections of 'the local' and 'the global' in youth music cultures. Using the story of the take-up and transformation of hip hop in Bristol as a case study, I build on the existing literature on youth, place, space and music (Bennett 2000; S. Cohen 1991; Elflein 1996; Kahn-Harris 2000; Shank 1994). While my primary focus is upon illustrating the details of the case study, I also briefly illustrate how Dürrschmidt's (2000) concept of the 'milieu' and Bourdieu's thoughts on the 'field of cultural production' (1993; Bourdieu and Wacquant 1992) offer tools which may help researchers to frame the complex interrelationships between global music cultures and local contexts. The notion of the milieu here is useful in capturing the particularities of local music cultures through which global genres can be adapted and transformed, while Bourdieu's arguments about the logic of the field of cultural production offer us a way of understanding the relationship between such localised music practices and the wider music industry.

My examination of hip hop in Bristol focuses on the way this global cultural form initially was copied and accepted by a community of young fans and musicians in the city and then dramatically modified to reflect the place in which it was being used, to the extent that it provided a template for what became known as 'trip hop'. I then suggest that as the excitement and music industry's celebration of the new genre waned, trip hop became the focus for criticism, whilst debates within the hip hop milieu in the United Kingdom became more conservative, rendering the movement less adaptable to radical change. Although it was only one element of the musical palette that has become important within Bristol's musical milieu, the development of hip hop in the city makes an informative case study, not least because it allows comparison with studies of its development in other cities and countries (Bennett 2000; Elflein 1997; Mitchell 1996; Gidley this volume). The discussion which follows divides the story of trip hop into three stages; adoption, transformation and retrenchment. Amongst other things the approach I adopt deals with musicians, DJs and fans interchangeably since the distinction between them is far from clear-cut and all contribute to the musical milieu.

SETTING THE SCENE

Bristol is home to a population of around 450,000, consisting of a variety of different communities living in close proximity. The mainly Bristolian working-class communities of Filton, Patchway and Southmead to the north of the city and Bedminster, Knowle West, Hartcliffe to the south are situated above and below the historically mainly Afro-Caribbean and Asian communities of St Pauls and Easton and then the middle class and artisan areas of Cotham, Redland and Clifton. Although Bristol has had its fair share of ethnic tension[1], the ethnic mix of the city and the proximity of different communities enabled the music culture of the late seventies to attract audiences and performers from a diverse set of backgrounds. Many early punks in Bristol were sons and daughters of Afro-Caribbean immigrants, while many white working-class kids were influenced by the reggae sound systems of the St Paul's area. Many of the city's reggae bands, such as Black Roots, Talisman and Restriction, as well as sound systems such as Roots Spot Crew, Kama Dread, Addis, Armagideon and Henri and Louis were made up of both black and white members. Meanwhile, the city also has had strong jazz, punk and indie/avant garde guitar scenes and some bands crossed the boundaries between such genres.[2] Describing Bristol as 'slackersville UK' Reynolds (1998: 315) has argued that a combination of cheap accommodation, a long established black population and a strong student and bohemian presence has made the town a fertile bed for 'genre-blending musical activity'. Many young people in the city drifted in and out of various music scenes and genres. In particular, the close geographical proximity of a wide mix of communities in the city seemed to encourage experimentation and mixing rather than a rigid adherence to particular styles (Webb 2006).

ADOPTING HIP HOP ESSENTIALS

Hip hop seeped into the consciousness of the city through a variety of channels, including national radio shows like John Peel's, local pirate stations like FTP (For the People), mix tapes from New York stations like Kiss FM that had been brought back by visitors to other cities and imported 12's stocked in independent record shops such as *Revolver*. Robert Del Naja (of Massive Attack) regularly went to London to buy reggae 12's and new hip hop cuts (Johnson 1996). Already a fan of the music, Del Naja had developed some skill as a graffiti artist, was thinking about becoming a rapper, and was starting to work with the sound system the Wild Bunch who later on became Massive Attack.

The sound of hip hop wasn't the only thing that was being bought into by Bristolians. The website for the city's Dug Out club includes video footage from the 1980s including a famous party at the Arnolfini, an arts centre in Bristol, in which DJ sets by the Wild Bunch are heavily focused on U.S. hip hop and accompanied by body popping and break dancing among the audience. The style, fashion and party scenes look as though they could have been shot in New York. As well as consuming hip hop in its musical form, a Bristolian club-going audience were consuming New York style trainers, sports clothing and hip hop jewellery.

The release of two U.S. made movies, Charlie Ahearn's *Wild Style* (1982) and Harry Belafonte's *Beat Street* (1984) made a significant contribution to the export of hip hop to an international audience (Elflein 1998; Bennett 2000). In Bristol, *Wild Style* started to interact with local musical and cultural knowledge, becoming a reference point in the specific context of ethnically mixed local music clubs like the Dug Out, in local fashion scenes dominated by particular individuals, shops and other institutions, and in the particular configuration of youth that were mixing in the social space of the city. Members of Massive Attack have stated, for example, that they watched the film *Wild Style* avidly for clues about fashion, graffiti and the musical style of the New York scene. Robert Del Naja of Massive Attack recounts the early 1980s period:

> The DJs (in Bristol) would go out and hunt for the same breaks they heard other DJs cut up in America or on records, all the classic breaks like 'Good Times', every DJ was doing that, every rapper was doing Sugarhill things and then getting into more modern stuff like Run DMC, Eric B and Rakim and Slick Rick.... And of course the breakdancers were breaking and graffiti artists were copying the Wild Style moves. (Johnson 1996: 110–12).

Other DJ crews in Bristol also bought wholesale into hip hop and the audiences for such DJs—who included *2Bad*, *3PM*, *UD4* and *City Rockers*—were massive. Large warehouse parties took place regularly, record shops like *Replay* and *Revolver* were selling new hip hop albums in the hundreds and some local clothing shops incorporated the changing trends in hip hop fashion.

However, towards the end of the 1980s the process of trying to mark themselves out from other artists led many Bristol musicians towards more innovative uses of the genre. Del Naja has described the feeling among members of the *Wild Bunch* that in order to stand out, they needed to produce something different from the numerous other hip hop DJ crews:

there were a million DJs around and a million rappers... there was so much copycat business that you wanted to do something to establish yourself as an individual again, and you couldn't do that in the same way that everyone else was doing, so being in the studio was something that had to be a progression. (Johnson 1996: 112)

The Wild Bunch recorded a single: 'The Look of Love' (1988) which featured a slow hip hop beat with a strong female vocal doing the Bacharach and David song. This was to become a template for further work by the crew. When another Bristol crew, Smith and Mighty, also released covers of Bacharach and David's 'Anyone Who Had a Heart' (1988) and 'Walk On By' (1988) the transformation of hip hop in the context of Bristol had begun in earnest. The soulful female vocal and the Bacharach and David filmic style cover version were the starting points here for a move away from pure hip hop to a style that started to weave in a moody, slightly melancholic aesthetic which looked to the mood of the post-punk sonics of *Joy Division* and *Public Image Ltd* and utilised the soul vocalists and reggae singers available and working in Bristol. It was a mix that reflected the traditional openness of musical communities in Bristol and the musical scenes that musicians like Rob Smith and Ray Mighty (of Smith and Mighty) had been a part of.

In trying to assess these developments and to understand their gestation we can turn to the work of Jörg Dürrschmidt (2000) and the phenomenology of Alfred Schütz (1970a, 1970b). On the basis of empirical work on the globalized lives of individuals living in the city of London, Dürrschmidt discussed ways in which their *Umwelten* (lifeworlds) are constantly disembedded and re-embedded (Dürrschmidt 2000). He uses the term *milieu* to describe the:

> relatively stable configuration of action and meaning in which the individual actively maintains a distinctive degree of familiarity, competence and normalcy, based on the continuity and consistency of personal disposition, habitualities and routines, and experienced as a feeling of situatedness (Dürrschmidt 2000: 18).

When looking at the unfolding of the processes that led to the musical creations of bands such as Massive Attack, Portishead, Mark Stewart and the Mafia it is clear that the Bristol music milieu included identifiable groups of people who were mixing socially in a limited number of venues and rehearsal spaces as well as playing each others' records, working with each other in a 'live' capacity and feeding off similar reference points. Many of these participants had been fans of the sounds of punk, reggae and jazz prior to their interest in hip hop, and this partly related to the eclectic musical history of the city. The knowledge of soul, funk and hip hop that formed an equally important influence can also be traced through the records being played by DJs in Bristol's club spaces from the late 1970s onwards (Brown 2002). The *relatively* stable milieu of this musical world consisted of musical reference points which were dis-embedded and re-embedded by the changing relevance of musical genres that moved into the social fabric of Bristol. Massive Attack offers a prominent example of this, with creative mixing and tension between various genres constituting a key feature of their sound. For example, elements of reggae, soul and hip hop are apparent on 'Blue Lines' and 'Protection', while post-punk, new wave, reggae and hip hop are interweaved on 'Mezzanine' and '100th Window' (See Chapman 1998a, 1998b; Hoskins 1998; Reynolds 1994; Dalton 2003).

Dürrschmidt expands on his notion of milieu by introducing the concepts of milieu structure, momentary milieu and extended milieu. These three elements provide the dynamism and fluidity of the milieu concept. Milieu structure refers to the stable configuration of relevancies, stocks of knowledge and dispositions that individuals have and that they maintain within tight social groups such as those associated with the workplace, locality, social groupings and family. Elements of Bristol's musical milieu had a fairly tight knit feel to them and notably, the Dug Out club in the late 1970s and early 1980s was a meeting point for the fairly particular group who would go on to become the artists and fans who were responsible for the trip hop sound. Other clubs, pubs, rehearsal spaces and studios acted in similar ways, bringing together groups of people who began to share similar musical reference points (e.g., pubs in the Montpelier district of the city such as the Montpelier, The Old England, The Cadbury House).

Dürrschmidt's second addition is the momentary milieu which refers to that which is current and transitory, but practically relevant at any one time. An example might be that of a classically trained pianist who is introduced by a friend to free and improvised jazz and a whole new way of approaching the piano. The individual then has a choice either to pursue this new milieu of understanding or to ignore it and continue to interpret the piano within the classical framework. In respect of our case study, we might focus here on the way in which hip hop in Bristol started to be mixed with the dynamics, tempo, effects and particularly the bass lines of reggae. During its initial 'arrival' hip hop took the form of a momentary milieu that was discovered by a section of the Bristol music making and fan community who chose to immerse themselves in it. They slowly started introducing it to a club going audience and gradually it became part of their milieu structure. Meanwhile, groups such as Massive Attack began to mix elements of the recently adopted genre with their in-depth understandings of reggae and splicing—both of which already were firmly embedded in the local milieu structure. As Massive Attack's career developed, a similar process occurred with the integration of Robert Del Naja and Grant Marshall's love of punk and post-punk—also already embedded within their milieu structure—with core ingredients of hip hop (notably in the 'Mezzanine' and '100th Window' albums).

Dürrschmidt's third element is the 'extended milieu'. This refers to the milieu that we are connected to through the ever increasing range of technology and global processes. These also expand our potential milieu. The influence firstly of radio and mix tapes on the Bristol population in the development of hip hop in the city, and secondly of artists travelling and sharing cultural production in different countries is an important part of this process. Equally important, as we shall see later, was the role of the broader U.K. music milieu in initially accepting and publicising the Bristol trip hop scene and then subsequently creating conditions of critique and decline through negative music press reviews, for example.

These theoretical descriptions, then, offer some useful tools for understanding our case study. I suggest that the milieu of hip hop felt its way into the U.K. but slotted in amongst other understandings of music and musical genres that were often particular to locations. Its arrival created a momentary milieu which influenced a large number of young people in Bristol's music and club scene at a particular time and then turned into part of their overall milieu structure. Hip hop slotted in amongst the reggae, punk, jazz and other traditions important to the musical milieux of the city and was then developed and used by the creative and fan community in a manner which incorporated such local influences.

TRANSFORMERS: FROM HIP TO TRIP

It is worth noting at this stage that there was considerable cross-over between 'fans' of music and 'musicians' in the Bristol scene I am describing and that the integration and participation of both was integral to the milieu that appropriated hip hop and transformed it into trip hop. Not only did some 'fans' of the music become 'musicians', but the mix of musicians and audience in the venues, clubs, bars and party spaces was central to the hip hop to trip hop party culture in Bristol. Many of those I interviewed within the Bristol hip hop milieu also stressed the eclecticism of their record collections and the breadth of their musical tastes. Hip hop fitted extremely well into such a structural milieu, since it specifically encouraged aspiring DJs to find samples from seemingly disparate styles of music that could be mixed together and that would fit with a base root hip hop beat or dub reggae bass line. Examples of this were the mixing of Tears for Fears' track 'Shout' with Grandmaster Flash's 'The Message' and of the soundtrack to *Planet of the Apes* with hip hop breaks (Monk and Canatella, 1997). The hip hop milieu, then, encouraged a degree of eclecticism, even at this early stage.

Somewhat consistent with Ben Gidley's discussion of the notion of youth as interculture (Gidley, this volume), audiences in the city of Bristol moved in and around a variety of styles. From my own fieldwork as a participant observer (Webb 2006), it was clear that the same people often could be found at reggae gigs, hip hop jams, indie gigs and even some punk gigs. A flavour of such eclecticism is provided by the following quote, from an inter-viewee who was a fan of the Bristol scene and who later (1990s) became a hip hop producer in the city (Purple Penguin and 100 Strong):

> In 1985, this was pre-sampler time when people were getting excited about drum machines and new technology. At this time I was mainly into Funk, Reggae, Punk and Jazz. I got involved in all sorts of live bands, some of which started to develop an indie feel. (Interview, 24.08.99)

Massive Attack, one of Bristol's most successful outfits had emerged at a time when punk, dub and hip hop had their own particular potency in Bristol. The band's first album, 'Blue Lines' (1991), offers a clear tem-plate of slowed down and simplified hip hop, but listen more carefully and you can hear the influences of soul, funk, reggae and string based film soundtracks. The contrast between 3D (as he was then known) and Tricky Kid mumbling in a west-country drawl and Shara Nelson's soulful vocal particularly on 'Safe from Harm' and 'Day Dreaming' is a notable fea-ture which became a template that Massive exported back to hip hop. The female vocalist offers a soulful style which complements the male rapper rather than playing the role of female rapper. As Massive Attack's career progressed their second album 'Protection' (1994) emphasised more of the stripped down, slow-mo hip hop adding different vocalists such as English indie darling Tracey Thorn. The album also forefronted their reggae roots with vocals from long time collaborator Horace Andy. These elements are further stretched on the third album 'Mezzanine' (1998). Here we find the new wave and punk sensibilities that both Robert Del Naja (3D) and Grant (Daddy G) had always admired and celebrated. These came to the fore with a more up-front guitar sound and a mood to match Joy Division or Public Image Ltd. These elements are as much a key to an understanding of Bristol as a musical city as they are to an understanding of the individual biographies, tastes and reference points of Massive Attack's members. In an interview with *Wire Magazine* in 1994, Massive Attack outlined their own understanding of where their particular brand of music comes from and what brought them together as a group:

> Daddy G: It's basically the whole punk thing, not strictly speaking punk, but through punk's amalgamation of reggae. Like I used to play the same sort of gigs as Mushroom and D and Nellie (Hooper) and there was a strong attachment from back then, back in the late 70's (Penman 1994)

Similar emphasis on the local context of Bristol is presented in Phil John-son's book *Straight Outa Bristol*, which emphasises the distinctiveness of the city which imported hip hop from America was moving into:

When hip hop took off in the early eighties it…was received within the club culture of the Dug Out, and other venues like the Dockland Settlement in St Paul's, into a scene where roots reggae, lover's rock and dub were already well-established, along with the late-punk sound of the Clash and the contemporary black music of soul and jazz that any club would have been playing as an incentive to dancers (Johnson 1996: 58–59).

In addition to this club culture and a distinct local variety of genre elements that hip hop was slotting into, it is also important to consider the role of the music industry and the way in which it was altered by what eventually was to be known as trip hop as a new genre and form. The U.K. industry and music press eventually accepted and even championed what became known as the 'Bristol sound', and included front covers and major interviews with Massive Attack, Portishead and Tricky. Interviews and reviews made reference to the 'trippy' nature of the music (discussing MA's love of Pink Floyd's 'Dark side of the Moon' for example), cannabis use and a general laid-back atmosphere associated with Bristol—something which led one commentator to describe the city as 'the graveyard of ambition' (Gillespie 2005). The term *trip hop*, according to Simon Reynolds (1998), was first coined by *Mixmag* journalist Andy Pemberton—and referred to a style that combined key elements of hip hop: breakbeats, looped samples and turntable manipulation, with a series of departures from the genre, including a contemplative, low key and self-effacing vocal and lyrical style, a slower tempo and the use of mood atmospheric samples and loping dub (reggae) base lines. For Reynolds, this genre blending was rooted in Bristol's particular musical architecture and the result was 'a distinctive Bristol sound, a languid, lugubrious hybrid of soul, reggae, jazz fusion and hip hop…' (Reynolds 1998: 316).

But consistent with the pattern of many popular music genres, as more and more additional bands, DJs and singers incorporated or copied the 'Bristol' prototype, the positive press coverage gradually transformed into critique. The music press started to deride the post-Massive Attack generation of bands who were making similar records, especially if they came from Bristol. The Bristol bands Alpha and Archive suffered from this journalist critique. This sense of derision is captured in Alex Needham's review for Alpha's second album in the NME (New Musical Express):

> *Bristolian trip hop. Yes, again.*… Six years after the Bristol boom, it would seem that the city is still a centre for drowsy, lush and gloomy pop… ultimately this is the record-as-sedentary-experience lurking in the background at a pretentious dinner party. If pop is about get up and go, *Alpha's* has unfortunately got up and gone (Needham 2001).

Archive suffered similarly, as this review of a gig in 1999—just before the release of their second album 'Take My Head'—illustrates:

> It rapidly becomes apparent that Archive are about as satisfying as the impenetrable architecture magazines that are bought to grace many a west London coffee table. They are saying nothing but in what they think is an archly cool way (*New Musical Express* 1999).

This negative music press had an effect on the way in which Bristolian musicians and fans alike perceived the continuation of the form that had become know as trip hop. Many of my interviewees discussed their dislike of the concept of trip hop, suggesting that they felt the label and the subsequent imitations by a range of artists from around the U.K. ultimately had negatively influenced the way they were covered in the music press (Webb 2006). In Bristol a combination of increasingly negative national coverage and local disquiet at the term trip hop impacted on the understandings of hip hop held by younger artists and audiences.

As hip hop in general was becoming a more and more important force within U.K. popular music as a whole, artists began to develop more rigid ideas of what form hip hop should take and where the boundaries of the genre should be drawn. The category 'U.K. hip hop' had originally started to develop around artists like Cookie Crew, MC Mello, London Posse, Demon Boyz, MC Einstein and others. These artists rapped in British accents but the rest of their art was much more directly influenced by hip hop's aesthetic than the trip hop sounds which had emerged from Bristol. As the status of trip hop in the music press declined, magazines focused on dance music culture began to reflect the growing influence of 'U.K. hip hop'. The magazine *Hip Hop Connection* became an important part of this trend, as did Tim Westwood's radio shows firstly on LWR and then on Radio 1. In turn, club nights in Bristol started developing more nights in tune with 'U.K. hip hop' and a variety of new artists and DJs emerged associated with this narrower definition of the genre (including 3PM, Aspects, Numbskullz and One Cut). U.K. hip hop had begun to replace the idea of trip hop, especially in the minds of club audiences who gravitated more to the good time, dancing and party atmosphere of a U.K. hip hop club night than the moody, slower and darker sound of trip hop. Bristol based record labels like Hombre started out running club nights that reflected this audience preference.

The work of Pierre Bourdieu (1993; Bourdieu and Wacquant 1992) offers a way of helping us to understand the complex relationships between the music industry and local music-making milieux which are illustrated by our case study. Milieux of musicians and fans in particular social spaces are involved with a set of structural forms outside of their immediate milieu that can be usefully described as a field. In our example, the field is that of the music industry which has a set of rules and understandings that the musician has to orientate him- or herself towards to firstly understand how to operate within it (e.g., contracts, copyright, distribution, promotion) and secondly to know how to change it if they want to do so. Fans are also involved in the field through interaction with the music industry's networks and by active involvement in the localised milieux through participation in gigs, DJ nights, buying records and CDs, contributing to forums and websites and inhabiting the local spaces of musical relevance. Bourdieu's notion of 'fields of cultural production' is a second layer to my account of milieux cultures. First we have the biographical and fine-grained understanding of the individuals in particular locations who are involved in the cultural production and consumption of music, and secondly we situate them within the wider industries that they work or play in; in this case the music industry. The field of cultural production that is the music industry, in Bourdieu's terms, is open to change from new actors in the field and from new developments. In our case the milieu of musicians using their knowledge of different musics developed their blending of hip hop, reggae, punk and soul into something new which, once accepted as such by the music industry, was labelled 'trip hop'. They were then engaged with the field that is the music industry in order to try and legitimate the form through record companies and the music press. For Bourdieu, struggles occur in fields over what is acceptable at any one time. In his words:

> the field of cultural production is the site of struggles in which what is at stake is the power to impose the dominant definition of the writer (or artist) and therefore to delimit the population of those entitled to take part in the struggle to define the writer (or artist).... An enlargement of the set of people who have a legitimate voice in literary (or artistic) matters may radically transform the established definition of the writer (or artist). (Bourdieu 1993: 42)

Within the music industry, struggles occur all the time for recognition of particular styles and aesthetics. For example within America different variations of hip hop vied for recognition and dominance, including Native Toungues, Five Percent Nation, Nation of Islam followers, Gangsta rap and so on. In the same way, trip hop may be said to have been involved in such a struggle for legitimacy within the broader field of the music industry as a new genre of dance music. Ultimately, however, the extent of the initial success of trip hop within the music industry marked the beginning of its downfall: once commercially successful and stylistically codified, it became heavily critiqued by the music press and then by musicians and fans alike. At the same time, the somewhat more rigid genre of U.K. hip hop began to gain currency within the broader cultural field of the music industry, a development which, in turn, led a substantial section of the musical milieu in Bristol to move away from trip hop and to engage with hip hop in a more, as they saw it, 'purist' way.

RETRENCHMENT

Jamie Hombre ran a record label in Bristol from the late 1990s through to 2003 called Hombre Records. Hombre became a barometer of opinion about hip hop in Britain and reflected a growing dismissal of the trip hop associated with Massive Attack, Portishead, Smith and Mighty and various artists related to the Cup of Tea record label.[3] Hombre was trying to establish a label that he felt would be as challenging and interesting musically as many of his predecessors in Bristol had been. He found that sections of the British music press and of the hip hop audience were very self-critical and concerned with defining their own genre through its production techniques, structure of beats and fluidity of rapping and emphasising the difference between hip hop and other genres like trip hop. He released a number of tracks which were interpreted critically by customers, musicians and audiences as reminiscent of the trip hop sound. Although he didn't fully accept this interpretation of the material he had released, the response prompted a change in direction:

> One Cut was the first release.... The first twelve-inch was mainly slow beats and instrumental. It got mixed up by a lot of people with trip hop and got slated a bit. DJs thought of it as trip hop and so the whole Bristol problem affected the release....Then I changed tack a bit and put out the Numbskullz. This did really well and it got good reviews as new British or U.K. hip hop. It made a modest profit? But it was definitely hip hop albeit a very British version. (Jamie Hombre, Interview, 30/07/01)

A critical response from the media, then, as well as from a younger audience of fans who were less familiar with the diverse musical culture of the city, started to change the perceptions and outputs of people like Hombre who were running small record labels. Hombre was prompted to focus more attention on other acts like the Numbskullz and Aspects. The milieu of musicians associated Massive Attack, Portishead and Reprazent, who now consisted of the elder statesman in the Bristol scene, had continued with the sort of experimentation that had led to trip hop in the first place (for example, Massive Attack's third album 'Mezzanine' and fourth '100th Window' still presented unusual combinations of sound that reflected the dimensions we have already discussed). The younger and newer hip hop generation, however, started to shift away from the culture of experimentation associated with bands like Massive Attack and towards the developing genre of UK hip hop, in which sound, production and stricter interpretations of what hip hop should be like tended to take precedence.

In a number of interviews with U.K. hip hop fans in Bristol (between1998 and 1999), my respondents deemed hip hop's authenticity to be marked out by 'tight' production (either in terms of the bass or the sharpness of a snare drum), quality of the vocal track and general consistency with a fairly narrow notion of hip hop (stripped down tracks with simple melody as a backing for the beats and rap). Equally important was the specificity of hip hop in terms of associated fashion and graffiti. Although ostentatious fashion such as large gold chains and jewellery tended only to be worn in an ironic sense (for example, *Goldie Looking Chain*), low key street sports wear such as hooded tops, baseball caps, low slung jeans and fairly stylish but non-flashy trainers were the norm.[4] This is not to say that the genre was regressive, but that it worked within strictly defined boundaries. Artists who strayed from those boundaries tended to be excluded. Just how tightly defined these boundaries were in musical terms can be seen in the following comments by Jamie from Hombre referring to what I thought was a U.K. hip hop track:

> The market is not ready for something like this yet. Its production isn't tight enough and the vocal is quite unusual for a U.K. hip hop track. It wouldn't sell to those DJs or fans. (Conversation with author, December 1999)

Jamie Hombre recognised that within U.K. hip hop, accent was also an important feature. One of his successful acts, Aspects, marked themselves out from the mainly London-centric U.K. hip hop scene by rapping in distinctly West country accents. Up until approximately 1998 and 1999, London accents had dominated the U.K. scene; however, labels like Jamie's succeeded in pursuing the Bristol accent as a marker of authenticity—something which changed perceptions with respect to one element of how U.K. hip hop had to sound and established the Bristol accent as an important part of the U.K. hip hop milieu. Nevertheless, the music as a whole remained fairly regimented with fine grained differences in production, samples used or instrumentation. U.K. hip hop then was fairly narrowly defined and there were clear limits to the extent of any variations if one was to be successful within this market segment.

CONCLUDING REMARKS

David Harvey in his discussion of dialectics and globalisation emphasizes that global flows will have great impact on environments that they are exported to but that the ideas that they hold will be transformed and modified in their use in different locations (Harvey 1996). The series of developments described in relation to this case study demonstrate the ways in which this worked in the case of hip hop in Bristol, at the same time as illustrating the subsequent feeding back into the music industry of the local transformation which came to be known as trip hop and, finally, the decline of this genre in favour of a very different interpretation—both in the broader field of the music industry and ultimately in Bristol itself. The present period will, no doubt, present further developments as U.K. hip hop becomes pressurised from new sub-genres in dance music such as grime, dub-step, variants of drum and bass, etc., and from global pressures, not least the dominance of the r&b variant of hip hop.

If we are to research and understand something as complex as hip hop as it resonates through and within the spatial geography and social milieux of the world, then we need to navigate a course which encompasses the field of the music industry and the interplay between this field and local milieux cultures. Crucially, moments of stability and the fixing of genres in terms of musical style are located within the context of the continual movement of forms especially in a more globally culturally mobile situation. When we look at the production of hip hop in various settings we must look at the individuals, their lifeworlds, the milieux of which they are a part and the broader field that they operate within. Using a combination of my development of Dürrschmidt's milieu and Bourdieu's approach to fields of cultural production, then, I have sought to develop some tools through which we may effectively research and understand processes such as those which surrounded the take-up and transformations of hip hop in Bristol. This combination I call *milieux cultures*.

NOTES

1. For example, Bristol had a bus boycott in 1963 because the bus company had barred 'coloured' bus workers. The boycott eventually led to black and Asian drivers and conductors working on the buses but was an example of the entrenched racism in the Britain of the time.
2. Bristol jazz artists included Andy Sheppard and Keith Tippett. Punk was highly influential in the city, through bands like The Cortina's, Disorder, Vice Squad, The Amebix, Chaos UK and Lunatic Fringe. The indie/avant garde guitar scene included The Blue Aeroplanes, The Brilliant Corners, and Strangelove. Some bands also crossed these scenes like the jazz and funk influenced Rip Rig and Panic and the early incarnation of the Pop Group.
3. A Bristol label that had many artists working within the trip hop genre, including Monk and Canatella, Statik Sound System, Purple Penguin, Receiver and Invisible Pair of Hands.
4. The prominence of such styles within hip hop was broadly consistent with national trends, something illustrated by the content of U.K. hip hop websites such as http://www.britishhiphop.co.uk/, http://www.ukhh.com/, http://www.b-boys.com/index.html and http://www.hijackbristol.co.uk/board/.

13 'Pin-up punks'

The reality of a virtual community

Eric Chamberlin

Subcultures are seductive. For insiders, subcultures provide a sense of cohesion and belonging. For social scientists they are social units with a size and relative autonomy that seems to invite study. Yet the term *subculture* as it was used in youth studies became so closely identified with the Marxist theories of Dick Hebdige's *Subculture: the Meaning of Style* and other works of the Centre for Contemporary Cultural Studies that it was difficult to separate the theory from the phenomenon. Furthermore as the 1990s progressed into the twenty-first century 'spectacular subcultures' (Hebdige 1979: 18) seemed to diminish in importance. The bordering of youth groups now seems less certain and the allegiance of participants is argued to be more tenuous, something which for some theorists has brought the whole notion of subculture into question (Bennett 1999; Muggleton 1997).

At the same time that youth culture has apparently shifted away from bounded subcultural groups, new expressions of youth identity have emerged through new communications technologies such as the Internet. The immediate tendency among academic researchers was to focus on the most exotic forms associated with these new technologies. 'Doug', one of the informants of Sherry Turkle's *Life on the Screen*, states that 'RL [real life] is just another window [on his computer's monitor]' (Turkle 1995: 13). This quote eloquently captures the potential for fluidity and multiplicity of identity available to Internet users. It also suggests that the net is yet another example of postmodern media's tendency to dissolve bordered and substantive culture and identity. However, while the net does have distinctive properties as a medium, the creation of fictitious personas and the playing out of different roles in different contexts are not limited to online communication nor do they characterize all of the interactions that occur on the Internet. For many users, including some participants in youth culture, windows are just another part of RL, and the cultures they participate in can exist both on and offline.

This chapter acknowledges that the general breakdown of collective boundaries has meant that subcultures are probably less prevalent within youth culture than they were in the past. However, rather than dismissing the notion of subculture, we use the term here in a similar way to theorists such as Hodkinson, who have chosen to rework the term more pragmatically as follows:

> While avoiding some of the term's previous implications, it will be used, essentially, to capture the relatively substantive, clearly bounded form taken by certain elective cultural groupings. This will be contrasted with an increasing tendency of late for theorists to emphasize that the saturation of society by media and commerce has led to the breakdown of collective boundaries. (2002: 9)

Through the work of Emile Durkheim we shall also examine some of the social forces that continue to sustain subcultures and lead to the creation of other related social phenomena. One such phenomenon consists of the active participants of an online community that is part of a niche market, soft-core pornography website, which we will refer to by the pseudonym Pin-Up Punks.[1]

THE SETTING

Launched in 2001, Pin-Up Punks presented itself as part of the alternative pornography movement stemming from the 'pro-sex' feminism espoused by Nadine Strossen (1995). Strossen's position is a response to the 'anti-pornography' feminism of Andrea Dworkin (1989). In common with other 'alterna-porn' websites, such as Heather Corrina's Scarlet Letters (2002), the models on Pin-Up Punks had a high level of creative control over their photo sets. Also in common with other 'alterna-porn' sites there was an effort to personalize and individualize the models. In the case of Pin-Up Punks this was achieved through the profiles of the models, online journals kept by the models and the comments the models made on the site's message boards and special interest groups. Unlike Scarlet Letters, Pin-Up Punks was a heavily marketed, for profit business, that generated revenues through memberships, merchandising and advertising. The personalization of the models was also part of a marketing strategy that presented the models as authentic. What the models 'authentically' represented was revealed by the metadata embedded in the header of the site's entrance page. Until August of 2003 it included the phrases 'naked punk chicks,' 'naked emo chicks,' and 'naked goth chicks.' The site was heavily, and successfully, marketed to youth and the alternative music scene. Most members ranged in age from eighteen through into their twenties, although a significant number were over thirty and a few over forty. The models were similarly aged with the oldest being thirty-five. European-Americans were the most common ethnic group but the share of international and multi-cultural members and models were on the rise during my research. Virtually all participants displayed a strong interest in non-mainstream music and culture.

The site acted as the main forum for a community that consisted of the paying members that chose to interact socially, the paid staff, and the paid models. For many participants the erotica became secondary to the social aspects of the site. Variants of the sentiment 'came for the women, stayed for the community' were common among the members. The site featured interactive journals, message boards, special interest subgroups, and also regional groups that provided opportunities for face-to-face interaction. These were all features added to the site at the demand of the paying membership as the community grew. Over the course of my research, photo albums, a webcam portal, and a chat room were added. The friendship networks on the site were very strong and the phrase 'like-minded people' was used constantly on the boards. Commitment to the community was high. Participants travelled considerable distances to attend various parties and events associated with the community, and people talked of being 'loyal' to the site. The longevity of membership and a high overall post-count were also valued and socially rewarded.

For this study, I immersed myself in the community. I posted on the general boards and in special interest groups for a total of nearly 900 messages over the course of a year.[2] I maintained a 'friends list' of both local and distant participants. I kept an interactive journal and posted comments to the journals of others. I became heavily involved with my local regional group and helped organize several dinner and bar meets, as well a gig at which an eclectic mix of local bands and DJ's performed.[3] Through my local group I was able to meet about twenty-five community participants face-to-face.

PIN-UP PUNKS AS PORNOGRAPHY

The focus of this chapter is the Pin-Up Punks community, not the erotic content of the website, but pornography is so controversial an issue that some discussion of its relationship to the community is necessary. The active participants accepted the idea of Pin-Up Punks as a female positive form of self-expression that was strikingly different from mainstream pornography, but there was an acute awareness that outsiders may have seen the site otherwise. 'Outsiders' included both paying members with no or minimal personal profiles, and non-members. The distrust of outsiders in the Pin-Up Punks community was more than disdain for 'lurkers.' There was a fear that those who did not share the community's values might be 'creeps' that would harass or harm the models or members. For this reason admittance to the local groups' online forums, where meeting times and locations were discussed, was very selective.

Participants frequently discussed the dangers of using a 'porn site' to discuss personal information, but there was a great deal of debate as to the appropriateness of the term *pornography* as applied to the site. Many preferred terms like *erotica* or *erotic art*. The marketing of the site presented it as highly female friendly. The staff even claimed the majority of the paying members were female. Only the staff knew the demographics of the site's anonymous members, but a May 2003 sample of 100 profiled members obtained through the site's 'find members' function revealed 81 men to 19 women. While some of the site's more active members were aware of this male majority, the site continued to be perceived as female friendly. The high degree of posting activity by the models may have been a part of this, as may the ruthless policing of the message boards by the staff. Comments deemed to be disrespectful to the models or other female participants were usually addressed by forcing the offender to have an anonymous account, thereby terminating his or her posting privileges. In the community this was called 'being zotted.' The site's owner once commented that he had suspended the posting privileges of 200 members, only two of whom had been women.

Another aspect of the site's marketing was that the models were presented as the sort of women that one might meet at a cool club night. There was an implied equality between the models and members. The models posted to their journals and the message boards, joined and participated in special interest forums, and attended local parties and gatherings with the members. Members sometimes posted nude or provocative pictures of themselves. There was even a special interest forum, the largest on the site, for males wishing to post photosets of themselves similar to the photosets of the female models. Inequities remained. While there was more than enough member-nudity to blur the line between exhibitionist and voyeur, models were paid for photographs and given free access to the site's features. Members, in contrast, voluntarily contributed photos, and paid for access to the site. Men were required to be more circumspect in their words and actions than women. All the members and models answered to a staff with a female majority, and the staff answered to a male owner and general manager.

For some members of my local group, these contradictions came into focus on the night the Pin-Up Punks stage show came to our city. The event took place at a small venue with a capacity of about two or three hundred patrons. The venue was known for hosting alternative bands and was familiar to all of us. It was an intimate club where the performers were frequently indistinguishable from the audience until they stepped up to the low stage and started performing. On this night, a dressing room was set-up next to the stage and the audience was forbidden to approach it. Many of the models mixed with the crowd before and after their burlesque-style performance, but there were more bouncers around than at a normal event for the venue. After the show a member sitting next to me laughed. He turned to me and said, 'This is *so* not what it's supposed to be'. About that time one of the other members present asked if he could take a picture of himself with the model he had been speaking with. With considerable embarrassment she told him that the models had to charge five dollars for every picture featuring any of them. The member next to me again laughed.

'Five dollars for a picture with a [Pin-Up Punk], they're supposed to be just like us, the kind of girls who would come to this club anyway'. The models clearly found charging money to online friends for photos very awkward, but they were under orders from the staff.

It is improbable that any exchange of a form of erotic intimacy for money can take place without the potential for feelings of exploitation, but who is exploited and to what degree are questions far too complex to be answered here. As a researcher,[4] I have always felt that the insider's perspective should be privileged. The community participants I met and spoke with, both models and members did not feel degraded and the models largely felt empowered. The embarrassment of the models in the above situation ended when another member pulled over a hundred dollars out of his wallet. He said something to the effect of 'the site needs to make money and I just got my pay check.' Once the issue of money was resolved both members and models took many pictures of each other. Despite its contradictions and inequalities Pin-Up Punks was a vibrant and growing community and it is to the subject of the community that we now return.

PIN-UP PUNKS AS A COMMUNITY

The term *community*, as applied to web based social groupings, is contested. This is partly due to the increased potential for multiple personas and fluid identities. Howard Rheingold questions whether 'relationships and commitments as we know them [are] even possible in a place where identities are fluid' (1993: 61). However, Nessim Watson responds by pointing out that such fluctuations of identity are by no means exclusive to the Internet (1997). In all cases, the participants from the Pin-Up Punks community that I met face-to-face appeared to be very much the people they presented themselves as online. Rather than construct fluid 'virtual' identities, they had tied their personas on the website to their everyday lives. Before I 'met' them in the traditional sense I often knew highly personal information about their lives, information that included intimate marital issues, personal anxieties, personal conflicts with parents, conflicts at work and sexual practices. Instead of utilizing the Internet's capacity for fluidity the participants were using it as venue for extreme honesty.

Pin-Up Punks was, and is, far from the only venue for 'true-to-life' personas on the web. The revelation of large amounts of personal information is consistent with the self-presentation strategies used by the authors of personal home pages in Joseph Dominick's 1999 study. Dominick noted the predominance of the strategy of 'ingratiation,' which involves the sharing of personal, and potentially embarrassing things about oneself with the goal of building friendship and trust (1999: 648). Denise Bortree's study of teenage girls' web logs revealed similar results (2005). She also observed that

the teenage girls in the ethnographic study accomplished [building rela-
tionships] through their blogs by sharing intimate thoughts, including
their frustrations, their disappointments and, at times, their despair.
(Bortree 2005: 32)

The active participants of Pin-Up Punks were seeking to broaden their
friendship networks and become part of the community. Therefore personal stories and intimate details of private life were presented, and ingratiation was by far the most common strategy. The level of self-revelation
on Pin-Up Punks was greater than one would expect during face-to-face
meetings, particularly between people who were just getting to know each
other. In the introduction to *Cybersociety 2.0* Steven G. Jones observes
that 'whereas it is true that the Internet overcomes distance, in some ways
it also overcomes proximity' (1998: xiii). Consistent with this, the lack
of physical presence or even vocal interaction on the Internet seemed to
embolden the self-revelation process. Yet, in the case of Pin-Up Punks
members, full participation, and social status, in the community required
both online and face-to-face interaction with other participants. This rein-
troduced proximity.

My local group was very new when I joined and had no official face-
to-face events. Few people knew each other prior to becoming community participants. When they did meet the level of initial formality was
unusually high for young Californians, particularly those involved with
alternative culture. The initial awkwardness of face-to-face interaction frequently re-emerged at larger events where there were numerous participants who had only 'met' online. At one such event a model confessed that
she had never been somewhere where so many people already knew who
she was. She found the experience quite intimidating. For most participants
the awkwardness faded as friendships developed both online and offline
components. Physical meetings were not limited to local groups. Members,
models, and staff travelled considerable distances to larger Pin-Up Punks
events. Some of these events were organized by the staff, some by members,
but all provided opportunities to add proximal communication to online
relationships. The combination of self-revelation and face-to-face socialization rapidly created strong friendship networks. These were at the core of
the community.

While face-to-face interaction was a significant aspect of the community, and was highly valued among the participants, the community was
international. Geographic realities prevented face-to-face meetings between
most participants. Watson notes that traditional definitions of community
involve notions of geographic proximity. She argues that the word *community* is etymologically related to the words *communication* and *com-
munion*, terms that do not necessarily require physical proximity (1997:
103–4). Responding to Howard Rheingold, who popularized the term *virtual community* in his book of the same name (1993), Watson also writes

that the 'distinction between "virtual" community and "real" community is unwarranted' (1997: 129). Certainly, the distinction between 'real life' and 'virtual' tended to be rejected on Pin-Up Punks, where new members often were criticized if they used the term *RL* or 'real life' to refer to offline time. A model once responded by referring to the personal revelations in her journal and her nude photos and asking how much more 'real' she could possibly be.

In her research on the rec.arts.tv.soaps newsgroup, Nancy Baym places emphasis on the importance to members of strategies to 'accomplish friendliness', through 'offering one another social support' (2000: 120–21). She also describes off topic tangents, where participants could discuss personal matters, as 'ritualized space for friendliness' (129). Such personal support was also a key feature of Pin-Up Punks, especially within participants' journals and certain special interest forums, such as the carefully screened parents' group. Late one night a model posted to the group about a moment of crisis in caring for her sick child. Several people on the parents' group that night offered sympathy and advice. The model again posted when her child fell asleep and several times over the next day to report on the child's progress and express gratitude for the kind words of her fellow parents.

SUBCULTURES ON PIN-UP PUNKS

Pin-Up Punks offered particularly rich opportunities to construct an online identity. How a participant filled out his or her profile and what special interest or regional groups they joined were particularly immediate examples of cultural associations and signifiers from which identity is constructed. Given the way that the site invoked punk, emo, goth, etc., in its marketing one would expect many of these associations to reflect subcultural affiliations, and some of them did. There were, for example, two gothic oriented groups, a punk group and a mod group. There are also opportunities to express such associations through one's profiled music preferences and interests. Most active members also posted pictures of themselves, which allowed for visual and stylistic signification, in the form of clothes or body modification, for example. Constructing a subcultural identity on Pin-Up Punks would have been very easy. For example, a participant might articulate a gothic identity by listing gothic and industrial bands as well as cerebral horror films among their 'favourites', discussing Anne Rice's vampire novels in the literature group, or being members of a pagan group. Initially, I expected to find an example of what Ted Polhemus called 'the gathering of the tribes' (1994: 128–29). Polhemus uses the phrase to describe increasing instances of subcultural participants who put aside perceived differences and gather at eclectic events of common interest. This was not what went on in the Pin-Up Punks community.

In my local group, two participants could be described as rockabillies, though they never used the word themselves. There was also a member of an emo music group, but the majority of the local participants, and participants in the community as a whole were far too eclectic in their tastes to group with any established subculture. The use of subcultural signifiers was only part of how participants constructed their online identities. The interest groups included cat owners, anime fans, graphic novel enthusiasts, sex industry workers, depressives, backpackers, Buddhists and Hindus, and an ever-expanding list of others. Instead of displaying subcultural affinities, the majority of members constructed highly individualized and eclectic identities. Those that did have subcultural affiliations were not allowed to be divisive in how they expressed them.

In one example, a new member of the site started a discussion thread on the general boards. He asked if there were any 'real' 'punk' or 'skinhead' girls on the site. A few members posted images from photosets of models they felt fit his criteria. Others asked him to define 'real.' The thread quickly deteriorated from there. The thread starter was called 'arrogant' and 'pretentious,' for even raising the issue of subcultural authenticity. What is most striking is that this was the only example of anyone trying to discuss issues of subcultural commitment or authenticity that I found anywhere on the site. I could not even find examples of such a discussion within the 'subcultural' special interest groups to which I subscribed. The members of the Pin-Up Punks community could be seen as demonstrating an increasing obsolescence of subculture as a theoretical model. The majority of participants did not fit into stylistically distinctive groups and there was far too much sharing of interests and social crossover between those participants who did fit into stylistic groups to describe the community as a gathering of subcultures.

PIN-UP PUNKS AS A SUBCULTURE

While Pin-Up Punks was not a gathering of subcultures, it is worth considering if it was a subculture in its own right. It was a 'real' rather than 'virtual' community and therefore, as Hodkinson puts it, 'relatively substantive' (2002). Hodkinson uses four indicators of substance to distinguish substantive subcultures from other youth scenes (28–33). The first of these is 'consistent distinctiveness' by which he means 'a set of shared tastes and values which is distinctive from those of other groups and reasonably consistent from one participant to the next (30).' Pin-Up Punks members, models and staff, shared a fondness for women who presented themselves as outsiders and were often tattooed or body pierced. They often had an affinity for pro-sex feminism. They enjoyed non-mainstream music and most seemed to see themselves as outsiders. These are consistent tastes and values, but a community so diverse as to include vegan *Star Trek* fans that love jazz and Hindu heavy metal fans cannot be regarded as consistently distinctive. The participants had some consistent tastes and values but not enough to meet this criterion. Hodkinson's second indicator, 'identity', is 'the extent to which participants hold a perception that they are involved in a distinct cultural grouping and share feelings of identity with one another' (30–31). The sense of community was quite strong so in this regard the community was substantive. The third indicator is commitment (31). This was demonstrated by the considerable time and effort that many participants dedicating to the community both online and off. Commitment was definitely present. The last indicator is autonomy. In essence the degree to which the community's sustaining 'infrastructure of events, consumer goods and communication' is internally controlled and 'retains a *relatively* high degree of autonomy' (32). The Pin-Up Punks community depended on the Pin-Up Punks business for its existence. The management of the business made this point clear on numerous occasions by not only removing participants but also threatening to disband regional groups if banned members were found attending regional events. While the business was interconnected with the community it was largely an external force. The community was not autonomous. We should, however, note that because the community was tied to one business, with one brand name and one set of defining set of images and tastes it had a degree of exclusivity and stability that was in its own way substantive.

Although Pin-Up Punks does not satisfy all of Hodkinson's criteria as a subculture, the presence of such strong self-identification and commitment reinforces its 'reality' as a community. There are striking parallels here in terms of both online and youth culture. The Pin-Up Punks community, like Watson's and Baym's examples, took the very Internet communication technologies so often represented as impersonal and distancing and used them to bring together a community of intimate friendships. Similarly, the community made use of the unbordered, less substantive nature of much of youth culture to create a clearly bordered community that was almost as substantive as a subculture. This suggests that while youth cultures are subject to social forces that fragment them and make them 'virtual' they are also subject to forces that unify them and make them 'real'.

POSTMODERNISM, DURKHEIM AND PIN-UP PUNKS

A possible understanding of these forces lies in a combination of postmodern and Durkheimian theory. Postmodernism gives us an understanding of forces that lead to the fragmentation of youth culture. Fredric Jameson describes postmodernism as the cultural logic of late capitalism. It is matrix or structure of contemporary culture and thought. Jameson connects the omnipresent market and the nature of postmodernist culture (1991: 4–5). Postmodernism is linked to our increasingly rapid bombardment by media images. The overwhelming and contradictory concepts presented by these images break down boundaries and definitions. Jameson often uses the word *schizophrenic* to describe cultural characteristics that result from this process and, in so doing, invokes and paraphrases Lacan (26). The schizophrenic nature of the cultural dominant can be seen in terms of incoherent decontextualized signifiers or images.

Historically, subcultures have seized on decontextualized signifiers and assembled them into new patterns as a mode of identity construction. Mods took the Italian motor scooter, and American soul music and combined them with the Union Jack (Chamberlin 1998). Punks did the same with sexual fetish clothing, the brightly coloured hair introduced by glam, and old school uniforms (Brake 1980). In these and numerous other cases, subcultural participants have distorted or destroyed the original signified meanings of these items by using them out of context. On Pin-Up Punks the process was taken further as participants further borrowed and mixed style, music and other forms of signification in ways that seemed 'schizophrenic' in relation to their previous subcultural associations.

The 'virtual' world of the Internet also seems very postmodern. It is very much a part of our rapid bombardment by media images and seems to put all images and information—whether factual or false, rational or ludicrous—on equal footing. Both Internet and youth culture seem not only subject to postmodern society's breakdown of meaning and structure, they seem to embrace it. Internet and youth cultures such as Pin-Up Punks rely on this postmodern fragmentation to provide them with the cultural 'spare parts' to build new cultural forms, but in the building process they also display substantiveness.

Baym, Watson and Hodkinson all observe the substantive nature of the communities they study. They quite rightly contrast their observations to the tendency of other theorists to emphasis fragmentation and lack of substance but they do not theorise very much as to the nature of the social forces that create this substantiveness. Bringing Emile Durkheim back into the discussion of youth culture can provide us with theories addressing this. Durkheim's theories are used in the work of Richard Cloward and Lloyd Ohlin (1960) and are also used extensively by Albert Cohen (1955). They use Durkheim to present ideas about lower-class criminal and deviant culture. I am using Durkheim to address the social strain and responses to the social strain of postmodern society. Durkheim can give us an understanding of the cost of postmodern fragmentation, and how cohesive communities can counter that cost.

Durkheim's work is concerned with belief systems[5] residing in the social sphere (1984: 329–30). The *common* or *collective consciousness* is the term Durkheim uses to describe the part of the social sphere in which belief systems reside. He observes that as societies grow from the localized or tribal level there is a thinning and abstraction of the collective consciousness caused by the abstraction of the objects to which it refers (1984: 230).

A weakening of social definitions weakens the collective consciousness. When the common consciousness is weakened, and other values fail to replace it, there is a state of dysfunction or 'anomie'. Anomie is the state of frustration and despair that occurs when desire is not controlled or guided by socially constructed belief systems. The causes of anomie are social, but it is experienced as an individual emotional state. Durkheim demonstrates the destructive and dysfunctional capacity of anomie by making anomie the central concept of his book *Suicide* (1952). The social maintenance of belief systems is primarily the function of the collective consciousness. Consequently a weakening of the collective consciousness that is not some-how compensated for will increase the overall level of anomie in a society (241–76).

Durkheim's ideas were first published over a century ago. To under-stand their significance to Pin-Up Punks, we need to see them in post-modern terms. The logic of the postmodern *cultural dominant* fragments the belief systems contained in the collective consciousness. From this we must conclude that anomie is very prevalent in postmodern society. Say-ing that anomie is very prevalent in postmodern society doesn't mean that all individuals suffer from it, or suffer from it equally. Despite this, we should note that postmodern anomie is generalized in its origin. It is based on a very broad breakdown of collective consciousness and, because of this, its source is not direct or specific. This means that it can be found throughout postmodern society not just among criminal subcultures dis-cussed by Cloward, Ohlin and Cohen. Yet there are many counter-anomic forces, sources of beliefs, which can overcome its affects for individuals and groups. These include professional ethics, religion and any other exposure to a set of beliefs that the individuals feels 'makes sense'. If the individual can successfully internalize a belief system anomie can be countered, but belief systems in contemporary society are many and conflicting. In the gaps between them anomie is experienced.

Subcultures also serve a counter-anomic function. They are systems of explicit and implicit beliefs assembled and recontexualized from the signifi-ers and concepts of the collective consciousness. Subcultures provide a kind of coherence and logic, albeit one that is often coded in music and style. While trying to read these implicit beliefs too precisely or without acknowl-edging the perspective of subcultural participants themselves is a mistake for which Dick Hebdige and the Birmingham School are often criticized, dismissing these implicit beliefs is equally wrong. Hodkinson also argues against such dismissal by citing 'a set of shared tastes and values' as part of his evidence for the substantiveness of subcultures. Indeed they are far too substantive to be viewed as a thing of the past.

Pin-Up Punks doesn't quite fit the model of subcultures as belief sys-tems. The beliefs common to Pin-Up Punks' participants were far too open-ended to be called a system. This was demonstrated through the lively and wide-ranging debates on the site's message boards. There was very little in the way of consensus on most issues, rather there was a dynamic of diverse tastes and opinions defining themselves in opposition or qualified agreement. This process of debate is the key to understanding the nature of Pin-Up Punks as subculturally influenced and internet-based community. Debate and discussion are the chief pastimes of many Internet communities, including Baym's. Through debate, participants in the Pin-Up Punks community constructed and refined their personal counter-anomic belief systems. The community did not provide an extensive belief system, but it did offer a safe zone or common ground for exploring values. In Durkheimian terms it was more specialized and focused version of the collective consciousness. In the community, participants were like-minded enough to be generally supportive of one another as they constructed identities and their underlying systems of explicit and implicit beliefs. When a participant logged onto the site and articulated an opinion, he or she might not have been certain of how it would be received, but they were certain of some things. A religious fundamentalist would not launch into a tirade about how anyone who views nude pictures on the web is going to go hell. The member would not be called a freak for having piercings and tattoos, nor would they be told that their self-worth depended on buying an expensive mainstream product. Instead they would probably receive legitimation of their own identity and beliefs.

The counter-anomic function of community collective consciousness provides a model for Pin-Up Punks and may be useful in understanding other communities both on and off the internet. It represents a shift in emphasis from the group to the individual in the counter anomic function rather than a new process. The belief systems of subcultures are not so complete as to prevent individual interpretations, and the shared beliefs articulated in the Pin-Up Punks community were a partial belief system. Nonetheless the belief system construction in Pin-Up Punks is a more individualistic process than that which occurs in a subculture. This shift was inevitable. The schizophrenia of the postmodern cultural dominant, which weakened the other belief systems, also made subcultures less credible as they were ever more rapidly exploited by the market and reduced to saleable images. This has not destroyed the phenomenon of subculture, but it does explain why it is less prevalent than in the past.

If Pin-Up Punks is at all representative of the current state of youth and alternative culture, we have reached a point where the subcultures of the past are often used as sources of signifiers and implied beliefs to be recontextualized on an individual basis. They continue to have impact and influence in this capacity and, for some, are useful as complete systems, but they are no longer as trusted as they once were.

NOTES

1. A pseudonym is necessary because some of the content of this chapter contradicts the marketing of the website. It is not my intention to harm the business hosting the community. During the course of my research many of the discussion forums were opened to search engines. This has forced me to paraphrase all online material, as direct quotes would reveal the identity of the website.
2. This is a fairly moderate posting level for an 'active' member. A high post count was a status symbol to a point. One member posted about 500 messages in a week. Some participants considered this excessive.
3. The gig promoted the site heavily, but was a fundraiser for a free speech charity and was organized entirely by the paying members of the site. It was not part of the model's stage show described latter.
4. The pornographic nature of the site initially prevented me from seeing it as a phenomenon worthy of study. I found it while searching the web for clues to better understand the changing relationship of youth to subculture. My first thought was that it was a tacky fetish site that represented a new low in exploitive youth marketing. Months later I found a link to Pin-Up Punks on Scarlet Letters, a site I respect. This prompted me to investigate further. I recognize that some readers will feel that I participated in the objectification women by conducting this study. Obviously I do not share this opinion. I believe that erotica can empower women. Pin-Up Punks is a less than perfect example of this but it is a valid example. If I didn't believe that I would never have conducted or published this research.
5. Durkheim uses the terms *ethics* and *morals*. I use 'belief systems' to remove the Judeo-Christian implications of those terms.

14 A 'bounded virtuality'
ICTs and youth in Alghero, Sardinia[1]

Silvia Ferrero

In the world of youth culture, information and communication technologies (ICTs) have sometimes been regarded as tools of liberation and democratization and as a new social space where young people can reconfigure their identity and the structures of authority of their social contexts. In some accounts, ICTs are conceived as spaces where visual and virtual communication becomes 'the connecting structure', to use Bateson's (1972) terms, between the inner world of youth and the external world. Some young people have developed a great ability to master ICTs. In so doing they also attempt to handle the process of social change and modernity, since a command of ICTs can represent an opportunity for a better future and a chance to overcome the social constraints and categories of their social environment.

Contrary to sociological literature that praises ICTs as tools of democratization for youth, this paper argues that ICTs can also become a source and symbol of frustration for young people. For the practices developed around new technologies can also reproduce the status quo, the social order and certain structures of authority and power. In other words, it is important to look at new technologies in relation to their 'embeddedness' (Miller and Slater 2000: 8), that is, the social context where they are used and experienced. In spite of the liberatory potential of ICTs, then, the way they are actually experienced is dependent upon questions of access and motivation. With reference to anthropological analysis of everyday practices of young people using ICTs in Alghero in Northern Sardinia, Italy this paper demonstrates how the institutional manipulation and appropriation of ICTs at a local level can be a source of frustration and disillusionment for young people. This study shows the resilience of social categories and attitudes rooted in the local context that constrain young people's expectations in relation to the use of ICTs and the Internet.

YOUNG PEOPLE AND ICTS

The introduction of ICTs in all aspects of human life has prompted academics to look at the effects of new technologies on the perceptions and actions of adults and children (McCluskey 1997; Negroponte 1995; Sefton-Green 1998). Studies on educational technologies, the Internet and the information economy have called for a re-thinking of concepts such as identity, subjectivity, authority, space, social change, modernity, culture and knowledge (Castells 1997; Turkle 1984; Virilio 1995). Above all, the concept of 'flexible selves' elaborated by Donna Haraway (1991) and Sherry Turkle (1984, 1997) has influenced for many years the ethnographic and experimental research on ICTs. For example, the notion that young people may change identity with ICTs and that their attitudes also change according to the institutional contexts in which they find themselves and use ICTs, appears consistently in sociological literature on the subject (Holmes and Glenn 1999; Newmann 1990). However, the literature on ICTs has also elaborated other hypotheses and scenarios.

For example, in the rethinking of social relations between adults, young people and ICTs some studies have also resurrected the idea of a 'generational distance' based on an asymmetry in the process of communication between adults and youth (Abbott 1996; Castellani 1993). Young people's ability to use a meta-language to affirm their own identities, individuality and uniqueness has long been studied in the social sciences. Through language youth generate new terminology and create verbal challenges and responses to the world of adults (Allison 1995; Hewitt 1989; Pilkington 1994). With the Internet and multimedia software youth have further acquired new devices of communication (Amthor 1991; Sefton-Green and Buckingham 1998). Thus, the 'communication gap' between adults and youth seems to have increased (Abbott 1996; 1998).

Some have described young people as masters of ICTs, something contrasted with the inability and unwillingness of adults to thoroughly engage with ICTs (Negroponte 1995). Studies on educational technologies, for example, speak of teachers' uneasiness at changing their teaching practices (c.f. Goodson and Marshall Mangan 1995), or to have their authority as knowledge-givers challenged in front of their students by means of ICTs (c.f. Macmillan et al. 1997; Singh 1993). In much of this literature, teachers are described as having uncomfortable relations with ICT skilled students and as nurturing feelings of delegitimization and disempowerment because of ICTs (cf. Kilian 1993; Warshauer 1998). Young people, the literature shows, display their knowledge and technical skills on ICTs with a readiness and quickness that enables them to challenge adults' traditional role as repositories of knowledge (Holmes and Glenn 1999; Buckingham 1990; Turkle 1997).

The relations between adults and young people seem to have become more complicated when it comes to ICTs, because ICTs have entered the game that youth play to separate their world from adults. In addition, in recent years we have witnessed cases of young people who have also succeeded in threatening the institutional contexts of working environments as well as financial and political establishments by means of ICTs. Research on young hackers and crackers shows, that young people's social practices with ICTs nowadays constitute a counter-culture against, and in opposition to, the middle-class establishment of adults (Nissen 1998).

However, youth's ability to master different types of software and hardware must not be considered only as expressions of young people's forms of counter-culture and resistance. As a matter of fact, in many situations knowledge on ICTs represents for young people an attempt to master modernity and social change (e.g. Miller and Slater 2000). A command of ICTs, in fact, means for many young people an opportunity for a better future and for overcoming the social and cultural constraints of their local context. For this reason, ICTs have also been conceived as tools of democratization and social emancipation, which increase the future job prospects of the socially disadvantaged.

A WORLD OF DIFFERENT REALITIES

However, understanding the relations between ICTs, young people and the social context in which they live, operate and interact is not such a straightforward process. Ethnographic research has demonstrated that it is important to look at the 'social envelope' in which individuals interact and live (Giacquinta et al. 1993). For example, studies on ICTs and children have largely shown that gender is an important element in the way girls and boys approach and use ICTs (Cockburn 1992; Thorne 1993; Vered 1998). Similarly, the space of interaction is crucial for generating different patterns of social behavior and attitudes towards ICTs. Research has shown that the public space of schools, while it is often considered as an institutional environment with gender equity (Buckingham and Sefton-Green 1998), often affects the possibilities, conditions and modalities in which ICTs are used and appropriated by girls and boys, adults and children, teachers and students (Frenkel 1990; Leveson 1998; Thorne 1993). Similarly, the domestic environment produces different patterns of use and relations with ICTs in the family (Silverstone and Hirsch 1992).

We may also consider that in some circumstances the use of ICTs is embedded in practices and discourses of class discrimination. For example, Carol Edwards, based in Atlanta, Georgia, highlights the negative and accumulative effects of racial, ethnic and class discrimination on young black people who come from disadvantaged areas and lack hope and prospects for their future (Edwards in Frenkel 1990). Edwards suggests that for these children new technologies do not represent opportunities of emancipation. On the contrary, their relevance is rejected because they are seen to stand as symbols of a white Western culture of domination. In these cases, the spirit of social emancipation associated with ICTs rapidly disappears. Certainly, the learning environment plays a crucial role in the way young people embrace education[2] and ICTs. If young people perceive schools as hostile environments or if teachers do not suitably adjust their communicative style and are not capable of challenging young people's anti-education culture in proper ways, ICTs can do little to change the negative attitudes towards education of these young people. Thus, to have a better understanding of the relations between ICTs and young people means to take into account the different conditions, modalities and spaces in which ICTs are used by, and made available to, young people. Similarly, we must understand to what extent local discourses of class, ethnicity, identity and power affect the social relations among peer groups and local people and how they impinge upon youths' perceptions and use of ICTs and education.

The following ethnographic study examines the different relations and interactions developed around ICTs among the students and teachers of two high schools in Alghero. The study illustrates feelings of inadequacy and anxiety among young people in relation to the pace of technological development as well as frustration towards the ways ICTs are manipulated and appropriated by teachers. Rather than tools of emancipation and social change, ICTs represent for these students a symbol of usurpation, class division and geographical isolation. Thus, in spite of general theories that praise the liberatory potential of ICTs in principle, it is the social context, the practices and the attitudes developed around ICTs by those who control and hold power over them that really matters.

It is, in fact, in the realm of the mundane, of everyday life, that we must see the consequences of ICTs in culture and society without falling into technological determinism and theoretical essentialism which are often found in the literature on new technologies.[3] Previous studies on ICTs have often centralized the importance of technological characteristics over the social context and its most relevant aspects that are presumed to be essential for interpersonal relations (e.g., Sproull and Kiesler 1986). For example, although the Internet may have effects on processes of communication (Jones 1997,1998; Strate et al. 1996) a 'virtual' culture cannot be entirely dissociated from 'real' life (Latour 1991; Jones and Kucker 1991; Robins 1995).

THE SITES OF RESEARCH: ALGHERO AND THE TWO SCHOOLS

Alghero is a small town on the Northern coast of Sardinia, an island off Southern Italy.[4] Its economy is based on tourism, a few agro-pastoral activities on the outskirts and employment in the local and central government administration as well as in the education sectors. In the 1960s Alghero, like many other towns in Southern Italy, witnessed a great development of its tourist industry, strong immigration flows from the outside and the hinterland and a consequent expansion of its urban areas. The process of urban redevelopment and expansion of Alghero generated various forms of social division and marginalization that still today have repercussions on the perceptions of identity and on the social relations among local people, particularly among youth. In Alghero space has strong connotations of class differentiation and identity. Where people live and socialize in the town discloses issues of social distinction (Ferrero 2002).

The politics of urban development of the 1960s produced a massive displacement of the poor inhabitants of the old center to new housing estates on the outskirts, which soon acquired the notoriety of 'neighborhoods for the poor' (Serusi 1981; Tansu 1982). In one clean move the politics of these urban changes created an elite center for the wealthy out of its historic center and peripheral lower class neighborhoods and ghettos on its outskirts. The social divide brought by past urban planning has catalyzed various processes of social differentiation among local people, which still today create social barriers of different kinds. Above all, feelings of powerlessness and lack of self-confidence are common experiences among the local youth who live in those areas. To a certain extent, the social interactions, relationships and dynamics among the students of the two schools where I conducted research in 2001 reflected such awareness (Ferrero 2005).

The tourist industry and commerce in Alghero were quite flourishing sectors and offered great potential for development. However, the frequent political upheavals with the local government and the monopoly exercised over some economic resources —particularly land—by a few elite groups in the town constituted a crucial deterrent for economic investments and opportunities, particularly for young people. Expressed by local people through the idiom of *immobilismo*, the inertia produced by the inefficiency of the economic and political system in Alghero, as well as a sort of inertia to change the economic and social relations in town, discouraged young people's involvement in entrepreneurial initiatives and produced feelings of exclusion and isolation. Access to ICTs in the town added to such feelings of isolation particularly for poorer families without ICTs at home. At the time of research there was in Alghero only one Internet café, one Internet point with only one computer, two public libraries with one Internet connection each, and two recreational youth centers with no computers.

The two schools where I conducted this study partially reflected local issues of social division and differentiation. The Pasini school,[5] situated in the old historic centre, was regarded as the school of the elite children and was a grammar school, mostly attended by young middle-class students. At the time of research it had thirty-three teachers and more than two hundred students. Local people held this school in high esteem for its historical role in the cultural formation of the local elite. The school hosted two streams of study, the more prestigious of which focused upon preparing mostly better off students for university and the other focused upon enabling students to enter the job market straight after they left school. The distinction between the two streams of study was subtly mapped onto questions of social differentiation among students and teachers and this had repercussions for the ways in which students perceived themselves and their relations with their peers. At the time of research, the Pasini school had seventeen computers distributed in each of the seventeen classrooms with an Internet connection that was always active. All computers were connected via a Local Area Network.

The second school was the Parietti school, located in the eastern side of the modern town, at the periphery of the modern center. A technical school offering two general programmes of study and four specialist programmes, the school had around six hundred and fifty students and seventy-one teachers at the time of the research, making it the largest school in the town. However, it was not universally popular in the locality because of its stern disciplinary atmosphere. At the time of this study the school had three large computer laboratories that were equipped with multimedia technologies and Internet connections. There were also thirty-one other computers distributed, one in each classroom. All computers had uninterrupted access to the Internet.

ICTS AND THE FRUSTRATION OF LOCAL YOUTH

In spite of the disparity of the technological appliances and facilities available in the two schools and the different patterns of interactions that developed around ICTs, the study reveals that ICTs were conceived in both schools with a strong sense of private ownership and possession. In both schools teachers and students treated ICTs as a sort of cultural capital and were convinced that management of ICT skills increased their prestige and social status. In other words, in both schools the question of an authoritarian control over ICTs, although it was motivated by different reasons and presuppositions, was implicitly geared towards maintaining an established hierarchy of relationships. Inevitably, students were caught, both in active and passive ways, within the practices and attitudes developed around ICTs.

At the Pasini school, for example, ICTs became embroiled in a game of competition among some teachers who wanted to affirm their status and prestige in the school as well as in the town. Since multimedia and ICTs were introduced into the educational activities of all schools in the town educational bodies in Alghero had organized an annual competition for the best multimedia projects, in which all schools at all levels participated. The content of the projects varied from educational subjects to issues related to the history, geography, archaeology and social characteristics of the town. The display of multimedia projects in this competition and in other events organized in town had become for all schools an important moment of confrontation and publicity and a good opportunity for the schools to attract new prospective students. At the Pasini school there was, in particular, one teacher of classics, Mr. Canu, who was very keen to participate in the competition. He had organized for three consecutive years an important multimedia project with his students of the fifth year of study, in which only a few students from other classes participated. The multimedia project was quite elaborate and required high skills and knowledge of sophisticated web design software and graphics.

At the time of this study, most of the computers distributed in the classrooms were quite old, with the exception of four computers that had a bigger memory and, therefore, could run the most up to date web-design software. Two of these computers were in the headmaster's office. The other two were in two different classrooms. One of the two classrooms was the fifth year class where Mr. Canu taught classics. The students of this class were in their final year of study. The other classroom was that of the students in the fourth year class and, although they belonged to the same stream of study, they had a different classics teacher. As mentioned above, a subtle discrimination among teachers tended to distinguish between the two streams of study in the school and value the classics stream as that of the privileged wealthy students. However, even within the same stream of study there were, nevertheless, further ways to create hierarchical divisions and distinctions among teachers and students. In a sort of unspoken social order, Mr. Canu's classes were regarded in the school as the classes of the richest children in town and the smartest of the school.

Although the claim that Mr. Canu's classes were the best ones in the school was questionable[6], many students were annoyed at this perceived inequality. The students who studied in the same stream but had different classics teachers were often caught in competition with Mr. Canu's classes. Many also disliked the fact that the multimedia project involved only the students of that classroom and that the best computers (i.e., the two that were left), as well as printers and scanners, were all taken into Mr. Canu's fifth year class for the project. The objections of the students demonstrate that they had some expectation that better access to computers might improve their education. However, the example shows that ICTs cannot be detached from the social context of their development. What is more, one could also argue that in this case ICTs became the vehicle through which students voiced dissatisfaction about inequalities in the school and the town more generally.[7]

The students of a fourth year classroom whose computer was transferred to Mr. Canu's room were frustrated by the knowledge they could do nothing to have their computer back. They knew that with the multimedia project the school would gain visibility and status in the town and that both the headmaster and Mr. Canu were very keen on this. Although ICT lessons were not compulsory in the school and most teachers did not use ICTs for their teaching, these students nonetheless often expressed their anger and frustration at the manipulation of the resources and the appropriation of their computer by Mr. Canu and, indirectly, by his students. In their angry discussions they often recalled the injustice of the abuses of power pursued in town by those who occupied positions of authority.[8] The students often drew parallels between this broader local situation and the ways in which computers in that school were appropriated and used by Mr. Canu and some of his students. Their discourse clearly showed that questions of social distinction and abuse of authority were issues that informed the ways young people related to their school and to the use of ICTs.

There were a few resistive responses to the injustice of the multimedia project. For example, a website against Mr. Canu was run by a group of students from different classrooms. This proved that there were far more computer-skilled students in the school than Mr.Canu and the headmaster realized. There were also cases of sabotage, whether in the form of equipment going missing from Mr Can's classroom or parts of the project being altered; for example, when students managed to hack into the central database on the intranet. However, although these were subtle manifestations of students' dissent and frustration, the reality of the majority of the students in the school was that they were indeed disenfranchized and there was little they could do about. It was there every day to remind them of Mr. Canu's perceived misuse of power and the privileged position of his students.

The last episode of injustice towards the students of that school occurred at the end of the academic year when students had their final examination before leaving school for good and were asked to present to a committee of external examiners their theses and projects. Mr. Canu's students benefited from updated multimedia software and hardware and had the opportunity to show off their multimedia projects unlike the students of the other fifth year classes who had not prepared their thesis using ICT facilities. This, again, gave Mr. Canu's students an advantage in front of the committee that the other students did not enjoy.

At the Parietti school a larger overall number of computers were available, but use of these by students was limited by the tight control exerted by the headmaster over the use of computer labs. In particular, the headmaster was not willing to let the students have free use of the Internet or to engage in creative use of ICTs. It was clear from my conversations with the headmaster and some of the teachers that ICTs were regarded as something of a threat to the old regime of teaching and the establishment of hierarchies of knowledge and power. For example, although the school ICT network had filters and anti-virus software installed on all computers, the headmaster had asked technicians to remove CD-roms and floppy disk drives from the computers in the classrooms to stop students using the computers for their own work. In so doing, he considerably reduced the potential use of these computers for the students. Behind various similar attempts to control students' use of ICTs lay a conviction that students would damage the image of the school outside through the Internet or that the ICT system of the school could be brought down by installing viruses on the computers of the school.

Students were not happy about this situation. Some commented that if they wanted to acquire proper computer skills and find a proper job they would have had to pay for private courses outside of school. Some others complained that it was ridiculous that they received only basic computer skills in word processing at the age of seventeen when they knew that even the kids of the elementary schools in the town were far more advanced with the use of some basic web-design software. Others lamented that the situation in their school vividly reminded them of the *immobilismo* in the town and the obstructive practices and attitudes of some bureaucrats in local public offices. In other words, they criticized the attitudes of some teachers and the headmaster who discouraged students' initiatives of self-learning with ICT. For example, they complained that they were not free to use the computer lab whenever they needed it and had to ask for permission to use it explaining how they were going to use it and what for. To a certain extent, this procedure was accepted and considered unavoidable by the students given the high number of students in the school. However, it meant that rather than being the tools for overcoming barriers of time and space ICT became tied down by the lengthy waiting times of the school's internal bureaucracy. What is more, the headmaster also often refused permission for their use and in so doing he boosted students' frustration and feelings of powerlessness.

The whole situation of ICTs at the Parietti school was a major source of frustration for many students, particularly for those who could not afford to buy a computer or expensive software of their own. As a matter of fact, many students of that school did not have a computer at home,[9] therefore, access to the computers of the school was regarded by these students as crucial for learning purposes and for keeping up-to-date on the use of the different software and ICT facilities available in the school. Hence, students became aware of the inadequacy of their computer skills in an era where multimedia and computers represented job opportunities and possibilities of change. They recognized the potential of the Internet but contrasted it with their own impotence and inability to fully master the technology because of traditional authoritarian relationships. It was also common for students to associate the use of the Internet and ICTs in that school with a type of sociality that reminded them of the *immobilismo* pursued in the town by a few elite groups. Furthermore, the headmaster appropriated the Internet and computers as new ways of maintaining relations of power in the school.

Over a period of time, the ongoing restrictions on students' access to ICTs appeared to have had an impact on their own motivation and enthusiasm. On many occasions I offered them the opportunity to work on multimedia projects, carry out research on the Internet and engage with ICTs in creative ways. However, they often turned these opportunities down.

For example, when I invited them to participate in European projects on the Internet and set up exchanges of research with other European students working on issues related to the local environment, history, archaeology and so on, they declined the opportunity. When I asked them why they did not want to work on these projects I was astonished that they referred to the social and cultural conditions that affected youth in Alghero. They claimed that there was no point in exchanging pieces of research with other European students and learning that there were so many opportunities 'out there' because they knew that the situation in their school and in the town was not so favorable for them. These projects would have been a sharp reminder of the bad conditions that prevailed not only in their school but also in Alghero. They also added that it was sad to think that their European counterparts could use ICTs more freely or imagine that they had better equipment than that available to them. With these comments students appeared to disclose deep-seated feelings of powerlessness with respect to their school system and local context

A similar situation arose when the students at the Parietti school were given a chance to learn some new ICT skills and turned it down. The headmaster organized a four-month course on which students could learn to design web sites by using the most recent web-authoring software. This was a good opportunity, especially for the students who complained about the poor ICT situation in the school and lamented that they could not afford to buy any computer and software for home. Nevertheless, the course collapsed due to lack of interest. When I inquired with some students about the failure of the course they explained that the course was organized in such a way that they could not actually interact freely with the software but had to follow the examples prescribed by the instructor. In other words, once again students perceived/experienced the layout of the course as a restriction, a limitation to their willingness to learn the new software at their own pace. Students felt that the determination of the headmaster to control the students' ways of using ICTs had also come to dominate and undermine that course and, therefore, to affect the teaching methods of the course instructor.[10]

The geographical limitation of the island also appeared to sap the confidence of the young people in my study. Expensive and infrequent transportation to the mainland discouraged young people from believing that they could participate in and benefit from the economic and cultural sectors of the mainland. The wish to have the latest versions of hardware was seen by these students as a sort of mirage. The only possibility was to have them sent from the Italian mainland with the inconvenience of long delays and increased expenditure for delivery. The search for new multimedia software or hardware was also difficult for students and attempts to crack, that is illegally copy, new releases of software were frustrated by linguistic problems as the manuals were written in English. In a nutshell, the condition of marginality experienced by the students of both schools was not only the outcome of some particularistic ways of manipulating and appropriating ICTs by teachers and the head masters but it was also determined by their condition as islanders and inhabitants of Alghero. The few opportunities of emancipation that local youth could envisage in their town impinged upon their hopes for the future, their self-esteem, belief that things could indeed change and, ultimately, the ways in which they acted and performed. Students' beliefs about local people's tendency to discriminate on the basis of social background and about the political and social inertia to change that pervaded among the economic and social elite of the town ultimately appeared to place significant limits on their ambitions.

In both schools the ways in which ICTs were used and manipulated by teachers and some students show that for the majority of students, they did not play the role of tools of democratization or empowerment. What was really striking, however, was the passive acceptance by the students in both schools of their condition. It appeared that the attitudes of headmasters and the manipulation of the school ICT resources by teachers had prompted feelings of powerlessness which ultimately affected their belief that they could act as proactive agents for their own future.

CONCLUSION

ICTs have a great potential for the intellectual and personal growth of young people. However, this study has shown that still nowadays ICTs can be drawn into local discourses of power and inequality. The main aim of this chapter was to reveal the pervasiveness of local categories and social practices rooted in the local context of Alghero and the resilience of such categories in domains such as the use of ICTs that are often regarded to be emancipatory. Furthermore, this paper demonstrated that, in spite of general theories that extol the contribution and effects of ICTs on people's perceptions of identity and the self, it is the social context, the practices and uses of ICTs and the structures of authority and power characterizing a particular context that may matter most.

When we talk about ICTs we look at the potential for action that this technology offers. We think of their 'virtuality', which projects on our imagination ideas of spaceless worlds or worlds apart into which empowered individuals can plunge and make new lives for themselves. However, this chapter has illustrated that for young people in Alghero things were different. ICTs and the Internet made young people realize the extent to which their 'virtuality' was in practice very limited both in terms of possibilities for action and in terms of physical, social and spatial boundaries. Although young people in Alghero were given the chance to use ICTs for concrete purposes and practices, their actions were nonetheless continuously embedded in the social practices, attitudes and discourses of their schools and the town. They felt excluded and undervalued in their aspirations to be recognized as subjects willing to engage in personal and creative work, hence above all as subjects with a right to enjoy ICTs in their own ways. All this represented a 'bounded virtuality' that reminded local youth of the social constraints and attitudes that they had to cope with daily.

Thus, when it comes to understanding the debates about youth, identity and ICTs one should be cautious of discourses of technological determinism or suggestions that ICTs are simple tools of democratisation. This paper has in fact shown that when dealing with youth, identity and ICTs there are many other issues to take into account which affect young people's social interactions and relation to ICTs.

NOTES

1. This research has been supported by an E.S.R.C. research studentship and the generosity of the University of London Scholarship Fund, the Sir Richard Stapley Educational Trust and the Radcliff-Brown Fund for Social Anthropological Research.
2. Studies on deprived areas and minority groups in the United States highlight the negative and cumulative effects of socio-economic and cultural discrimination on children by teachers and in the school environment in general (Frenkel 1990; Oakes 1985). Negative educational experiences, these studies explain, generate disillusionment, low self-esteem and feelings of mediocrity as well as lack of assertiveness among children.
3. In this respect, it is interesting to look at the debates against technological determinism (e.g., Williams 1974) and the work of the Frankfurt School on media and new technologies (e.g, Adorno and Horkheimer 1972; Habermas 1987; Marcuse 1984), which, on the contrary, depict a pessimistic scenario where new technologies shape and limit people's freedom of critical thinking and speech.
4. Sardinia is an island in the Eastern half of the Mediterranean Sea, off the West coast of the Italian mainland. With its 24,090 square kilometers and a population of 1.650.000 inhabitants, Sardinia is the second largest island of the Mediterranean after Sicily.
5. For reasons of anonymity the real names of the two schools are disguised as well as names of places and persons.
6. I found the students' perceptions of Mr. Canu's class somewhat confusing since many students in the school were from wealthy families and, furthermore, Mr. Canu's class included some students from modest backgrounds. This illustrates to some extent that the episode was partly a matter of perception, something encouraged by Mr. Canu's persistent praising of his students as the best and most privileged of the school.
7. In these cases, the students introduced understandings of local inequalities even though they had little immediate bearing on the inequalities within the school. The students employed different ways of expressing their frustration towards Mr. Canu's privileged access to school resources. These included direct criticism of him as well as generalized comments about social inequalities in the town. I have no reason to believe that Mr. Canu's behavior was driven by anything other than wanting to provide the best for his own classes.

8. The other teachers in the school were also upset about the situation but they were very cautious not to reveal their disapproval.
9. This differed from the other school where many students had computers at home.
10. Surprisingly, in spite of the general enthusiasm generated at the beginning, many students dropped out of the web-design course, often attributing their disillusionment to the personal approach taken by the headmaster to the course.

15 Identity and structure in online gaming

Young people's symbolic and virtual extensions of self

Nic Crowe and Simon Bradford

Popular debates about computer games rage as the media literacy of young people increases apace. Adults fail to grasp the allure of the gaming environment, dismissing it as frivolous or, invariably, dangerous; indeed, cyber space has considerable potential for fomenting new moral panics centred on this novel aspect of young people's leisure lives. However, computer games are central to the lives of many young people. Online gaming—the ability to play against other gamers across the Internet—has only added to the form's potency. Well established in the computer games platform, net-play is now a major feature of every next-generation gaming console. A U.K. survey highlighted that 82 per cent of nine- to nineteen-year-olds have at least one games console, and that 70 per cent play computer games online. The survey also acknowledged that most young people spend nearly as much time playing video/computer games as they do with homework (Livingstone and Bober 2005: 10).

In this chapter we investigate the practices of young people within the virtual worlds of online gaming communities, considering how young people construct and maintain virtual identities within virtual social systems. We examine how those identities interact with the virtual environment and the structures and institutions that are developed to allow groups and individuals to operate within its 'culture'. We suggest that the distinction between *virtual* and *material* 'existence' is not clear-cut and oppositional but porous and mutually defining—a shifting dynamic rather than a rigid division. Online games, particularly the virtual worlds of role-playing games, sit at the interface between these two planes. The virtual world of online games offers young people a 'spectacular space' (similar in some ways to shopping malls and street corners, yet simultaneously quite different) in which they can undertake creative identity work. Importantly, game worlds have a particular capacity in enabling participants to interact with others in a form *mediated* by the game itself. This, we argue, makes these games potentially powerful settings for young people to exercise agency in marking out and playing with identity. The use of avatars (character images within the game that young people adopt and 'become' while in the game environment) also permits young people to appear in a form chosen by them. Thus, in the virtual world, 'material' cultural codes of body and conduct constituted by gender, class and race can, apparently, be effaced, opening up interesting and creative possibilities for participants. Thus, online gaming is an important and under-researched space in which young people engage in new practices of 'leisure and pleasure'.

MMORPGS: THE CASE OF RUNESCAPE

So-called MMORPGs (Massively Multiplayer Online Role-Playing Games) offer a unique gaming experience in which users assume the role of 'citizen' within a virtual world. We focus here on 'Runescape'. This game is not based on spatial progression—in which the player solves puzzles, or overcomes other characters, unlocking access to additional areas or different/ better equipment (the convention in games such as 'Tomb Raider')—but on gaining *experience* through in-game tasks or challenges (centred on fighting or working, for example). As the characters undertake their activities so their experience in that area grows and their ability to perform certain tasks increases (in *Runescape* only the best cooks are able to cook shark, or the most experienced miners can prospect and mine gold). Some citizens opt to become specialists—armour smiths or magicians—whilst others develop a more rounded character. There are quests—or adventures—to be undertaken but in *Runescape* these are not necessarily central to the game dynamic and many users simply become skilled craftspeople earning a living from their virtual labours.

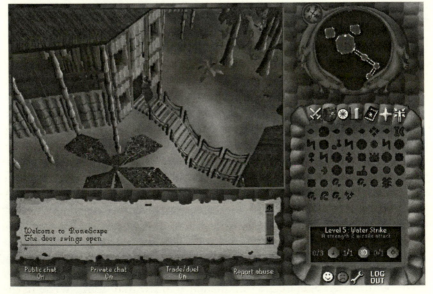

Figure 15.1 Runescape screenshot (courtesy Jagex LTD).[2]

Runescape differs from the more traditional gaming structure in that, depending on how they choose to interact with the world, gamers are not bound by either linear plot or function. The worlds themselves are sophisticated multiplayer interactions. The larger worlds such as 'Norrath' the land of the most popular game, *Everquest*, boasts an area so large that it would take eight hours to walk its virtual length, and it has a population larger than Miami (Hertz 2002: 96). *Everquest's* virtual currency has a higher exchange rate against the dollar than the yen and high-level characters are regularly bought and sold on e-Bay for thousands of dollars. In contrast, *Runescape* offers young people a less complex, although arguably no less challenging, experience. A smaller Java-based world with over 240,000 regular users, *Runescape* is the product of a small U.K. 'bedroom' developer and, thus, far more user-responsive in terms of its growth and development. *Runescape* citizens often express 'ownership' of the game and regard its future development as a partnership. Unlike similar games, *Runescape* is free and does not require the purchase of an initial disk followed by a monthly subscription. Potential users simply log on, register, create a character and can be playing within five minutes. Citizens can upgrade to 'member status' unlocking additional parts of the world for $5 per month. This instant accessibility seems to make it very attractive to younger people. Yee (2002) estimates the average age of an *Everquest* player to be approximately twenty-six. Jagex, *Runescape's* creator, claims to have a player base of 'a wide age range from 8 to 50 years olds ... (which) is 90 per cent : 10 per cent, male:female' (Jagex 2006). However, our research indicates that the vast majority of users are eleven to sixteen, drawn from Europe, America and Australasia. Usage is contingent on the time of day *Runescape* is accessed.

GAMING IDENTITIES IN RUNESCAPE'S VIRTUAL SPACE

Runescape offers a range of geographical locations, including towns, forests and dungeons, within which users live their virtual lives. The narrative borrows heavily from the Western Fantasy tradition[1], a genre that drives many of the structures and institutions—fighting, magic, guilds and klans—of the game dynamic. Significantly, it provides an arena that allows character skill development within conventions in which young people are already culturally competent—a 'bricolage' of familiar cultural forms—and as such it is instantly accessible.

> I used to watch Xena on TV. When I found Runescape I thought shit, I am like Xena or something (Ares'girl, 16).
> Games like Runescape reminds me of stuff like 'Lord of the Rings' and Warhammer games, you get to use magic n stuff... (Oliver, 13).

But for many, the virtual world (like its material other) simply provides an opportunity to hang out and be noticed:

For me, going online or to a (clan) meet is like going out on Friday night. I want the noobs (new gamers) to know I am there. I put on my best armour so they know Jazz is on the board... usually it's just a good place to meet my sisters, to be seen, you know (Jazzygirl, 14).

In these worlds (and for users like 'Jazzygirl') the virtual playground is a highly interactive space. Indeed, at its very essence virtuality *requires* interactivity (Stallabrass 1993: 83).

Game interaction has been seen in terms of the relationship between player and environment (Jenkins 1995; Poole 2000; Wolf 2001). As Fuller and Jenkins (1995) note, the main function of a video game is the creation of 'spectacular spaces' that must be explored by central characters. Actors within these spaces solve the problems created by the environments so that they can go on to what further spectacle awaits them. The real and the virtual are not essentially linked, even though there is an assumption that as technology advances, the games have become more 'realistic'. Yet, the virtual is not simply a technological construction but is fundamentally *cultural*. It is not the technology itself that initiates and sustains the willingness of users to treat the virtual environment *as if* it were real. Rather, it is the extent to which the interface between technology and gamer acts as a means of expression for each player, '...a representation of a person can be manipulated within the representation of a real or imagined environment, both of which can be manifested through the use of various technologies including computers' (Reid 1994: 3).

In other words, virtual worlds (like other worlds) exist neither solely in the technology used to represent them, nor in the minds of the user or participant, but in the relationship between subjectivity, social processes and practices and the technologically generated representations which gamers assemble through their game playing. Poole (2000) considers this in terms of a symbolic interaction between various semiotic modes. Games operate on the level of 'icon' where objects, rather than being granted real physical attributes, exist principally as symbols: visual frames of reference whose significance is learnt like rules. The illusion of reality lies not in the game itself but in the users' willingness to treat the manifestations of their imaginings as if they were real, mirroring the continuous mediation of the material world by cultural and social practices.

Of course inhabitants of virtual worlds do not simply interact with the game environment. The vibrancy of these games emerges because they necessitate interactions with other users. Within game systems, notions of realism and identity take on a deep significance. Users' looks, their gender and race as represented by their choice of avatar, name, skills and characteristics; the way that they interact and speak and the language they use represents their virtual 'face', mediating interaction with others. Unlike the material world, these characteristics are, arguably, less constrained by biological or social forces. However, this has led to a (sometimes erroneous) tendency to see cyberspace as a means of liberation from the fixed identity of the material world (Massey 2005: 94). We suggest that distinctions between 'material' and 'virtual' are extremely subtle in the ways that they contribute to 'user identities'.

The idea that identity is discursive and constituted in material, social and cultural practices has a long history that circumscribes Freud, Mead, Goffman and Foucault amongst others. Suler points out that '…many people walk around in their [face to face] lives wearing 'masks' that are quite different than how they think and feel internally' (2000: para.2).[3] Turkle notes that people have always assumed shifting social roles in the past when placed in different social situations but that 'involvement with families and communities kept such cycling through under fairly stringent control' (1995: 179). Arguably, the virtual displaces some of the limits on identity construction, or as Lyles puts it, 'untainted by the social markers of race, class, ethnicity, and sex… identities can emerge' (1996: 114). This is not to say that that virtual identity is somehow separate from 'real life', merely that the former may be an alternative that compliments the latter. As Suler notes, the virtual offers gamers the chance to concentrate on a particular characteristic that they may not be able to express in the real world. Virtual identity in *Runescape*, with its emphasis on role-playing and skills development resonates with this.

Castranova observes that in virtual worlds a user's virtual identity performs a social role and consequently 'the process of developing… capital seems to invoke exactly the same risk and reward structures in the brain that are invoked by personal development in real life' (2001: 16). Filiciak stresses the emotional attachment between gamer and avatar, noting that virtual self '…is closer to the image of ourselves than the one we present (in the material world) which is governed by requirements and expectations of real life' (2003: 92–93). However, although virtuality may remove some control and consequential elements of the material world, cultural and societal forces that help us make sense of material existence remain constant; we always come from somewhere. Logging into *Runescape*, a young person can choose to be male or female, black or white, to work or not. Yet their understanding of what it actually means to be a man or a woman, a black or a white character, the role and function of work—or indeed the contrast between work and leisure—is shaped by their cultural experience. Virtual identity is not a blank canvas and virtual space remains a discursive arena *already shaped* by the social and cultural. It offers not liberation from the material world, but rather an intriguing interface between two planes of existence as the following quote suggests:

'Sassy' is really my mate Sam. We all know she is a guy but when we are on Runie we treat him as a girl. I don't care that he is my girlfriend on Rune, she looks good and she has class armour. If she looks good then I look good. Most of the time I actually forget that she is Sam (Sir Max Power, 18).

In virtual worlds like *Runescape*, players can change their physical appearance and virtual persona at will. Material identity remains hidden behind a virtual mask but virtual identity can articulate a number of discursive positions. These may co-exist or, perhaps, conflict with the player's actual material world. In everyday life, many physical characteristics are unalterable, and this fixity underpins a range of social opportunities, social constraints and social institutions.[4] Identity is inscribed on the physical body (Foucault 1977, 1978; Bourdieu 1984) and as Reid (1994) notes, 'social structures based on bias towards... differing portions of humanity depend on the ease to which we can assess each others bodies and ascribe identity to physical form' (1994). Once the fixity of physical form is stripped away by the absence of constraint that virtual worlds afford, cultural meaning can be *virtually* manipulated at will. In these circumstances, the physical self adopts the role of symbol and becomes a kind of virtual *cyborg*. This manifests a constructed and embodied self *beyond* the physical, existing in a world where identity is, at least partially, self-defined rather than determined. This is the ultimate late modernity, in which identity, however transitory, is not *given* but *made* (Bauman 1997:71).

HANGING OUT IN VIRTUALITY: PUBLIC AND PRIVATE SPACES

Book (2003) argues that virtual worlds might serve a similar function to tourist locations in that they allow participants to escape from their everyday life and break 'the constraints of the self'. *Runescape* has a number of popular settings where 'citizens' go to hang out. Some players simply use these as a meeting place and divorce their virtual self from the activity around them.

> I don't bother with the quests and stuff... but I like to come here and enjoy the scenery... we just come here to meet and chat, its nice up on the cliffs looking over the ocean. I meet my sisters and we just hang out (Katspaw, 14).

Like material meeting spaces the virtual world acts almost as a tourist location, a place to escape from real life into a fantasy environment where one can simply enjoy the 'sights' and chat to friends. In *Runescape*, however, we can also see how the tourist analogy operates on a sophisticated level where players use locations within the world to add depth to their virtual experience.

One of my favourite places on Rune is the Braxton Waterfall. You can just sit back by the river and relax.... I could watch the water for hours it's so pretty... not that many people come here so it's a great place just to be, you know (Axegrrl, 16).

Axegrrl's observations are interesting. She feels the need for a place where she can escape from the everyday world of *Runescape* (having, presumably *already* escaped the everyday world of the material) to have time to herself. She treats the virtual world *as though* it was real. *Runescape* characters are simply avatars that cannot 'sit' and indeed the 'waterfall' is little more than a photo with a few pixels that suggest movement. However for Axegrrl this represents a real location that induces peace, tranquillity and a palpable sense of relaxation.

How this operates becomes clearer when we consider Axegrrl's approach to her role within the *Runescape* world. She described how she spends the first part of her gaming session at 'work', mining and smithing. It is through this activity that she generates income with which she is able to buy armour, food, clothes and so on. For her, these activities carry the genuine status of 'working'. Often these 'work' locations attract many users, so she seeks quieter places to chat or wind down from the stresses of work, in the same way she might do after school. There is yet another tension between the real and the virtual here. Axegrrl and Jazzygirl, like most other players, both admit to playing the games on their own in a bedroom. They are already in their own private space yet they still feel the need to seek out *private* virtual space within the *public* arena of the virtual world. Privacy it seems is not a simple matter of logging off. It is important to both of them that they remain connected to the interactivity of the virtual even in the desire to remove themselves from interaction with others. Axegrrl admits to having never seen a real waterfall or sat by a real river, so the virtual also creates a symbolic experience of how an event in real life might actually feel. This cyber-experimentation is deep rooted throughout the virtual world. Despite having never fished in real life, Jar-o-Mayo (16) says, '... there's nothing like sitting or fishing on the beach at Karamaja after a hard days fighting'.

These players demonstrate a desire to re-create the 'real' material world *within* the virtual, but in ways that might not be possible in the material world. They regard their main in-game activity as 'work', which is then contrasted with leisure time spent at vacation settings. Work space and leisure space are kept quite distinct. As neither of these players have jobs in 'real-life', *Runescape* provides them with an arena in which they can act out an experience of what they *think* it is like to be an adult worker. They assign different and distinct spaces to each activity so that the two contrasting realms of work and play remain separate. During one session, for example, Axegrrl becomes annoyed when another player attempts to sell her lobster.

Figure 15.2 Runescape screenshot (courtesy Jagex LTD).

It was a good price but he pissed me off. The noob couldn't see that we are trying to relax here, if he wants to sell his stuff he should go to somewhere like Draynor or the (fishing) Guild, that's where people buy lobbies (Axegrrl, 16).

What irritates Axegrrl here is that the world of work (more specifically someone else's work) impinges on her leisure space. It is little surprise therefore that players like Axegrrl seek out quieter spaces to escape and relax but, evidently, it is sometimes a struggle to keep the two worlds apart. As we will see, however, some players hang out in more visible ways.

RESPECT, POSITION AND POWER: SUSTAINING A STABLE VIRTUAL WORLD

For some players the busy trade locations on *Runescape* are ideal places to hang out; a little like the spaces created in town centres and malls in the material world. For these players, the distinction between work and leisure in the virtual spaces of *Runescape* is not important. One group talked about their in-game work and leisure activities:

I don't see why people go to the waterfall, what's the point, no-one's there. We hang out in Varrok, in the bar or on the square... people can see you there (Rune Thief 7, 14).

What's the point of getting Rune or Dragon if you can't show the noobs you have got it...? When I got my dragon battle I went straight to Lummy and the noobs kept following me about wanting to see it. That was the best, I really felt the don (Laura Cool, 14).

Again, virtual space becomes the arena in which respect is enacted and maintained (Sennett 2003: 59), and in which a 'virtual meritocracy' emerges (Young 1958). Only the best and wealthiest players can wear Rune, Dragon or God Armour. To progress to these levels of achievement the players will have invested many hours developing in-game activity skills and this affords respect. Armour is a symbol of experience and worth within the virtual world and is worn at all times. Unlike Axegrrl and Jar-o-Mayo these characters do not differentiate between work and leisure, they have celebrity status and their role is 'to be seen'. However, as the number of Rune wearing inhabitants has grown, this process has been subverted by some of the very best players who now choose to wear the lowest grade of armour—bronze. This is a form of symbolic resistance to the norms of the virtual world, and the players' status within the arena is highlighted through their transgression. They do not wear the best armour because their characters have strong fighting skills— this in itself affords them status since high level combat statistics are achieved through investing many hours on developing fighting skills. It also, of course, reinforces their notoriety within *Runescape* society, adding virtual capital to their celebrity status.

This hierarchy of players is central to the structural fabric of *Runescape*. But these power relations are not simply products of the game dynamic itself. They have emerged through in-game struggle and consensus, constructed through the dynamic of a *virtua-culture*. Although combat achievement and armour afford respect and status this need not necessarily have been so. There is nothing in the 'rules' of *Runescape* that dictates that this is a game requirement, but the culture has evolved in this manner because combat has been valued over other skills and become the criterion against which a successful player is defined. Like its material life counterpart, virtua-culture represents a system of shared and contested meanings that are embedded and expressed in cultural forms and practices. As such, a virtual hegemony is at work. Whilst the norms and structure give the appearance of being somehow 'natural' to the virtual world—perhaps even part of the rules of the game—they are driven by an elite which enjoys a consensual status: the virtual meritocracy. These players influence and shape the *Runescape* world and their authority seldom appears challenged.

The shops only charge you 300gp, but she's got everyone paying 1k per shark, I dunno how she does it. I mean, like most guys I don't take orders from a 16 year old girl, but I am so not going to argue with Bronzequeen no matter who she is in RL (Sassy Sammy, 17).

This process operates to fix and maintain prices of key items within the *Runescape* world. Status-conferring armour is one example. By controlling the production and distribution of armour one also succeeds in controlling a stratifying structure within the virtual world. Stratification is maintained through careful manipulation of the gaming dynamic itself and we might assume that market forces would eventually prevail. As more players reach the required competence to mine or smith Rune, the market becomes flooded with Rune items and the price will fall. However, player development cannot keep pace with game development. Players need to invest many hundreds of hours of game play in the single skill before they reach the required level to perform the most advanced tasks. Most gamers interviewed play an average of 3 hours a night and this game play is spread over a number of different activities. Since the virtual world is dynamic, by the time players reach the required competence the world has moved on with new armour to make or more powerful spells to master. The top levels of competence always remain *just beyond* average players, and even though many players aspire to them, few manage to arrive. Consequently, controlling interests remain in the hands of a minority.

Far from frustrating the ordinary player this system is not only accepted but actively embraced. Hegemony is constituted precisely by the unchallenged relations and predominance of elite power in the '…"spontaneous" consent given by [the masses]… to the general direction imposed on social life by the dominant fundamental group…' (Gramsci 1971: 12). The power of the elite lies in its 'normalisation'. Virtual hegemony is sustained because of the perceived benefit to the virtua-culture. *Runescape*'s economy involves both currency and barter transactions. A fixed and stable pricing system allows economic structures to function smoothly and elite authority secures consent because it adds structure and stability to virtual economics. As such, elite interests become 'universalised'.

> The way the game fixes the prices is important to me because I don't use gold pieces (gp) much, I like to trade goods. I get coal for 1000gp a cert and can trade it for lobster certificates 'cause they also sell for 1000gp. You can cook them and sell them for 2k at Edgeville. I wanted to become a smith but I am never going to reach a high enough level so it's easier to mine coal and then trade it. Everyone needs coal… its easy money (Sherminator 112, 16).

> … I don't know how we get the prices but everyone knows them and you always know if you are getting ripped off (Kayonobe, 16).

These players are absolutely aware of what constitutes a fair price for their goods. Sherminator112's observation is interesting. He realises how hard it is to reach the required level and has developed a compromise through specialising in a high demand, yet attainable and lucrative, skill—

coal mining. When interviewed he was wearing the best armour and weapons available on *Runescape* (his helmet alone would have cost 2 million gold pieces). Some citizens have, apparently, found that concentrating on low cost, yet essential, items is an effective path to the acquisition of virtual capital. Mining is a time consuming task. Sherminator112 estimates that he has invested over 2000 mining hours in his armour, but since essential items are not made obsolete by game development he realised he had time to build up funds. The process of acquisition, effectively, remains hidden. Because the system does not openly declare itself, the players believe that prices are fixed by the game itself and not subject to internal manipulation, a further example of the invisibility—and effectiveness—of hegemonic power practices.

Although some citizens are happy to work within prevailing structures and practices, there are others who are more aware of extant power relations:

> BronzeQueen controls lobster fishing and the price of lobby certs. I was in the (fishing) Guild and there was this guy trying to sell his certs for 1.5k and everyone was telling him they are only worth 1k... so like he's arguing with everyone and being a total noob about it. Then BronzeQueen comes in with Bronze and just says 'they are 1k'... but he tells her to f off, so she just gets the fishing clan to occupy all the fishing spots so he can't fish no more. It was like that for weeks, the clan just didn't move (Sassy Sammy, 17).

Both Bronze and BronzeQueen are longstanding and well-respected citizens, demonstrated by the way they are able to mobilise a clan of other players to 'protect' their fishing operation. The crime of the 'noob' was not that he wanted to get more money for his goods but rather, in doing so, he was seen to challenge BronzeQueen's authority and destabilise an established trading equilibrium. Clearly this was not to be tolerated either by the clan or, interestingly, the other fishers. Even within the virtual world, BronzeQueen is able to exercise *real* authority in the way that the she closes down an important trading location, acquiring substantial consent in doing so.

BronzeQueen's position reflects a Weberian authority. She is nothing if not *charismatic* and has the capacity to respond to the multiple social anxieties and risks associated with citizenship of a world in which access to resources can be quickly barred and whose acquisition offers the best route to security. BronzeQueen engenders a conviction on the part of followers that she has some (almost divine?) quality, perhaps the capacity for revelation which itself contributes to social and economic stability. She is charismatic, and the medievalist narrative genre in which *Runescape* exists is amenable to BronzeQueen drawing on a representation of quasi-traditionalist legitimacy. Her position as 'queen' resonates with a timeless historical past that, apparently, is immune to criticism. Charisma and tradition are clearly significant elements of a virtual cultural capital, sustaining and advancing the position of *Runescape* elites.

NETWORKS AND THE CONSTRUCTION OF THE 'SOCIAL'

Whilst power works in an individualised modulation, *Runescape* practices also illustrate subtle demarcations of a 'networked' power that creates the sense of a 'virtual-social'. Virtual status is based on stratified networks of interaction between gamers, reflecting those in the material world. As well as sustaining (virtual) social order, networks function as a source of trust and reciprocity that can offer a virtual ontological security (Giddens 1991:36) forming the 'natural' ground of day-to-day virtual life and stable parameters to identity. This is a security in which virtual identities can be made potentially productive. We have already noted the *disciplined* way in which gamers engage in *Runescape*'s virtual division of labour. BronzeQueen, and others' 'sovereign' authority rests on creating a balance through which a valued position within the wider virtual world is maintained by deploying various *stabilising practices* such as setting fish prices, whilst also ensuring that their bands of followers stay sufficiently loyal to be immediately mobilised to enforce this position.

A complicated tension operates in *Runescape*'s power dynamic which is perhaps most easily understood in the context of the 'clan' system. Clans— or *klans* as some are known on *Runescape*—are co-operative networks in which small groups of players share common and well defined goals. Formalised and disciplined with a recognised internal structure, clans invariably have their own ritual practices, symbols and distinctive styles. They are self-sufficient units having their own high level miners, smiths and cooks who furnish the clan with whatever services they need. Some, such as the Rune Monks, have dedicated their virtual lives to good and they protect citizens from player-killers in the wilderness areas. Others, like the Silver Knights, are highly organised bands of marauders that steal and pillage their way across the *Runescape* world. There are even gender specific klans for example the 'Sisters of Battle' whose goal is spelt out in their motto 'striking a blow for gender equality across the *Runescape* world'. A common feature of all these differing groups is that they seldom comprise individuals who know each other in real life and their existence is constituted by the virtual.

Most players are invited to join a clan within hours of logging into the game. Klan membership is a key means of stimulating inter-player interaction and supplants the family as the key social institution of the virtual world, offering a source of trust and mutuality. Membership legitimates not only the virtual self, but also an individual's virtual sociality—role and function within the virtua-culture—adding purpose and meaning to virtual existence. Klans provide space in which the virtual individual can elaborate a self-identity by ensuring safety and stability in what is, potentially, a dangerous environment. Like 'material' identity, virtual identity is fundamentally social. Even players who detach themselves from the game dynamic speak of the virtual self as part of a collective. Katspaw, for example, sees her virtual meetings as a 'meeting of the "nogame Klan"' rather than simply catching up with a few friends online.

> We're a bit like the Shark gurls in Cathaby 'cept we don't do nothing. People will look for us at Taverley... they expect to see us there... I get PMs (private messages) from people I don't really know saying 'hey saw your sisters at the benches, where were you?'... dey kno where to find us (Katspaw, 14).

Meeting is an intimate bonding experience with 'sisters', not just friends. The desire to 'belong' emerges in friendship groups and gangs throughout the material world but the significance of these klans is that they bring young people together in spite of differences that would not, perhaps, be tolerated in the material world. Members of these virtual groups do not share the material geo-demographic characteristics that bring young people together in the material world. Virtual geography and interest supplant material bonding criteria. We see, for example, how BronzeQueen holds her clan together in almost military obedience based on virtual, rather than physical, presence.

CONCLUSIONS: BACK TO LIFE, BACK TO REALITY

Parker (2004) argues that the 'realism' of games lies not in accurate re-creation of the material world as an aesthetic, but in its re-working of material social processes. Stallabras rejects video games as '...capitalist and deeply conservative...' in tricking players into imitating idealized markets and sweatshop labour through repetitive manipulation of game objects and numbers (1993: 104). Since all contemporary cultural forms are arenas in which culture is both produced and reproduced we might argue that *Runescape* is, unsurprisingly, an agent of social reproduction. Yet for the young people of *Runescape*, virtual identity can offer a mechanism to experiment with the institutions and structures of the material world relatively free from the (real or imagined) constraints of those institutions and structures. Such a view echoes Willis et al. (1990), in which young people use commercial cultural forms to 'establish their presence, identity and meaning' (1990: 2). As such we suggest that *Runescape* represents a site of grounded aesthetics, 'whereby meanings are attributed to symbols and practices and where symbols and practices are selected, re-selected, highlighted and recomposed to resonate further appropriated and particularized meaning (21).

At the juncture between production and reproduction young people are both objects and subject agents. Katz notes that 'in the interchange, the social relations of production and reproduction that characterize a particular social formation at a given historical moment and geographical location are encountered, reproduced, altered, and resisted' (2001: 6). For Katz, it is young people's geographies that are crucial in this. For the young people involved in this study *Runescape* becomes a playground in which they can partially strip away cultural experiences (of gender or race, for example) and become relatively free to experiment with a range of discursive positions. There exists the possibility to symbolically experience another gender or race, what it is like to be an adult, to work, to have a position of influence, or to simply sit by a waterfall and enjoy the 'view'.

But the virtual exists within the real insofar as it is set against and measured by the cultural practices of the material world. The two worlds are porous, although the real becomes mutated—unmade and remade—by the virtual and vice versa. The virtual self does not exist in a cultural vacuum but has fashioned cultural experience to meet the requirements of virtual existence. If the traditional fixity of meaning (associated with the 'body: 'race' or 'sex', for example) can no longer be relied upon, then different criteria have been woven into the institutions and structures of virtual world. Space and activity within the virtual are subject to a new range of forces, even if some of these are indeed borrowed from the material. More importantly, success and status are now defined in new ways. Cultural attributes that are valued in the material world—gender or race, for example—do not necessarily represent cultural capital in the virtual, and the maintenance of position and status draw on different systems of value and belief.

NOTES

1. In contrast to many of the 'Eastern' influenced games (the Final Fantasy series) and genres (martial art based beat-em-ups) popular on console platforms.
2. Please note that, although reproduced here in black and white, the actual Runescape game is in full color.
3. Although such a view implies that there is a 'real' self hidden behind the mask—a concept rejected by writers such as Foucault and Hall—the analogy is nevertheless appropriate to virtual space. Inspired by Scott McCloud's concept of 'masking' in comics, Jim Bumgardner, the creator of *Palace*—one of the first and most developed of the graphical chat-based worlds—argued that the appeal of his world was that the avatars enable people to maintain partial anonymity behind its mask.
4. We acknowledge, however, the radical deconstruction of the physical body implied by Foucault's work *and* recognise the problems associated with taking this position to its 'end-point' (e.g., Hall 1996b: 11).

Bibliography

Abbott, C. (1996) 'Young People Developing a New Language: The Implications for Teachers and for Education of Electronic Discourse', Euro Education 96, Denmark: Aalborg.

Abbott, C. (1998) 'Making Connections: Young People and the Internet', in J. Sefton-Green (ed.) *Digital Diversion. Youth Culture in the Age of Multimedia*, London: UCL Press.

Abdulaziz, Mohamed H., and Osinde, K. (1997). 'Sheng and Engsh: Development of Mixed Codes Among the Urban Youth in Kenya', *International Journal of the Sociology of Language*, 125: 43–63.

Abrams, M. (1959) *The Teenage Consumer*, London: Press Exchange.

Ackroyd, P. (2001) *London: The Biography*, London: Vintage.

Adorno, T. (1941) 'On Popular Music', in T. Adorno (1991) *The Culture Industry*, London: Routledge.

Adorno, T. and M. Horkheimer (1972) *Dialectic of Enlightenment*, New York: Continuum.

Agar, M. (1996) *The Professional Stranger* (2nd ed.), San Diego, CA: Academic Press.

Alexander, C. (2000) The Asian Gang: Ethnicity, Identity, Masculinity, Oxford: Berg.

Allison, J. (1995) 'Talking of Children and Youth Language, Socialization and Culture', in V. Amit-Talai and H. Wulff (eds.) *Youth Culture: A Cross-Cultural Perspective*, London, New York: Routledge.

Amico, S. (2001) '"I Want Muscles": House Music, Homosexuality and Masculine Signification', *Popular Music*, 20 (3): 359–78.

Amthor, G. (1991) 'Interactive Multi-Media in Education', *T.H.E. Journal* (suppl.), September: 2–5.

Anderson, N. (1923) *The Hobo: The Sociology of the Homeless Man*, Chicago: University of Chicago Press.

Andreini, L. (1985) Le Verlan: Petit Dictionnaire Illustré, Paris: Veyrier.

Antifaschistisches Autorenkollektiv (1996) *Drahtzieher im braunen Netz*, Hamburg: Konkret Literaturverlag.

Appadurai, A. (1986) 'Introduction: Commodities and the Politics of Value', in A. Appadurai (ed.) *The Social Life of Things: Commodities in Cultural Perspective*, Cambridge: Cambridge University Press.

Austin, J. (1998) 'Knowing Their Place: Local Knowledge, Social Prestige, and the Writing Formation in New York City', in J. Austin and M. Willard (eds.) *Generations of Youth: Youth Cultures and History in Twentieth-Century America*, New York: NYU Press.

Back, L. (1996) *New Ethnicities and Urban Cultures*, London: UCL Press.

Back, L. (2002) 'The Fact of Hybridity', in D. T. Goldberg and J. Solomos, (eds.) *A Companion to Racial and Ethnic Studies*, Oxford: Blackwell.

Backer, S. (2000) 'Right-wing Extremism in Unified Germany', in P. Hainsworth (ed.) *The Politics of the Extreme Right—From the Margins to the Mainstream*, London: Pinter.

Baker, H. (1993) *Black Studies: Rap and the Academy*, Chicago: University of Chicago Press.

Ball, R. (1990) 'Lexical Innovation in Present-Day French: la Français Branché', *French Cultural Studies*, 1 (1): 21–35.

Banks, M, Lovatt, A., O'Connor, J. and Raffo, C. (2000) 'Risk and Trust in the Cultural Industries', *Geoforum*, 31: 453–464.

Barnes, A. (2004) 'Iron Maiden's Eddie Heads the All-Time Classic T-shirt Chart' *The Independent on Sunday*, 21 November.

Bateson, G. (1972) Steps to an Ecology of Mind: A Revolutionary Approach to Man's Understanding of Himself, New York: Ballantine.

Baulch, E. (2003) 'Gesturing Elsewhere: The Identity Politics of the Balinese Death/ Thrash Metal Scene', *Popular Music*, 22(2): 195–216.

Bauman, Z. (1992b) 'Survival as a Social Construct', *Theory, Culture and Society*, 9(1): 1–36.

Bauman, Z. (1997) *Postmodernity and its Discontents*, Cambridge: Polity Press.

Bauman, Z. (2001) *The Individualized Society*, London: Polity.

Bausinger, H. (1984) 'Media, Technology and Daily Life', *Media, Culture and Society*, 6: 343–51.

Baym, N. K. (2000) Tune In, Log On: Soaps, Fandom, and Online Community, Thousand Oaks, CA: Sage.

Bazin, H. (1995) *La Culture Hip Hop*. Paris: Desclee de Brouwer.

Beck, U. (1992) Risk Society: Towards a New Modernity, London: Sage.

Beck, U. and Beck-Gernsheim, E. (2000) *Individualization*, London: Sage.

Becker, H. (1963) Outsiders: Studies in the Sociology of Deviance, New York: Free Press.

Bennett, A. (1999) 'Subcultures or Neo-Tribes? Rethinking the Relationship Between Youth, Style and Musical Taste', *Sociology*, 33 (3): 599–617.

Bennett, A. (2000) Popular Music and Youth Culture: Music, Identity and Place, Basingstoke, U.K.: Macmillan.

Bennett, A. (2003) 'The Use of Insider Knowledge in Ethnographic Research on Contemporary Musical Scenes', in A. Bennett, M. Cieslik and S. Miles (eds.) *Researching Youth*, London: Palgrave.

Bennett, A. (2005) *Culture and Everyday Life*, London: Sage.

Bennett, A. (2006) 'Punk's Not Dead: The Significance of Punk Rock for an Older Generation of Fans', *Sociology*, 40(1): 219–35.

Bennett, A. and Kahn-Harris, K. (2004) *After Subculture*, Basingstoke, U.K.: Palgrave.

Best, B. (1997) 'Over-The-Counter-Culture: Retheorizing Resistance in Popular Culture' in S. Redhead, D. Wynne, and J. O'Connor (eds.) *The Clubcultures Reader: Readings in Popular Culture Studies*, Oxford: Blackwell.

Bethune, C. (1999) *Le Rap: Une Esthetique Hors la Loi*, Paris: Éditions Autrement.

Bocock, R. (1993) *Consumption*, London: Routledge.

Bocquet, J. L. and Pierre-Adolphe, P. (1997) *La Rapologie*, Paris: Mille et Une Nuits.

Böhse Onkelz (2005) *Homepage*. Online. Available at http://www.onkelz.de/ (accessed 21 June 2006).

Book, B. (2003), 'Travelling through Cyberspace: Tourism and Photography in Virtual Worlds'. Online. Available at http://ssrn.com/abstract=538182 (accessed 16 June 2003).

Born, G. (2000) 'Music and the Representation/Articulation of Sociocultural Identities' in G. Born and D. Hesmondhalgh (eds.) *Western Music and Its Others: Difference, Representation and Appropriation in Music*, Berkeley, CA: University of California Press.

Bortree, D. (2005) 'Presentation of Self on the Web: An Ethnographic Study of Teenage Girls' Weblogs', *Education, Communication and Information*, 5 (1): 25–39.

Bourdieu, P. (1977) *Outline of a Theory of Practice*, Cambridge: Cambridge University Press.

Bourdieu, P. (1981) 'Men and Machines', in K. Knorr-Cetina and A. Cicourel, (eds.) *Advances in Social Theory and Methodology: Towards an Integration of Micro and Macro Sociologies*, London and Boston: Routledge and Kegan Paul.

Bourdieu, P. (1984) Distinction: A Social Critique of the Judgement of Taste, London: Routledge.

Bourdieu, P. (1986) 'The Forms of Capital', in J. E. Richardson (ed.) *Handbook of Theory of Research for the Sociology of Education*, New York: Greenwood Press.

Bourdieu, P. (1993) *The Field of Cultural Production*, Cambridge: Polity Press.

Bourdieu, P. (1996) 'Understanding', *Theory, Culture and Society* 13(2), 17–27.

Bourdieu, P. and Wacquant, L. (ed.) (1992) *An Invitation to Reflexive Sociology*, Cambridge: Polity Press.

Bradby, B. (1993) 'Sampling Sexuality: Gender, Technology and the Body in Dance Music', *Popular Music*, 12 (2): 155–76.

Brake, M. (1980) The Sociology of Youth Culture and Youth Subcultures, London: Routlege and Kegan Paul.

Brake, M. (1985) Comparative Youth Culture: The Sociology of Youth Cultures and Youth Subcultures in America, Britain and Canada, London: Routledge.

Breitbart, M. (1998) 'Dana's Mystical Tunnel: Young People's Designs for Survival and Change in the City', in T. Skelton G. Valentine (eds.) *Cool Places: Geographies of Youth Culture*, London: Routledge.

Brown, A. R. (2003a) 'The Problem of 'Subcultural Markets': Towards a Critical Political Economy of the Manufacture, Marketing and Consumption of Subcultural Products', paper presented at *Scenes, Subcultures or Tribes?* Conference, University of Northampton, U.K., 21–23rd September.

Brown, A. R. (2003b) 'Heavy Metal and Subcultural Theory: A Paradigmatic Case of Neglect', in D. Muggleton and R. Weinzierl (eds.) *The Post-Subcultures Reader,* Oxford and New York: Berg.

Brown, C. (2002) *Bovver*, Blake, U.K.: Blake Publishing.

Bucholtz, M. (2002) 'Youth and Cultural Practice', *Annual Review of Anthropology*, 35: 525–52.

Buckingham, D. (1990) Watching Media Learning. Making Sense of Media Education, London: Falmer Press.

Bull, M. (2005) 'No Dead Air! The iPod and the Culture of Mobile Listening', *Leisure Studies*, 24 (4): 343–55.

Bureau, M.-C. (1999) 'Activités Artistiques et Espace Urbain: Professionnalisation et Création d'activités', Séminaire de recherche du Centre d'études de l'emploi—Extraits du rapport, in M. C. Bureau, C. Leymarie, E. M'bia and R. Shapiro (1999) *Activités Artistiques, et Metissage: Dynamique de Creation, Professionnalisation et Inscription Urbaine*. Document de travail du CEE 99/40.

Büsser, M. (2001) Wie klingt die Neue Mitte? Rechte und Reaktionäre Tendenzen in der Popmusik, Mainz: Ventil Verlag.

Cagle, Van M. (1995), Reconstructing Pop/Subculture: Art, Rock, and Andy Warhol, London: Sage.

Calio, J. (1998) *Le Rap: Une Réponse des Banlieues*, Lyon: Entpe Aléas.
Camarillo, A. (1985) Chicanos in California: A History of Mexican-Americans in California, San Francisco: Boyd and Fraser.
Campbell, C. (1995) 'The Sociology of Consumption', in D. Miller (ed.) *Acknowledging Consumption: A Review of New Studies*, London: Routledge.
Capps, L. and Ochs, E. (2001) *Living Narrative: Creating Lives in Everyday Storytelling*, Cambridge, MA: Harvard University Press.
'Captain Dan' (2005) *Monster Energy Pit Blog*. 16 August 2005. Available http://www.warpedtour.com/pit/8-15/index.html (accessed 4 February 2006).
Cardeña, I. (2003) 'On Humour and Pathology: The Role of Paradox and Absurdity for Ideological Survival', *Anthropology and Medicine*, 10(1):115–42
Carrington, B. and Wilson, B. (2004) 'Dance Nations: Rethinking Youth Subcultural Theory', in A. Bennett and K. Kahn-Harris (eds.), *After Subculture: Critical Studies in Contemporary Youth Culture*, London: Palgrave.
Cartledge, F. (1999) 'Distress to Impress?: Local Punk Fashion and Commodity Exchange' in R. Sabin (ed.) *Punk Rock: So What? The Cultural Legacy of Punk*, London: Routledge.
Castellani, A. (1993) 'Ritratto di giovane inquieto. Immagini e stereotipi della condizione giovanile in Italia', in M. Canevazzi (ed.) *Ragazzi senza tempo. Immagini, conflitti delle culture giovanili*, Genova: Costa e Nolan.
Castells, M. (1997) The Information Age: Economy, Society and Culture. Vol. 2, The Power of Identity, Cambridge MA: Blackwell.
Castells, M. (2001) *The Internet Galaxy*, Oxford: Oxford University Press.
Castranova, E. (2001) *Virtual Worlds: A First-Hand Account of Market and Society on the Cyberian Frontier*. Online. Available at http://papers.ssrn.com/sol3/papers.cfm?abstract_id=294828 (accessed 5 June 2006).
de Certeau, M. (1986) *Heterologies: Discourse on the Other*, trans. B. Massumi, Minneapolis: University of Minnesota Press.
Chamberlin, E. (1998) 'Mods and the Revival of the Subculture: A Durkheimian and Semiotic Analysis Based on Insider Research', unpublished thesis, New York University.
Chambers, I. (1976) 'A Strategy for Living', in S. and T. Jefferson (eds.) *Resistance Through Rituals: Youth Subcultures in Post War Britain*, London: Hutchinson.
Chambers, I. (1985) *Urban Rhythms: Pop Music and Popular Culture*, Basingstoke, U.K.: Macmillan.
Chandler, D. and Roberts-Young, D.(1998) 'The Construction of Identity in the Personal Homepages of Adolescents', Online. Available at http://www.aber.ac.uk/media/Documents/short/strasbourg.htm (accessed 20 January 2006).
Chaney, D. (1996) *Lifestyles*, London: Routledge.
Chapman, R. (1998a) 'Massive Attack: Mezzanine (Album Review)', *Mojo Magazine*, May 1998.
Chapman, R. (1998b) 'Dark Side of the Spliff: Massive Attack', *Mojo Magazine*, May.
Charlton, M. and K. Newmann. (1990) 'Theoretical and Methodological Frame of Reference', in M. Carlton and B. Bachmair (eds.) *Media Communication and Everyday Life*, Munich: K.G. Saur.
Chatterton, P. and Hollands, R. (2003) Urban Nightscapes: Youth Cultures, Pleasure Spaces and Corporate Power, London: Routledge.
Childs, D. (1995) 'The Far Right in Germany since 1995', in L. Cheles, R. Ferguson, and M. Vaughan (eds.) *The Far Right in Western and Eastern Europe*, Harlow, U.K.: Longman.
Cieslik, M. (2001) 'Researching Youth Cultures: Some Problems with the Cultural Turn in British Youth Studies', *Scottish Youth Issues Journal*, 2: 27–47

Clarke, G. (1981) 'Defending Ski-Jumpers: A Critique of Theories of Youth Subcultures', in S. Frith and A. Goodwin (eds.) (1990) *On Record: Rock, Pop and the Written Word*, London: Routledge.

Clarke, J. (1976a) 'The Skinheads and the Magical Recovery of Community', in S. Hall and T. Jefferson (eds), *Resistance through Rituals*, London: Routledge.

Clarke, J. (1976b) 'Style', in S. Hall, and T. Jefferson, (eds.) *Resistance Through Rituals: Youth Subcultures in Post-War Britain* London: Hutchinson.

Clarke, J., Hall, S., Jefferson, T. and Roberts, B. (1976) 'Subcultures, Cultures and Class: A Theoretical Overview', in S. Hall and T. Jefferson (eds.) *Resistance Through Rituals: Youth Subcultures in Post War Britain*, London: Hutchinson.

Cloward, R. and Ohlin, L. (1960) *Delinquency and Opportunity: A Theory of Delinquent Gangs*, Glencoe, IL: Free Press.

Cockburn, C. (1992) 'The Circuit of Technology. Gender, Identity and Power', in R. Silverstone and E. Hirsch (eds.) *Consuming Technologies: Media and Information in Domestic Spaces*, London/New York: Routledge.

Cohen, A. K. (1955) *Delinquent Boys: The Culture of the Gang*, Glencoe, IL: Free Press.

Cohen, L. (2003) A Consumer's Republic: The Politics of Mass Consumption in Postwar America, New York: Alfred A. Knopf.

Cohen, P. (1997) Rethinking the Youth Question: Education, Labour and Cultural Studies, London: Macmillan.

Cohen, Sara. (1991) Rock Culture in Liverpool: Popular Music in the Making, Oxford University Press.

Cohen, Stanley. (1972) *Folk Devils and Moral Panics*, London: MacGibbon and Kee.

Cohen, Stanley. (1987) *Folk Devils and Moral Panics: The Creation of Mods and Rockers*, 3rd ed., Oxford: Basil Blackwell.

Colegrave, S. and Sullivan, C. (2001) (eds.) *Punk. A Life Apart*, London: Cassell.

Collins, M (2004) The Likes of Us: A Biography of the White Working Class London: Granta.

Corrina, H (2002) *The Scarlet Letters*. Available at http://www.scarletletters.com (accessed 1 December 2002)

Cullum-Swan, B. and Manning, P. K. (1994) 'What Is a T-shirt? Codes, Chronotypes, and Everyday Objects' in S. H. Riggins (ed.) *The Sociology of Things: Essays on the Social Semiotics of Objects*, Berlin and New York: Mouton de Gruyter.

Cusick, P. (1983) The Egalitarian Ideal and the American School, New York: Longman.

Dalton, S. (2003) 'Massive Attack Take a Stand' *The Scotsman*, February 2003.

DCMS (2001) *Creative Industries Mapping Document*. London: Department of Media, Culture and Sport. Online. Available HTTP: <http://www.culture.gov.uk/global/publications/archive_2001/ci_mapping_doc_2001.htm> (Accessed 8 January 2006).

Deleuze, G. and Guattari, F. (1986) *Kafka: Toward a Minor Literature*, Minneapolis: University of Minnesota Press

Denski, S. and Sholle, D. (1992) 'Metal Men and Glamour Boys: Gender Performance in Heavy Metal', in S. Craig (ed.) *Men, Masculinity and the Media*, London: Sage.

Desforges, L. (1998) 'Checking Out the Planet: Global Representations/Local Identities and Youth Travel', in T. Skelton and G. Valentine (eds.) *Cool Places: Geographies of Youth Cultures*, London: Routledge.

DfEE (2001) *Transforming Youth Work*. London: Department for Education and Employment.

Doane, M.A. (1982) 'Film and the Masquerade: Theorising the Female Spectator', *Screen*, 23 (3-4): 74-87.

Dokumentation der Opfer rechter Gewalt (2004) Online Documentation of Victims of Right-Wing Violence. Available HTTP: <http://www.opfer-rechter-gewalt.de/> (accessed 26 May 2006)

Dominick, J. (1999) 'Who Do We Think You Are? Personal Home Page and Self-Presentation on the World Wide Web', *Journalism and Mass Communication Quarterly*, 76 (4): 646–58.

Donovan, J. (1993) 'An Introduction to Street Gangs', in Gang Investigators Association (ed.) *Gang Training Seminar Handbook*, Sacramento, CA: Gang Investigators Association.

Dornbusch, C. and Raabe, J. (2004a) 'Rechtsrock fürs Vaterland', in A. Röpke and A. Speit (eds.) *Braune Kameradschaften. Die neuen Netzwerke der militanten Neonazis*, Berlin: C. H. Links.

Dornbusch, C. and Raabe, J. (eds.) (2004b) *RechtsRock. Bestandaufnahme und Gegenstrategie*, Münster : Unrast.

Dornbusch, C. and Speit, A. (2004) 'Mode für den "nationalen Widerstand"', in A. Röpke and A. Speit (eds.) *Braune Kameradschaften. Die neuen Netzwerke der militanten Neonazis*, Berlin: C. H. Links.

Du Bois-Reymond, M. (1998) '"I Don't Want to Commit Myself Yet": Young People's Life Concepts', *Journal of Youth Studies*, 1(1): 63–79.

Du Gay, P. (ed.) (1997) *Culture of Production / Production of Culture*, Milton Keynes: Open University Press.

Duncombe, S. (1998) 'Lets All Be Alienated Together: Zines and the Making of an Underground Community', in J. Austin and M. Willard (eds.) *Generations of Youth: Youth Cultures and History in Twentieth-Century America*, New York: NYU Press.

Durkheim, E. (1952) *Suicide, A Study in Sociology*, London: Routledge and Kegan Paul.

Durkheim, E. (1984) *The Division of Labor in Society*, New York: Free Press.

Dürrschmidt, J. (2000) *Everyday Lives in the Global City*, London: Routledge.

Dworkin, A. (1989) *Pornography: Men Possessing Women*, New York: Dutton

Dyson, M. E. (1993) *Reflecting Black: African American Cultural Criticism*, Minneapolis: University of Minnesota Press.

Eberwein, M. and Drexler, J. (2002) *Skinheads in Deutschland—Interviews* (5th ed.), Augsburg: Sonnentanz-Verlag.

Eckert, P. (1988) 'Adolescent Social Structure and the Spread of Linguistic Change', *Language in Society* 17: 183–208.

Elflein, D. (1998) 'From Krauts with Attitudes to Turks with Attitudes: Some Aspects of Hip-Hop History in Germany', *Popular Music*, 17(1): 17–93.

Elle (2003) 'Rock Sexy: Fashion's Going Mental About Metal...', September, p. 25.

Evans, K. and Furlong, A. (1997) 'Metaphors and Youth Transitions: Niches, Pathways, Trajectories and Navigations', in J. Bynner, L. Chishom, and A. Furlong (eds,) *Youth, Citizenship and Social Change in a European Context*, Aldershot, U.K.: Ashgate.

Evens, S.M. and Boyt, H.C. (1992) *Free Spaces: The Sources of Democratic Change in America*, Chicago: University of Chicago Press.

Farin, K. and Seidel, E. (2002) *Skinheads*, Munich: C.H. Beck.

FCO (1999) Britain's Popular Music Industry: A Nation of Great Music, London: Foreign and Commonwealth Office.

Featherstone, M. and Hepworth, M. (1991) 'The Mask of Ageing and the Postmodern Life Course', in M. Featherstone, M. Hepworth, and B.S. Turner (eds.) *The Body: Social Process and Cultural Theory*, London: Sage.

Ferguson, J. (1982) 'Jim Ferguson's Fashion Notebook', in N. Knight (ed.) *Skinhead*, London: Omnibus Press.

Ferrero, S. (2002) 'Knowing Your Place: Discourses of Diversification and Other-ness through Space in Alghero, Sardinia', in *Identity and Space Envisioning*, Binghamton: Global Publications

Ferrero, S. (2005) 'Empowering the Subject: State Education Reform and Trust in Sardinia', unpublished thesis, Goldsmiths College, University of London.

Filiciak, M, (2003) 'Hyperidentity: Postmodern Identity Patterns in Massively Multiplayer Online Role-Playing Games', in M.Wolf, and B.Perron, (eds.) *The Video Game Theory Reader*, New York: Routledge.

Finnegan, R. (1989) *The Hidden Music Makers: Making Music in an English Town*. Cambridge: Cambridge University Press.

Fornäs, J. (1995) 'Youth, Culture and Modernity', in J. Fornäs and G. Bolin (eds.) *Youth Culture in Late Modernity*, London: Sage.

Fornäs, J. and Bolin, G. (eds.) (1995) *Youth Culture in Late Modernity*, London: Sage.

Fornäs, J. Lindberg, U. and Sernhede, O. (1995) *In Garageland: Rock, Youth and Modernity*, London: Routledge.

Forrest, E. (1994) 'Generation X', *The Sunday Times*, 10 July: 17.

Forschungsgruppe Wahlen (2004) *Landtagswahl in Sachsen, 19 September 2004*, Mannheim: Forschungsgruppe Wahlen (Report)

Forsyth, A. J. M. (1997), 'A Quantitative Exploration of Dance Drug Use: The New Pattern of Drug Use of the 1990s', unpublished PhD thesis, University of Glasgow.

Foucault, M. (1977) *Discipline and Punish: The Birth of the Prison*, Harmond-sworth: Penguin Books.

Foucault, M. (1978), The History of Sexuality: An Introduciton, Vol. 1, Harmond-sworth: Penguin Books.

Fountain, N. (1988) Underground: The London Alternative Press 1966–74, Lon-don: Comedia/Routledge.

Fowler, D. (1992) 'Teenage Consumers? Young Wage-Earners and Leisure in Man-chester, 1919–1939', in A. Davies and S. Fielding (eds.) *Workers' Worlds: Cultures and Communities in Manchester and Salford, 1880–1939*, Man-chester: Manchester University Press.

Frenkel, K. (1990) 'Women and Computing', *Communication of the ACM*, 33 (11): 34–46.

Frith, S. (1983) Sound Effects: Youth, Leisure and the Politics of Rock, London: Constable.

Frith, S. (1995) 'The Stockton Conference: Recollections and Commentaries', in W. Straw, S. Johnson, R. Sullivan, and P. Friedlander (eds.) *Popular Music: Style and Identity*, Montreal: The Centre for Research on Canadian Cultural Industries and Institutions.

Frith, S. (1996) *Performing Rites*, Oxford: Oxford University Press.

Fuller, M. and Jenkins, H. (1995) 'Nintendo® and New World Travel Writing: A Dialogue', in S. Jones (ed.) Cybersociety: Computer-Mediated Communica-tion and Community, Thousand Oaks, CA: Sage.

Furlong, A. and Cartmel, F. (1997) *Young People and Social Change: Individualiza-tion and Risk in Late Modernity*, Buckingham, U.K.: Open University Press.

Gianquinta, J., Bauer, J. and Levin, J. (1993) *Beyond Technology's Promise: An Examination of Children's Educational Computing at Home*, Cambridge: Cambridge University Press.

Giddens, A. (1991) Modernity and Self-Identity: Self and Society in the Late Mod-ern Age. Cambridge: Polity.

Gillespie, G. (2005) *The Naked Guide to Bristol*, Bath: Naked Guides Limited.

Gillespie, M. (1995) *Television, Ethnicity and Cultural Change*, London: Routledge.

Gilroy, P. (1987) *There Ain't No Black in the Union Jack: The Cultural Politics of Race and Nation*, London: Hutchinson.

Gilroy, P. (1993a) *The Black Atlantic: Modernity and Double Consciousness*, London: Verso.

Gilroy, P. (1993b) *Small Acts: Thoughts on the Politics of Black Cultures*, London: Serpent's Tail.

Gilroy, P. (2001) *Between Camps: Nations, Cultures and the Allure of Race*, London: Penguin.

Gilroy, P. (2003) 'The Sounds in the Streets', *Street Signs*, 1 (6): 3–6.

Goodson, I. and J. Marshall Mangan. (1995) 'Subject Cultures and the Introduction of Classroom Computers', *British Educational Research Journal*, 21 (5): 613–28.

Goodwin M H. (1990) *He-Said-She-Said: Talk as Social Organization Among Black Children*, Bloomington IN: Indiana University Press

Goyvaerts, D. L. (1996) 'Kibalele: Form and Function of a Secret Language in Bukavu (Zaire)', *Journal of Pragmatics*, 25: 123–43.

Gramsci, A. *(1971) Selections from the Prison Notebooks*, London: Lawrence and Wishart

Gross, R. L. (1990) 'Heavy Metal Music: A New Subculture in American Society' *Journal of Popular Culture*, 24 (1): 119–29.

Grumke, T. and Wagner, B. (eds.) (2002) *Handbuch Rechtsradikalismus–Personen–Organisationen–Netzwerke vom Neonazismus bis in die Mitte der Gesellschaft*, Opladen: Leske and Budrich.

Guide, The (2004) 'Michael Holden Isn't Sure What Not to Wear', Guardian 16–22 October, p. 21.

Gunn, J. (1999) 'Goth Music and the Inevitability of Genre', *Popular Music and Society*, 23(1): 31–50.

Gunn, J. (in press) 'Dark Admissions: Gothic Subculture and the Ambivalence of Misogyny and Resistance', in M. Bibby and L. Goodlad (eds.) *Goth: Undead Subculture*, Durham, NC: Duke University Press.

Gutiérrez, Gonzalez, N. (1993) *Qué Trabajos Pasa Carlos: La Construcción Interactiva del Albur en Tepito*, Tuxtla Gutiérrez: Instituto Chiapaneco de Cultura.

Habermas, J. (1987) *The Theory of Communicative Action, vol. 1. Reason and the Rationalization of Society*, Cambridge: Polity Press.

Haiman, J. (1998) *Talk is Cheap: Sarcasm, Alienation, and the Evolution of Language*, New York: Oxford University Press.

Hall, Stanley (1904) *Adolescence: Its Psychology and Its Relations to Physiology, Anthropology, Sociology, Sex, Crime and Education*, 2 vols, New York: D. Appleton.

Hall, Stuart (1987) 'Minimal Selves', in *Identity: The Real Me*, ICA Documents 6, London: ICA: 44-46

Hall, Stuart (1988) 'New Ethnicities', in K. Mercer (ed.) *Black Film, British Cinema*, ICA Documents 7, London: ICA, 27–31.

Hall, Stuart (1994) *The Question of Cultural Identity: The Polity Reader in Cultural Theory*, Cambridge: Polity.

Hall, Stuart (1996a) 'Who Needs "Identity"?' in S. Hall and P. Du Gay (eds.) *Questions of Cultural Identity*, London: Sage.

Hall, Stuart (1996b) 'On Postmodernism and Articulation: An Interview with Stuart Hall', in D. Morley and K. H. Chen (eds.) *Stuart Hall: Critical Dialogues*, London: Routledge.

Hall, Stuart (2001) 'The Multicultural Question', in B. Hesse (ed.) *Unsettled Multiculturalism*, London: Zed Books

Hall, Stuart and Jefferson, T. (eds.) (1976) *Resistance Through Rituals: Youth Subcultures in Post-War Britain*, London: Hutchinson.

Halliday, M (1976) 'Anti-Language', *American Anthropologist*, 78 (3): 570–84.

Hamabata, M.M (1986) 'Ethnographic Boundaries: Culture, Class and Sexuality in Tokyo', *Qualitative Sociology*, 9 (4): 354–71.

Hammersley, M. and Atkinson, P. (1995) *Ethnography: Principles in Practice* (2nd ed.), London: Tavistock.

Hancock, I. (1984) 'Shelta and Polari' in P Trudgill (ed.) *The Languages of the British Isles*, Cambridge: Cambridge University Press.

Haraway, D. (1991) 'Situated Knowledge: The Science Question in Feminism and the Privilege of Partial Perspectives', in D. Haraway (ed.) *Simians, Cyborgs, and Women: The Reinvention of Nature*, New York: Routledge.

Hargreaves, A. and McKinney, M. (eds.) (1997) *Post-Colonial Cultures in France*, London: Routledge.

Harris, K. (2000) "Roots'?: The Relationship Between the Global and the Local Within the Global Extreme Metal Scene', *Popular Music*, 19(1): 13–30.

Harris, K. (2001) 'Transgression and Mundanity: The Global Extreme Metal Music Scene', unpublished PhD thesis, Goldsmiths College, University of London.

Harvey, D. (1989), The Condition of Postmodernity: An Enquiry into the Logics of Social Change, Oxford: Basil Blackwell.

Harvey, D. (1996) *Justice, Nature and the Geography of Difference*, Oxford: Blackwell.

Heartfield, J. (2005) 'Abolish the DCMS: A Cultural Critic Argues That Arts Funding Should Not Be a Matter For Government'. Available at http:///wwww.spiked-online.com/Articles/00000000551F.htm (accessed 6 January 2006).

Heat (2003) 'Star Style: Rock T-shirts', 20-26 September: 50–51.

Hebdige, D. (1974a) 'Aspects of Style in the Deviant Subcultures of the 1960s', unpublished MA thesis, Centre for Contemporary Cultural Studies, University of Birmingham.

Hebdige, D. (1974b) 'Reggae, Rastas and Rudies: Style and the Subversion of Form', Stencilled paper 24, Centre for Contemporary Cultural Studies, Birmingham: University of Birmingham.

Hebdige, D. (1976) 'The Meaning of Mod', in S. Hall and T. Jefferson (eds.), *Resistance Through Rituals: Youth Subcultures in Post-War Britain*, London: Hutchison.

Hebdige, D. (1979) *Subculture: the Meaning of Style*, London: Methuen

Hebdige, D. (1982) 'This is England! And They Don't Live Here', in N. Knight (ed.) *Skinhead*, London: Omnibus Press.

Hebdige, D. (1983) '"Ska Tissue': the Rise and Fall of Two Tone', in S. Davis and P. Simon (eds.) *Reggae International*, London: Thames Hudson

Hebdige, D. (1987) Cut 'n' Mix: Culture, Identity and Caribbean Music, London: Routledge

Hebdige, D. (1988) Hiding in the Light: On Images and Things, London: Routledge.

Henderson, S. (1993) 'Young Women, Sexuality and Recreational Drug Use: A Research and Development Project', Final Report for Lifeline, Manchester: Lifeline.

Hertz, J. C. (2002) 'Gaming the System: Multi-player Worlds Online' in L. King (ed.), *Game On: The History and Culture of Video Games*, London: Laurence King Publishing.

Hesmondhalgh, D. (2005) 'Subcultures, Scenes or Tribes? None of the Above', *Journal of Youth Studies*, 8 (1): 21–40.

Hessisch/Niedersächsische Nachrichten/HNA (2006). Online edition. Available at http://www.hna.de/ (accessed 26 May 2006).

Hetherington, K. (1998) *Expressions of Identity: Space, Performance, Politics*, London: Sage.

Hetherington, K. (1998) 'Vanloads of Uproarious Humanity: New Age Travellers and the Utopics of the Countryside' in T. Skelton and G. Valentine (eds.) *Cool Places: Geographies of Youth Culture*, London: Routledge.

Hewitt, R. (1986) *White Talk, Black Talk: Inter-Racial Friendship and Communication Amongst Adolescents*, London: Cambridge University Press.

Hewitt, R. (1989) 'Creole in Classroom: Political Grammar and Educational Vocabularies', in R. Grillo (ed.) *Social Anthropology and the Politics of Language*, London: Routledge.

Heyl, B.S. (2001) 'Ethnographic Interviewing', in P. Atkinson, A. Coffey, S. Delamont, J. Lofland and L. Lofland (eds.) *Handbook of Ethnography*, London: Sage.

Hodkinson, P. (2002) *Goth. Identity, Style and Subculture*, Oxford: Berg.

Hodkinson, P. (2003) 'Net.Goth: Internet Communication and (Sub)Cultural Boundaries', in D. Muggleton and R. Weinzierl (eds.) *The Post-Subcultures Reader*, Oxford: Berg.

Hodkinson, P. (2005) 'Insider Research in the Study of Youth Cultures', *Journal of Youth Studies*, 18 (2): 131–49.

Hodkinson, P. (2006) 'Subcultural Blogging: Online Journal Interaction and Group Involvement among UK Goths', in A. Bruns and J. Jacobs (eds.) *Uses of Blogs*, New York: Peter Lang.

Hoggart, R. (1958) The Uses of Literacy: Aspects of Working Class Culture. Harmondsworth, U.K.: Penguin.

Holland, S. (2004) Alternative Femininities: Body, Age and Identity, Oxford: Berg.

Holmes, D. (1996) 'The Education Dynamics of Cyberspace Exploration', in R. Pose (ed.) *Teaching Communication Skills in a Technological Era, Australian Communication Conference 1996*, vol. 1 Research paper (A): 133–141, Melbourne: Monash University 16–17 September.

Holmes, D. and Glenn, R. (1999) 'Adolescent CIT Use: Paradigm Shifts for Educational and Cultural Practices?', *British Journal of Sociology of Education*, 20 (1): 69–78.

Hoskins, B. (1998) 'Massive Attack: Mezzanine (Album Review)'. *Rolling Stone*, May. Howard, S. (ed.) (1998) *Wired-Up: Young People and the Electronic Media*, London: UCL Press.

Hunt, S. (2005) *The Life Course: A Sociological Introduction*, Basingstoke, U.K.: Palgrave.

Hunter, S. (2004) 'Those About to Rock: Confessions of a Teenage Heavy Metal Freak', *The Guardian Weekend*, 29 April: 16–22.

Huq, R. (2005) 'Subculture RIP?', in H. Maitland (ed.) *Navigating Difference: Cultural Diversity and Audience Development*, London: Arts Council of England.

Huq, T. (2006) Beyond Subculture: Pop, Youth and Identity in a Postcolonial World, London: Routledge.

Husbands, C. (1991) 'Militant Neo-Nazism in the Federal Republic of Germany in the 1980s', in L. Cheles, R. Ferguson, and M. Vaughan (eds.) *Neo-Fascism in Europe*, Harlow: Longman.

Husbands, C. (1995) 'Militant Neo-Nazism in Germany', in L. Cheles, R. Ferguson, and M. Vaughan (eds.) *The Far Right in Western and Eastern Europe*, Harlow, U.K.: Longman.

Hutchins, E. (1995) *Cognition in the Wild*, Cambridge, MA: MIT Press.

Infratest-Dimap (1998) Wahlreport Landtagswahl Sachsen-Anhalt 1998, Berlin: Infratest-Dimap. (Report)

Ingold, T. (2001a) 'From the Transmission of Representations to the Education of Attention', in H. Whitehouse (ed.) *The Debated Mind: Evolutionary Psychology Versus Ethnography*, Oxford: Berg.

Ingold, T. (2001b) 'Beyond Art and Technology: The Anthropology of Skill' in M.B. Schiffer (ed.) *Anthropological Perspectives on Technology*, Albuquerque: University of New Mexico Press.

Jackson, P. (2004) Inside Clubbing: Sensual Experiments in the Art of Being Human, Oxford: Berg.

Jackson, P., Stevenson, N. and Brooks, K. (2001) *Making Sense of Men's Magazines*, Cambridge: Polity.

Jagex (2006) *Jagex Software*. Available at http://www.jagex.com/corporate/index.ws (generated 1 March 2006).

James, A. (1986) 'Learning to Belong: the Boundaries of Adolescence', in A. P. Cohen (ed.) *Symbolising Boundaries: Identity and Diversity in British Cultures*, Manchester: Manchester University Press.

Jameson, F. (1991) *Postmodernism, or, the Cultural Logic of Late Capitalism'*, Durham, NC: Duke University Press.

Jenkins, R. (1983) *Lads, Citizens and Ordinary Kids: Working Class Youth Life-Styles in Belfast*, London: Routledge and Kegan Paul.

Jenkins, R. (1995) *Social Identity*, London: Routledge.

Johnson, P. (1996) *Massive Attack, Portishead, Tricky and the roots of `Trip-Hop': Straight Outa Bristol*, London: Hodder and Stoughton.

Jones, S. (1988) *Black Youth, White Culture: The Reggae Tradition from JA to UK*, Basingstoke, U.K.: Macmillan

Jones, S. (ed.) (1995) *Cybersociety: Computer Mediated Communication and Community*, London: Sage.

Jones, S. (1997) *Virtual culture*, London: Sage.

Jones, S. (ed.) (1998) *Cybersociety 2.0 : Revisiting Computer-Mediated Community and Technology*, Thousand Oaks, CA: Sage.

Jones, S. and Kucker, S. (2001) 'Computers, the Internet, and Virtual Cultures', in J. Lull (ed.) *Culture in the Communication Culture in the Communication Age*, London: Routledge.

Jordan, J. (1998) 'The Art of Necessity: The Subversive Imagination of the Anti-Road Protest and Reclaim the Streets', in G. McKay (ed.) *DiY Culture: Party and Protest in Ninties Britain*. London: Verso.

Kahn-Harris, K. (2006) *Extreme Metal: Music and Culture on the Edge*, Oxford: Berg.

Katz, C. (2001) 'Vagabond Capitalism and the Necessity of Social Reproduction', in *Antipode* 33(4): 708–27, Online. Available HTTP: http://web.gc.cuny.edu/Psychology/faculty/Katz.pdf (30 June 2006)

Kendall, L. (1999) 'Recontextualizing Cyberspace: Methodological Considerations for On-Line Research', in S. Jones (ed.), *Doing Internet Research: Critical Issues and Methods for Examining the Net*, London: Sage.

Kilian, C. (1993) 'On-line Education. The Forum of Anarchy', *Technos* 2 (3): 27–28.

Kimberlee, R.H. (2002) 'Why Don't British Young People Vote at General Elections?', *Journal of Youth Studies*, 5(1): 85–98.

Kissling, E.A. (1991) 'Street Harassment: The Language of Sexual Terrorism', *Discourse and Society*, 2: 451–460.

Kissling, E.A. and Kramarae, C. (1991) 'Stranger Compliments: The Interpretation of Street Remarks', *Women's Studies in Communication*, 14: 75–93.

Klein, N. (1999) *No Logo: Taking Aim At the Brand Bullies*, New York: Picador.

Knight, N. (ed.) (1982) *Skinhead*, London: Omnibus Press.

König, H.-D. (ed.) (1998) *Sozialpsychologie des Rechtsextremismus*, Frankfurt/Main: Suhrkamp.

Kopytoff, I. (1986) 'The Cultural Biography of Things: Commoditization as Process', in A. Appadurai (ed.) *The Social Life of Things: Commodities in Cultural Perspective*, Cambridge: Cambridge University Press.

Kühnl, R., Rilling, R. and Sager, C. (eds.) (1969) *Die NPD: Struktur, Ideologie und Funktion einer neofaschistischen Partei*, Frankfurt/Main: Suhrkamp.

Kwaku (2004) 'Christina Aguilera Ate Our Music!', *Black Information Link*, 30 January 2004

Labov, W. (1972a) *Sociolinguistic Patterns*, Philadelphia: University of Pennsylvania Press.

Labov, W. (1972b) 'The Linguistic Consequences of Being a Lame', in W. Labov (ed.) *Language in the Inner City*. Philadelphia, Pennsylvania: University of Pennsylvania Press.

Laing, D. (1985) *One Chord Wonders: Power and Meaning in Punk Rock*, Milton Keynes: Open University Press.

Lapassade, G (1996) *Le Rap ou La Fureur de Dire*, Paris: Loris Talmart.

Laqueur, W. (1984) *Young Germany: A History of the German Youth Movement* (2nd ed.), New Brunswick, NJ: Transaction.

Latour, B. (1991) 'Technology in Society Made Durable', in J. Law (ed.) *A Sociology of Monsters*, London: Routledge.

Laughey, D. (2006) *Music and Youth Culture*, Edinburgh: Edinburgh University Press. Leblanc, L. (1999) *Pretty in Punk: Girls' Gender Resistance in a Boys' Subculture*, London: Rutgers University Press.

Leblanc, L. (2002) '"The Punk Guys Will Really Overpower What the Punk Girls Have to Say": The Boys' Turf', in C.L. Williams and A. Stein (eds.) *Sexuality and Gender*, Oxford: Blackwell.

Leveson, N.G. (1998) 'Educational Pipeline Issues for Women'. Available at http://www.ai.mit.edu/people/ellens/Gender/pipeline.html (accessed 18 May 2000).

Lincoln, S. (2004) 'Teenage Girls "Bedroom Culture": Codes Versus Zones', in A. Bennett and K. Khan-Harris (eds.), *After Subculture: Critical Studies in Contemporary Youth Culture*, London: Palgrave.

Linde, C. (2000) 'The Acquisition of a Speaker by a Story. How History Becomes Memory and Identity', in *Special issue on History and Subjectivity, Ethos*, 28 (4): 608–32.

Lipsitz, G. (1994) 'We Know What Time It Is: Race, Class and Youth Culture in the Nineties', in A. Ross and T. Rose (eds.) *Microphone Fiends: Youth Music and Youth Culture*, London: Routledge.

Livingstone, S. (2002) *Young People and New Media*, London: Sage.

Lowles, N. (2001) 'Goldesel des White Power—ISD Records', in Searchlight, Antifaschistisches Infoblatt, Enough Is Enough (eds.) *White Noise—Rechtsrock, Skinhead-Musik, Blood & Honour—Einblicke in die internationale Neonazi-Musik-Szene*, Münster: Unrast.

Lowles, N. and Silver, S. (2001) 'Vom Skinhead zum Bonehead', in Searchlight, Antifaschistisches Infoblatt, Enough Is Enough (eds.) *White Noise—Rechtsrock, Skinhead-Musik, Blood & Honour—Einblicke in die internationale Neonazi-Musik-Szene*, Münster: Unrast.

Lurie, A. (1992) *The Language of Clothes*, (2nd, rev. ed.), London: Bloomsbury.

Lyles, C. (1996) 'CyberFaith: Promoting Multiculturalism Online', in R. Holeton (ed.) *Composing Cyberspace: Identity, Community and Knowledge in the Electronic Age*, Boston: McGraw-Hill.

Macdonald, N. (2001) *The Graffiti Subculture: Youth, Masculinity and Identity in London and New York*, Basingstoke: Palgrave.

MacDonald, R. and Marsh, J. (2005) *Disconnected Youth?* Basingstoke: Palgrave.

MacInnes, C. (1967) 'Old Youth and Young', *Encounter*, September.
MacKay, H. (ed.) (1997) *Consumption and Everyday Life*, London: Sage.
MacRae, R. (2004) 'Notions of "Us and Them": Markers of Stratification in Club-
    bing Lifestyles', *Journal of Youth Studies*, 7 (1): 55–71.
Macmillan, R.B., Liu, X. and Timmons, V. (1997) 'Teachers, Computers, and the
    Internet: The First Stage of a Community-Initiated Project for the Integra-
    tion of Technology into the Curriculum', *The Alberta Journal of Educational
    Research*, 18 (4): 222–34.
Maffesoli, M. (1996) *The Time of the Tribes: The Decline of Individualism in the
    Mass Society*, London: Sage.
Malbon, B. (1998) 'Clubbing: Consumption, Identity and the Spatial Practices of
    Every-Night Life', in T. Skelton and G. Valentine (eds.), *Cool Places: Geogra-
    phies of Youth Cultures*, London: Routledge.
Malbon, B. (1999) *Clubbing: Dancing, Ecstasy and Vitality*, London and New
    York: Routledge.
Marcuse, H. (1967) 'Ziele, Formen und Aussichten der Studentenbewegung', *Das
    Argument*, 1: 389–408
Marcuse, H. (1984) *One-Dimensional Man*, Boston MA: Beacon Press.
Martín, A. (2005) 'Historia de las Lecturas Infantiles. Las aleluyas: Primera lec-
    tura y primeras imagines para niños (Siglos XVII–XIX)', *CLIJ*, 179 (Febru-
    ary): 44–53
Martin, L. and Segrave, K. (1993) *Anti-Rock: The Opposition to Rock 'n' Roll*,
    New York: Da Capo.
Martin, P. J. (2004) 'Culture, Subculture and Social Organization', in A. Bennett
    and K. Kahn-Harris (eds.), *After Subculture*, Basingstoke, U.K.: Palgrave.
Martin, S. E. (1989) 'Sexual Harassment: The Link Joining Gender Stratification,
    Sexuality, and Women's Economic Status', in J. Freeman (ed.) *Women: A
    Feminist Perspective* (4th ed.), Mountain View, CA: Mayfield Publishing.
Massey, D. (1998) 'The Spatial Construction of Youth Cultures', in T. Skelton
    and G. Valentine (eds.) *Cool Places: Geographies of Youth Cultures*, Lon-
    don: Routledge.
Massey, D. (2005) *For Space*, London: Sage.
May, T. (1993) *Social Research: Issues, Methods and Process*, Buckingham, U.K.:
    Open University Press.
McCluskey, E. (1997) 'Net in the Classroom: Teachers Provide Access, Despite
    Sense that They're Tilting at Windmills', in M. O'Reilly and associates (eds.)
    The Internet and Society. Harvard Conference on the Internet, Cambridge
    MA: Harvard University Press.
McGowan, L. (2002) *The Radical Right in Germany—1870 to the Present*, Har-
    low: Pearson
McHugh, K.E. (2003) 'Three Faces of Ageism: Society, Image and Place', *Ageing
    and Society*, 23(2): 165–85.
McKay, G. (1998) *DiY Culture: Party and Protest in Nineties Britain*, London:
    Verso
McRobbie, A. (1980) 'Settling Accounts with Subcultures: A Feminist Critique', in A.
    McRobbie (2000), *Feminism and Youth Culture* (2nd ed.), London: Macmillan.
McRobbie, A. (1989) 'Second Hand Dresses and the Role of the Rag Market', in
    A. McRobbie (ed.) *Zoot Suits and Second Hand Dresses: An Anthology of
    Fashion and Music*, London: Macmillan.
McRobbie, A. (1994) *Postmodernism and Popular Culture*, London: Routledge.
McRobbie, A. (1998) *British Fashion Design*, London: Routledge.
McRobbie, A. (1999) *In the Culture Society: Art, Fashion and Popular Music*, Lon-
    don: Routledge.

McRobbie, A. (2000) *Feminism and Youth Culture* (2nd ed.), London: Macmillan.

McRobbie, A. and Garber, M. (1976) 'Girls and Subculture: An Exploration', in S. Hall and T. Jefferson (eds.) *Resistance Through Rituals: Youth Subcultures in Post-War Britain*, London: Hutchison.

Mayol, P. (1997) *Les Enfants de la liberté: Etudes sur l'autonomie sociale et la cultures des jeunes*, Paris: L'Harmattan.

Mendoza-Denton, N. (1996) 'Muy Macha: Gender and Ideology in Gang-Girls' Discourse about Makeup', *Ethnos*, 61 (1–2): 47–63.

Mendoza-Denton, N. (1997) 'Chicana/Mexicana Identity and Linguistic Variation: An Ethnographic and Sociolinguistic Study of Gang Affiliation in an Urban High School', unpublished PhD thesis, Stanford University.

Mendoza-Denton, N. (1999) 'Fighting Words: Latina Girls, Gangs, and Language Attitudes', in D. Leticia Galindo & M. D. Gonzales (eds.) *Speaking Chicana: Voice, Power, and Identity*, Tucson: University of Arizona Press.

Mendoza-Denton, N. (in press) *Homegirls: Language and Symbolic Practice in the Making of Latina Youth Styles*, Oxford: Blackwell.

Merkl, P. (1997) 'Why are they So Strong Now? Comparative Reflections on the Revival of the Radical Right in Europe', in P. H. Merkl and L. Weinberg (eds.) *The Revival of Right-Wing Extremism in the Nineties*, London: Frank Cass.

Merle, P. (1999) *Le Dico du Français Branché*, Paris: Seuil.

Merton, T. (1938) 'Social Structure and Anomie', *American Sociological Review*, 3 : 672–82.

Merton, R. (1972) 'Insiders and Outsiders: A Chapter in the Sociology of Knowledge', in R. Merton (ed.) *Varieties of Political Expression in Sociology*, Chicago: University of Chicago Press.

Middleton, R. (1990) *Studying Popular Music*, Buckingham: Open University Press.

Miles, S. (1995) 'Towards an Understanding of the Relationship Between Youth Identities and Consumer Culture', *Youth Policy*, 51: 35–42.

Miles, S. (2000) *Youth Lifestyles in a Changing World*, Buckingham: Open University Press.

Miles, S., Dallas, C. and Burr, V. (1998) 'Fitting In and Sticking Out': Consumption, Consumer Meanings and the Construction of Young People's Identities', *Journal of Youth Studies*, 1 (1): 81–96.

Miller, D. and D. Slater (2000) *The Internet. An Ethnographic Approach*, Oxford: Berg.

Mitchell, T. (1996) *Popular Music and Local Identity: Rock, Pop and Rap in Europe and Oceania*, Leicester: Leicester University Press.

Mock, B.. (2005) 'Race: Unwanted Poster', in *Pittsburgh City Paper Online*, Pittsburgh: Steel City Media. Available at http://www.pittsburghcitypaper.ws/scripts/printIt.cfm?ref=5304 (accessed 15 January 2006).

Monti, D. (1994) *Wannabe: Gangs in Suburbs and Schools*, Oxford: Blackwell.

Moore, E. (2004) 'Explaining the Correlation between Social Identity and Language Use: The Community of Practice', paper delivered at the BAAL/CUP Language and Identity Seminar, University of Reading, 5–7th July.

Moreno-Álvarez, G. (2001) 'El Uso del Albur en La Frontera', unpublished MA thesis, Las Cruces: New Mexico State University.

Morrill, C, Adelman, M., Musheno, M. and Bejarano, C. (2000) 'Telling Tales in School: Youth Culture and Conflict Narratives', *Law & Society Review*, 34 (3): 521–65.

Mr Roboto Project, The (2006) 'Official Membership Packet'. Available at http://www.therobotoproject.org/member/member_packet.html (accessed 15 January 2006)

Muggleton, D. (1997) 'The Post-Subculturalist', in S. Redhead, D. Wynne, and J. O'Connor (eds.) *The Club Cultures Reader*, Malden, U.K.: Blackwell.

Muggleton, D. (2000) *Inside Subculture: The Postmodern Meaning of Style*, Oxford: Berg.

Muggleton, D. and Weinzierl, R. (2003) *The Post-Subcultures Reader*, Oxford and New York: Berg.

Mungham, G. and Pearson, G. (eds.) (1976) *Working Class Youth Culture*, London: Routledge and Kegan Paul.

National Institute of Justice (1995) 'Research in Brief, Prosecuting Gangs: A National Assessment', available at http://www.ajp.usdoj.gov/nij/pubs-sum/151785.htm (12/12/2006).

Nayak, A. (2003) *Race, Place and Globalization: Youth Cultures in a Changing World*, Oxford: Berg.

Neale, S. (1980) *Genre*, London: British Film Institute.

Needham, A. (2001), 'Alpha (Album Review)', *New Musical Express*, March.

Negroponte, N. (1995) *Being Digital*, New York: Alfred A. Knopf.

Negus, K. (1999) *Music Genres and Corporate Cultures*, London: Routledge.

Newmann, D. (1990) 'Opportunities for Research on the Organizational Impact of School Computers', *Educational Researcher*, 19 (3): 8–13.

New Musical Express (1999) 'Archive (gig review)', September.

Nini, S. (1993) *Ils Disent que Je Suis Une Beurette*, Paris: Fixot.

Nissen, J. (1998) 'Hackers: Masters of Modernity and Modern Technology', in J. Sefton-Green (ed.) *Digital Diversion. Youth Culture in the Age of Multimedia*, London: UCL Press.

Nixon, S. (1997) 'Circulating Culture', in P. Du Gay (ed.) *Production of Culture/ Cultures of Production*, London: Sage.

Oakes, J. (1985) *Keeping Track: How Schools Structure Inequality*, New Haven: Yale University Press.

Oakley, A. (1981) 'Interviewing Women: A Contradiction in Terms', in H. Roberts (ed.) *Doing Feminist Research*, London: Routledge and Kegan Paul.

Oakley, A. (1998) 'Gender, Methodology and People's Way of Knowing: Some Problems with Feminism and the Paradigm Debate in Social Science', *Sociology*, 32 (4): 707–31.

Obalk, M., Soral, A. and Pasche, A. (1984) *Les mouvements de mode explique aux parents*, Paris: Robert Laffont.

Oevermann, U. (1998) 'Zur soziologischen Erklärung und öffentlichen Interpretation von Phänomenen der Gewalt und des Rechtsextremismus bei Jugendlichen. Zugleich eine Analyse des kulturnationalen Syndroms', in H.-D. König (ed.) *Sozialpsychologie des Rechtsextremismus*, Frankfurt/Main: Suhrkamp.

Office of the Deputy Prime Minister (2003) 'Learning to Listen: Action Plan for Children and Young People 2003/04', Available at http://www.odpm.gov.uk/index.asp?id=1123203 (accessed 16 January 2006).

O'Flaherty, W.D. (1980) *Women, Androgynes, and Other Mythical Beasts*, London: The University of Chicago Press.

Olnick, Jeffrey K., & Robbins, J. (1998) 'Social Memory Studies: From "Collective Memory" to the Historical Sociology of Mnemonic Practices', *Annual Review of Sociology*, 24: 105–40.

Osgerby, B. (1998) *Youth in Britain Since 1945*, Oxford: Blackwell.

Osgerby, B. (2004) *Youth Media*, London: Routledge.

Paoletti, J.B. and Kidwell, C.B. (1989) 'Conclusion', in C.B. Kidwell and V. Steele (eds.) *Men and Women: Dressing the Part*, Washington, D.C.: Smithsonian Institution Press.

Paredes, A. (1993) *Folklore and Culture on the Texas-Mexican Border*, Austin, TX: University of Texas.

Park, R. E. (1925) *The City*, Chicago: University of Chicago Press.

Parker, K. (2004) *Free Play: The Politics of the Video Game*. Available at http://www.reason.com/0404/fe.kp.free.shtml (accessed 16 January 2005).

Parsons, T. (1949) 'Age and Sex in the Social Structure of the United States', in T. Parsons (ed.) *Essays in Sociological Theory*, New York: Free Press.

Pearson, G. (1983) *Hooligan: A History of Respectable Fears*, London: Macmillan.

Pearson, G. (1994) 'Youth Crime and Society', in M. Maguire, R. Morgan, and R. Reiser (eds.) *The Oxford Handbook of Criminology*, Oxford: Clarendon Press.

Penman, I. (1994) 'MassiveAttack', *TheWire*, May.

Peterson, R. and Bennett, A. (2004) 'Introducing Music Scenes', in A. Beenett and R. Peterson (eds.), *Music Scenes: Local Translocal and Virtual*, Nashville: Vanderbilt University Press.

Peukert, D. (1983) 'Die "Wilden Cliquen" in den zwanziger Jahren', in W. Breyvogel (ed.) *Autonomie und Widerstand: Zur Theorie und Geschichte des Jugendprotestes*, Essen: Rigidon.

Pfahl-Traughber, A. (2002) 'Die Entwicklung des Rechtsextremismus in Ost- und West-Deutschland im Vergleich', in T. Grumke and B. Wagner (eds.) *Handbuch Rechtsradikalismus—Personen—Organisationen—Netzwerke vom Neonazismus bis in die Mitte der Gesellschaft*, Opladen: Leske and Budrich.

Pierre-Adolphe, P., Mamoud, M. and Tzanos, G. (1995) *Le Dico de la Banlieue*, Boulogne: La Sirene.

Pilkington, H. (1994) *Russia's Youth and Its Culture: A Nation's Constructors and Constructed*, London: Routledge.

Pilkington, H. (2004) 'Youth Strategies for Global Living: Space, Power and Communication in Everyday Cultural Practice', in A. Bennett and K. Kahn-Harris (eds.) *After Subculture: Critical Studies in Contemporary Youth Culture*, London: Palgrave.

Pini, M. (1997a) '"Other Traces": A Cultural Study of Clubbing and New Modes of Femininity', unpublished PhD thesis, Goldsmiths College: University of London.

Pini, M. (1997b) 'Women and the Early British Rave Scene', in A. McRobbie (ed.) *Back to Reality? Social Experience and Cultural Studies*, Manchester: Manchester University Press.

Pini, M. (2001) *Club Cultures and Female Subjectivity: The Move from Home to House*, Basingstoke, U.K.: Palgrave.

Polhemous, T. (1994) *Street Style*, New York: Thames and Hudson.

Poole, S. (2000) *Trigger Happy, the Inner Life of Video Games*, London: Fourth Estate.

Poster, M. (1997) 'Cyberdemocracy: the Internet and the Public Sphere', in D. Holmes (ed.) *Virtual Politics: Identity and Community in Cyberspace*, London: Sage.

Pötsch, S. (2002) 'Rechtsextreme Musik', in T. Grumke and B. Wagner (eds.) *Handbuch Rechtsradikalismus—Personen—Organisationen—Netzwerke vom Neonazismus bis in die Mitte der Gesellschaft*, Opladen: Leske & Budrich.

Rampton, B. (1995) *Crossing: Language and Ethnicity among Adolescents*, London: Longman

Rampton, B. (1999) 'Sociolinguistics and Cultural Studies: New Ethnicities, Liminality and Interaction', *Social Semiotics*, 9 (3): 355–73.

Rattansi, A. and Phoenix, A. (1997) 'Rethinking Youth Identities: Modernist and Postmodernist Frameworks', in J. Brynner, L. Chisholm, and A. Furlong (eds.) *Youth, Citizenship and Social Change in a European Context*, Aldershot, U.K.: Ashgate.

Reay, D. and Lucey, H. (2000) '"I Don't Really like It Here but I Don't Want to Be Anywhere Else": Children and Inner City Council Estates', *Antipode*, 32 (4): 410–28.

Recordstore.co.uk (2004) Available at http://www.recordstore.co.uk/teeshirtstore/result.jsp (accessed: 30 June 2006)

Redhead, S. (1990) *The End of Century Party: Youth and Pop Towards 2000*, Manchester: Manchester University Press.

Redhead, S. (1993) 'The Politics of Ecstacy' (sic) in S. Redhead (ed.) *Rave Off: Politics and Deviance in Contemporary Youth Culture*, Aldershot, U.K.: Avebury.

Redhead, S. (1997) *Subcultures to Clubcultures—An Introduction to Popular Cultural Studies*, Oxford: Blackwell.

Reed, A. (2005) '"My Blog Is Me": Texts and Persons in UK Online Journal Culture (and anthropology)', *Ethnos*, 70 (2): 220–42.

Reid, E. (1994) *Cultural Formations in Text-Based Virtual Realities*, unpublished MA Thesis, University of Melbourne. Available at http://www.aluluei.com/cult-form.htm (accessed 30 June 2006).

Reynolds, S. (1994) 'Trip-Hop Don't Stop: Massive Attack and Portishead', *Melody Maker*, September.

Reynolds, S. (1998) *Energy Flash*, London: Macmillan.

Reynolds, S. and Press, J. (1995) *The Sex Revolts. Gender, Rebellion and Rock'n'Roll*, London: Serpent's Tail.

Rheingold, H. (1993) *The Virtual Community: Homesteading on the Electronic Frontier*, Reading, MA: Addison-Wesley.

Rietveld, H. (1998) *This is Our House: House Music, Cultural Spaces and Technologies*, Aldershot, U.K.: Ashgate.

Roberts, H. (1981) *Doing Feminist Research*, London: Routledge & Kegan Paul.

Roberts, R. (1971) *The Classic Slum*, Manchester: Manchester University Press.

Robins, K. (1995) 'Cyberspace and the World We Live In' in M. Featherstone (ed.) *Cyberspace/Cyberbodies*, London: Sage.

Roccor, B. (2000) 'Heavy Metal: Forces of Unification and Fragmentation within a Musical Subculture', *The World of Music*, 42 (1), 83–94.

Rock, P. (2001) 'Symbolic Interactionism and Ethnography', in P. Atkinson, A. Coffey, S. Delamont, J. Lofland and L. Lofland (eds.) *Handbook of Ethnography*, London: Sage.

Rogers, P. (2006) 'Are You Normal? Young People's Participation in the Renaissance of Public Space—A Case Study of Newcastle Upon Tyne, UK', *Children, Youth, Environments*, 16 (2), 105–126.

Röpke, A. and Speit, A. (eds.) (2004) *Braune Kameradschaften. Die neuen Netzwerke der militanten Neonazis*, Berlin: Ch. Links Verlag.

Rose, T. (1994) *Black Noise: Rap Music and Black Culture in Contemporary America*, Hanover, NH: Wesleyan University Press

Rosen, C. (2004–2005) 'The Age of Egocasting', *The New Atlantis*, 7, Fall 2004/Winter 2005: 51–72.

Roseneil, S. (1993) 'Greenham Revisited: Researching Myself and My Sisters', in D. Hobbs and T. May, (eds.) *Interpreting the Field: Accounts of Ethnography*, Oxford: Claredon Press.

Ross, A. (1994) 'Introduction', in A. Ross and T. Rose (eds.) *Microphone Fiends: Youth Music and Youth Culture*, London: Routledge.

Roth, M. (2000) 'Building Punk Community: The Tale of *Mr. Roboto*', *Here Be Dragons*, Issue 7, Pittsburgh.
Rutherford, J. (1997) 'Young Britain', *Soundings: A Journal of Politics and Culture*, 6: 112–25.
Sardiello, R. (1998) 'Identity and Status Stratification in Deadhead Subculture', in J. Epstein (ed.) *Youth Culture: Identity in a Postmodern World*, Malden, MA: Blackwell.
Savage, J. (1992) *England's Dreaming: Sex Pistols and Punk Rock*, London: Faber and Faber.
Scheuch, E.K. and Klingemann, H.-D. (1967) 'Theorie des Rechtsradikalismus in westlichen Industriegesellschaften', *Hamburger Jahrbuch fürWirtschafts- und Gesellschaftspolitik*, 12 (1967): 11–19
Schilling-Estes, N. (2005) '"Backwards Talk" in Smith Island, MD: Linguistics Forms and social functions', paper presented at SECOL LXXII, Raleigh, NC, 7–9 April.
Schröder, B. (1997) I*m Griff der rechten Szene—Ostdeutsche Städte in Angst*, Reinbek/Hamburg: Rowohlt.
Schütz, A. (1970a) *On Phenomenology and Social Relations*, Chicago: Chicago University Press.
Schütz, A. (1970b) *Reflections on the Problem of Relevance*, New Haven and London: Yale University Press.
Schütz, A. (1976) *Collected Papers II: Studies in Social Theory* (4th ed.) A. Brodersen (ed.), The Hague: Martinus Nijhoff.
Searchlight, Antifaschistisches Infoblatt, Enough Is Enough (eds.) (2001) *White Noise—Rechtsrock, Skinhead-Musik, Blood & Honour—Einblicke in die internationale Neonazi-Musik-Szene*, Münster: Unrast.
Sefton-Green, J. (1998) *Digital Diversions. Youth Culture in the Age of Multimedia*, London: UCL Press.
Sefton-Green and Buckingham (1998) 'Digital Visions: Children's Creative Uses of Multimedia Technologies', in J. Sefton-Green (ed.) *Digital Diversion. Youth Culture in the Age of Multimedia*, London: UCL Press.
Sennett, R. (2003) *Respect: The Formation of Character in a World of Inequality*, London: Allen Lane.
Serusi, A. (1981) *Cosa Possiedono i Poveri. Indagine di Sociologia Urbana. I part*, unpublished thesis, Universita degli Studi di Sassari. Facoltà di Giurisprudenza, Sassari (Italy).
Shank, B. (1994) *Dissonant Identities: The Rock 'n' Roll Scene in Austin, Texas*, Hanover, NH: Wesleyan University Press.
Shaw, A, (1980) 'Researching Rhythm and Blues', *Black Music Research Journal*, 1: 71–79.
Shedden, J. (2002) 'Fantastic Clothes Take Me Back to When Punk Made My Day' *Guardian, Money*, Saturday, 6 July.
Shields, R. (1992) 'The Individual, Consumption Cultures and the Fate of Community', in R. Shields (ed.) *Lifestyle Shopping: The Subject of Consumption*, London: Routledge.
Shuker, R. (1998) *Key Concepts in Popular Music*, London: Routledge.
Shuman, A. (1986) *Storytelling Rights. The Uses of Oral and Written Texts by Urban Adolescents*, Cambridge: Cambridge University Press
Shumway, D. (1992) 'Rock and Roll as a Cultural Practice', in A. DeCurtis (ed.) *Present Tense: Rock and Roll and Culture*, Durham, NC: Duke University Press.
Siegler, B. (1991) *Auferstanden aus Ruinen... Rechtsextremismus in der DDR*, Berlin: Edition TIAMAT

Silver, S. (2001) 'Das Netz wird gesponnen—Blood & Honour 1987–1992', in Searchlight, Antifaschistisches Infoblatt, Enough Is Enough (eds.) *White Noise—Rechtsrock, Skinhead-Musik, Blood & Honour—Einblicke in die internationale Neonazi-Musik-Szene*, Münster: Unrast.

Silverstone, R. and E. Hirsch, (1992) *Consuming Technologies: Media and Information in the Domestic Spaces*, London: Routledge.

Simpson, M. (1994) *Male Impersonators: Men Performing Masculinity*, London: Cassell.

Singh, P. (1993) 'Institutional Discourse and Practice. A Case Study of the Social Construction of Technological Competence in the Primary Classroom', *British Journal of Sociology of Education*, 14 (1): 39–58.

Skeggs, B. (2001) 'Feminist Ethnography', in P. Atkinson, S. Coffey, S. Delamont, J. Lofland, and L. Lofland (eds.) *Handbook of Ethnography*, London: Sage.

Skelton, T. and Valentine, G. (eds.) (1998) *Cool Places: Geographies of Youth Cultures*, London: Routledge.

Smith, J. (2001) 'Globalizing Resistance: The Battle of Seattle and the Future of Social Movements', *Mobilization: An International Journal*, 6 (1): 1–19.

Song, M. and Parker, D. (1995) 'Commonality, Difference and the Dynamics of Discourse in In-Depth Interviewing', *Sociology*, 29 (2): 241–56.

Southall, A. (1988) 'The Segmentary State in Africa and Asia', *Comparative Studies in Society and History*, 30 (1): 52–82

Speit, A. (ed.) (2002) *Ästhetische Mobilmachung—Dark Wave, Neofolk und Industrial im Spannungsfeld rechter Ideologien*, Münster: Unrast

Sproull, L. and S. Kiesler (1986) 'Reducing Social Context Cues: Electronic Mail in Organisational Communication', *Management Science*, 32: 1492–512.

Stacey, J. (1988) 'Can There Be a Feminist Ethnography?', *Women's Studies International Forum*, 11 (1): 21–27.

Stahl, G. (2001) 'Tracing Out an Anglo-Bohemia: Music Making and Myth in Montreal', *Public*, 22/23: 99–121.

Stallabras, J (1993) 'Just Gaming: Allegory and Economy in Computer Games', *New Left Review*, 198: 83–106.

Stanley, L. and Wise, S. (1983) *Breaking Out: Feminist Consciousness and Feminist Research*, London: Routledge and Kegan Paul.

Steele, V. (1989) 'Appearance and Identity', in C.B. Kidwell and V. Steele (eds.) *Men and Women: Dressing the Part*, Washington, D.C.: Smithsonian Institution Press.

Stevenson, N. (1995) *Understanding Media Cultures*, London: Sage.

St. John, G. (2003) 'Post-Rave Technotribalism and the Carnival of Protest', in D. Muggleton and R. Weinzierl (eds.) *The Post-Subcultures Reader*, Oxford: Berg.

Stone, C.J. (1999) *The Last of the Hippies*, London: Faber and Faber.

Stöss, R. (1991) *Rechtsextremismus in der Bundesrepublik. Entwicklung, Ursachen und Gegenmassnahmen*, Wiesbaden: Verlag für Sozialwissenschaften

Stöss, R. (2004) 'Der Nährboden für rechte Netzwerke. Rechtsextreme Einstellungen und ihre Ursachen', in S. Braun and D. Hörsch (eds.) *Rechte Netzwerke — eine Gefahr*, Wiesbaden: Verlag für Sozialwissenschaften.

Stöss, R. and Niedermayer, O. (1998) *Rechtsextremismus, politische Unzufriedenheit und das Wählerpotential rechtsextremer Parteien in der Bundesrepublik im Frühsommer 1998*, Berlin: Free University Berlin. (Research Report)

Stöss, R. and Niedermayer, O. (2005) *Rechtsextreme Einstellungen in Berlin und Brandenburg*, Berlin: Free University Berlin. (Research Report)

Strate, L.R. Jacobson and S.B. Gibson (1996) 'Meaning: Cybercommunication and Cyberculture', in L. Strate, R. Jacobson,, and S.B. Gibson (eds.) *Communication and Cyberspace*, Cresskill, NJ: Hampton Press.

Stratton, J. (1985) 'On the Importance of Subcultural Origins', in K. Gelder and S. Thornton (eds.) (1997) *The Subcultures Reader*, London: Routledge.

Straw, W. (1991) 'Systems of Articulation, Logics of Change: Communities and Scenes in Popular Music', *Cultural Studies*, 5 (3): 368–88.

Straw, W. (2001) 'Scenes and Sensibilities', *Public*, 22/23: 245–57.

Strossen, N. (1995) *Defending Pornography: Free Speech, Sex, and the Fight for Women's Rights*, New York: Scribner.

Stuart-Smith, J., Timmins, C. and Wrench, A. (in press) 'Empirical Evidence for Gendered Speech Production: /s/ in Glaswegian', in J. Cole and J.I. Hualde (eds.) *LabPhon 9: Change in Phonology*, Berlin: Walter De Gruyter.

Suler, J. (2000) *Identity Management in Cyberspace*. Available at http://www.rider.edu/~suler/psycyber/identitymanage.html (accessed 5 November 2003).

Suttles, G. D. (1968) *The Social Order of the Slum: Ethnicity and Territory in the Inner City*, Chicago: Chicago University Press

Sweetman, P. (2004) 'Tourists and Travellers? "Subcultures", Reflexive Identities and Neo-Tribal Sociality', in A. Bennett and K. Kahn-Harris (eds.) *After Subculture*, Basingstoke: Palgrave.

Swidler, A and Arditi, J. (1994) 'The New Sociology of Knowledge', *Annual Review of Sociology*, 20 (1): 305–29.

Tansu, G.M. (1982) *Cosa Possiedono i Poveri. Indagine di Sociologia Urbana Nel Centro Storico di Alghero*, II part., unpublished thesis, Universita degli Studi di Sassari. Facoltà di Giurisprudenza, Sassari (Italy).

Thoday, P. (1995) *Le Franglais*, London: Althone.

Thompson, M. (1979) *Rubbish Theory: The Creation and Destruction of Value*, Oxford: Oxford University Press

Thorne, B. (1993) *Gender Play: Girls and Boys in School*, New Brunswick, NJ: Rutgers University Press.

Thornton, S. (1994) 'Moral Panic, the Media and British Rave Culture', in A. Ross and T. Rose (eds.) *Microphone Fiends: Youth Music and Youth Culture*, London: Routledge.

Thornton, S. (1995) *Club Cultures: Music, Media and Subcultural Capital*, Cambridge: Polity.

Thrasher, F. (1927) *The Gang*, Chicago: Chicago University Press.

Toynbee, J. (2000) *Making Popular Music*, London: Arnold.

Tsitsos, W. (1999) 'Rules of Rebellion: Slamdancing, Moshing, and the American Alternative Scene', *Popular Music*, 18 (3): 397–414.

Turkle, S. (1984) *The Second Self: Computers and the Human Spirit*, London: Granada.

Turkle, S. (1995) *Life on the Screen: Identity in the Age of the Internet*, New York: Simon and Schuster.

Turkle, S. (1997) 'Computational Technologies and Images of the Self', *Social Research*, 64 (3): 1093–1111.

Turner, V. (1982) *From Ritual to Theater: The Human Seriousness of Play*, New York: PAJ Publications

Valentine, G., Skelton, T. and Chambers, D. (1998) 'Cool Places: An Introduction to Youth and Youth Cultures', in T. Skelton and G. Valentine (eds.), *Cool Places: Geographies of Youth Cultures*, London: Routledge.

Van Zoonen, L. (1994) *Feminist Media Studies*, London: Sage.

Verdelhan-Bourgade, M. (1990) 'Communiquer en Français contemporain: Quelque Part ça m'interpelle,' Phénomènes Syntaxiques en Français branché', *La Linguistique* 26(1): 53–69.

Vered, K. O. (1998) 'Blue Group Boys Play *Incredible Machine*, Girls Play Hop-scotch: Social Discourse and Gendered Play at the Computer', in J. Sefton-Green (ed.) *Digital Diversions. Youth Culture in the Age of Multimedia*, London: UCL Press.

Verfassungsschutz, Bundesamt für (1996–2005) *Verfassungsschutzbericht 1996–2004*, Cologne: Bundesamt für Verfassungsschutz. Also online in English. Available at http://www.verfassungsschutz.de/en/en_publications/annual_reports/ (accessed 21 May 2006).

Verfassungsschutz des Landes Brandenburg (2001) *"National befreite Zonen"—Kampfruf und Realität*, Potsdam : Innenministerium Brandenburg.

Virilio, P. (1995) *The Art of the Motor*, Minneapolis: University of Minnesota Press.

Wagner, B. (2002) 'Kulturelle Subversion von rechts in Ost- und Westdeutsch-land: Zu rechtsextremen Entwicklungen und Strategien', in T. Grumke and B. Wagner (eds.) *Handbuch Rechtsradikalismus. Personen— Organi-sationen—Netzwerke vom Neonazismus bis in die Mitte der Gesellschaft*, Opladen : Leske and Budrich.

Waibel, H. (1996) *Rechtsextremismus in der DDR bis 1989*, Cologne: PappyRossa.

Wai-Teng Leong, L. (1992) 'Cultural Resistance: The Cultural Terrorism of British Male Working-Class Youth', *Social Theory*, 12: 29–58.

Wall, M. (2001) *Run to the Hills: Iron Maiden The Authorised Biography* (rev. ed.), London: Sanctuary.

Walser, R. (1993a) *Running with the Devil: Gender, Power and Madness in Heavy Metal Music*, Middletown, CT: Wesleyan University Press.

Walser, R. (1993b) 'Forging Masculinity: Heavy Metal Sounds and Images of Gender', in S. Frith, A. Goodwin and L. Grossberg (eds.) *The Music Video Reader*, New York: Routledge.

Warschauer, M. (1998) 'Online Learning in Socio-Cultural Context', *Anthropol-ogy and Educational Quarterly*, 29 (1): 68–88.

Watson, N. (1997) 'Why We Argue About Virtual Community: A Case Study of the Phish.Net Fan Community', in S. Jones (ed.) *Virtual Culture: Identity and Communication in Cybersociety*, Thousand Oaks, CA: Sage.

Wax, R. (1971) *Doing Fieldwork: Warnings and Advice*, Chicago: University of Chicago Press.

Weaver, J. and Daspit, T. (2001) 'Rap (in) the Academy: Academic Work, Educa-tion and Cultural Studies', *Taboo: the Journal of Culture and Education*, Fall/Winter: 7–13.

Weaver, J., Dimitriadis, G. and Daspit, T. (2001) 'Hip Hop Pedagogies and Youth Cultures: Rhythmic Blends of Globalization and the Lost Third Ear of the Academy', *Taboo: The Journal of Culture and Education*, Fall/Winter: 103–31.

Webb, P. (2004) 'Interrogating the Production of Sound and Place: The Bristol Phenomenon from Lunatic Fringe to World-Wide Massive', in S. Whiteley, A. Bennett, and S. Hawkins (eds.), *Music, Space and Place: Popular Music and Cultural Identity*, London: Ashgate Press.

Webb P. (2005) 'Bristol', in J. Shepherd, D. Horn and D. Laing (eds.) *Encyclopedia of Popular Music of the World 4—Locations Volume*, London: Continuum Press.

Webb P. (2006) 'Global Cuts: An Investigation into Localised Dance Music Pro-duction', unpublished PhD thesis, University of the West of England.

Weil, K. (1992) *Androgyny and the Denial of Difference*, London: University Press of Virginia.

Weinstein, D. (1991) *Heavy Metal: The Music and its Culture*, New York: De Capo Press.

Weinzierl. R. and Muggleton, D. (2003) 'What is 'Post-Subcultural Studies' Anyway?', in D. Muggleton and R. Weinzierl (eds.) *The Post-Subcultural Studies Reader*, Oxford: Berg

Weiss, M. (2001) 'Begleitmusik zu Mord und Totschlag', in Searchlight, Antifaschistisches Infoblatt, Enough Is Enough (eds.) *White Noise—Rechtsrock, Skinhead-Musik, Blood & Honour—Einblicke in die internationale Neonazi-Musik-Szene*, Münster: Unrast.

Wellman, B. (1997) 'An Electronic Group Is Virtually a Social Network', in S. Kiesler (ed.) *Culture of the Internet*, Mahwah New Jersey: Lawrence Erlbaum..

Welsh, I. (2000) 'New Social Movements', *Developments in Sociology*, 16: 43–60.

Whyte, W. F. (1943) *Street Corner Society: The Social Structure of an Italian Slum*, Chicago: Chicago University Press.

Willens, H., Würtz, S. and Eckert, R. (1994) *Analyse frendenfeindlichers Straftäter*, Bonn: Bundesministeriun des Inneren.

Williams, R. (1974) *Television: Technology and Cultural Form*, London: Schocken Books.

Williams, R. (1977) *Marxism and Literature*, Oxford: Oxford University Press.

Williamson, M. (2001) 'Vampires and Goths: Fandom, Gender and Cult Dress', in W.J.F. Keenan (ed.) *Dressed to Impress: Looking the Part*, London: Berg.

Willis, P. (1977) *Learning to Labour: How Working Class Kids Get Working Class Jobs*, Aldershot, U.K.: Gower.

Willis, P. (1978) *Profane Culture*, London: Routledge and Kegan Paul.

Willis, P. (1980) 'Notes on Method', in S. Hall (ed.) *Culture, Media and Language*, London: Hutchinson.

Willis, P., Jones, S., Canaan, J. and Hurd, G. (1990) *Common Culture: Symbolic Work at Play in the Everyday Cultures of the Young*, Milton Keynes, U.K.: Open University Press.

Willis, T. (1993) 'The Lost Tribes: Rave Culture', *The Sunday Times*, 18 July 1993.

Wise, S. and Stanley, L. (1987) *Georgie Porgie: Sexual Harassment in Everyday Life*, London: Pandora.

Wolf, M. (2001) *The Medium of The Video Game*, Austin: University of Texas Press.

Woodhouse, A. (1989) *Fantastic Women: Sex, Gender and Transvestism*, London: Macmillan.

Wulff, H. (1995) 'Inter-Racial Friendship: Consuming Youth Styles, Ethnicity and Teenage Femininity in South London', in V. Amit-Talai and H. Wulff (eds.) *Youth Culture: a Cross-Cultural Perspective*, London, New York: Routledge.

Yee, N (2002) *The Norrathian Scrolls: A Study of Everquest*. Available at http://www.nickyee.com/eqt/home.html (accessed 30 June 2006).

Young, M. (1958) *The Rise of the Meritocracy*, Harmondsworth, U.K.: Penguin.

Young, J. (1971) *The Drugtakers: The Social Meaning of Drug Use*, London: Paladin.

Young, T. (1985) 'The Shock of the Old', *New Society*, 14 February: 246.

Selective discography

Alpha (1997) 'Come from Heaven', Melankolic.

Böhse Onkelz (1984) 'Der nette Mann', Rock-o-Rama.

Böhse Onkelz (1987) 'Onkelz wie wir', Metal Enterprises.

Böhse Onkelz (1991) 'Wir ham noch lange nicht genug', Bellaphon Records.

Böhse Onkelz (1992) 'Heilige Lieder', Bellaphon Records.

Böhse Onkelz (1998) 'Viva los tioz', Virgin Records.

Lady Sovereign (2005) 'Cha Ching', [Promo Single], 679 Recordings.

Massive Attack (1991) 'Blue Lines', Circa Records.

Massive Attack (1994) 'Protection', Circa Records.

Massive Attack (1998) 'Mezzanine', Circa Records.

Massive Attack (2003) '100th Window', Virgin Records.

Monk and Canatella (1997) 'Monk and Canatella', Cup of Tea Records.

Smiley Culture (1985 [1984]) 'Cockney Translation', 12" Single, Fashion Records.

Smith and Mighty (1988a) 'Anyone', 12" Single, Three Stripe Records.

Smith and Mighty (1988b) 'Walk On By', 12" Single, Three Stripe Records.

The Streets (2002) 'Original Pirate Material', Vice/Atlantic Records.

The Wild Bunch (1988) 'Friends and Countrymen', 12" Single, 4th and Broadway Records.

Volkszorn (2004) 'Der ewige Jude', Micetrap Records NJ.

Contributors

Andy Bennett is Professor in the Department of Communications, Popular Culture and Film at Brock University. He has published three books, including *Popular Music and Youth Culture: Music, Identity and Place* (Macmillan 2000), as well as a number of edited and co-edited collections, including *Remembering Woodstock* (Ashgate 2004) *After Subculture* (Palgrave 2004) and *Music Scenes* (Vanderbilt University Press 2004) and numerous journal articles and book chapters. Andy is a Faculty Associate of the Center for Cultural Sociology at Yale University, an Associate of PopuLUs, the Centre for the Study of the World's Popular Musics at Leeds University, and a member of the Board for the European Sociological Association Network for the Sociology of the Arts.

Simon Bradford is Senior Lecturer in the School of Sport and Education at Brunel University and is Director of the Centre for Youth Work Studies at the University. He joined Brunel University in 1985 after working for thirteen years in residential social work and youth and community work. His main research interests lie in the evaluation of social policy initiatives affecting young people and communities, youth culture, the organisation of professional work in the 'public services' and aspects of young people's citizenship. He is author of numerous journal articles on youth work and youth policy.

Dunja Brill holds a PhD in Media and Cultural Studies (University of Sussex), an MA in International Journalism (Napier University), and an MSc in Psychology (University of Bonn). She used to be involved in the German alternative music scene as a freelance writer for various magazines (e.g. *Sonic Seducer* and *Black*). Her research interests include subcultures, gendered media representations, and alternative music. She has taught at the University of Sussex and at Humboldt-University Berlin, and currently pursues a research project on constructions of violence, gender, race and class in 'extreme' music. She is also working on a book about gender and eroticism in the Goth subculture.

Andy Brown is Senior Lecturer in Media Communication at Bath Spa University College, UK. His research interests include popular music, media and niche consumerism, television and audience studies and racism and identity politics. He is currently researching the New Wave of Heavy Metal. Previous publications include *Political Languages of Race and the Politics of Exclusion* (Ashgate 1999).

Eric Chamberlin holds an interdisciplinary Master's degree from New York University where he wrote on the mod subculture past and present. He presented another paper on the mod subculture at Kansas State University while earning a second Master's degree in library and information science from the University South Carolina. His research is concerned with the group dynamics of elective identities. He participates in Renaissance era reenactment as a hobby. This is his first published work.

Nic Crowe is a lecturer in Youth and Community with the Centre for Youth work Studies at Brunel University, West London. Previously he was a community worker in London and a youth worker in Surrey. Before joining Brunel, he was head of Media and Film at the Holy Cross School in Kingston. The focus of his PhD thesis is young people's identity in online gaming and his research interests include video games, Internet culture and ideas of cyber-community.

Wolfgang Deicke is Tutor in Politics at Ruskin College, Oxford. A political sociologist by trade, his research interests lie with social movements and identity politics, especially those of the far right in post-war Europe. Wolfgang is currently completing a PhD thesis on 'Continuity and Change in the Austrian Freedom Party in Vienna, 1956–2001' in the Department of Politics, International Relations and European Studies (PIRES) at Loughborough University.

Silvia Ferrero is an independent researcher. Her research interests include issues of class, ethnicity and identity in relation to youth, management organisation, and information and communication technologies in educational institutions. She studied for her PhD in anthropology at Goldsmiths College, University of London. She has worked predominantly on the Mediterranean region, particularly Sardinia, Italy. She is a director and consultant of Eight & Eight Ltd for which she has carried out research projects in the field of multiculturalism in transnational and educational environments.

Ben Gidley is a research fellow at the Centre for Urban and Community Research, which is attached to the Sociology department at Goldsmiths College, London. He has worked on a number of research projects, mainly in London, around issues of youth, ethnicity, migration, social exclusion and community development, including the ethnographic evaluation of the Home Office's Positive Futures youth engagement programme.

David Hesmondhalgh is Professor of and Media and Music Industries at the University of Leeds. He is the author of *The Cultural Industries* (2nd ed., 2007), and editor of several books, including *Media Production* (2006), *Understanding Media: Inside Celebrity* (with Jessica Evans, 2005), and *Popular Music Studies* (with Keith Negus, 2002).

Paul Hodkinson is Lecturer in Sociology at the University of Surrey. His research interests focus on young people's relationship to commerce, media and new technologies. In particular he has researched and written about the relationship between individual and collective identities within youth culture. Such issues are explored via a comprehensive reworking of the notion of subculture in his book, *Goth. Identity, Style and Subculture* (2002 Berg), a publication which gave rise to national media reviews and interviews. He has also published various journal papers and chapters focused upon the implications of different forms of media use for patterns of identity and community among young people.

Rupa Huq is Senior Lecturer in Sociology at Kingston University. Her research interests are mainly concentrated in the areas of youth, ethnicity and popular music. Her international experience spans advising the Council of Europe and working with the British Council in settings from India to Finland. She has been a parliamentary candidate, music journalist and practicing DJ amongst other things. Her book *Beyond Subculture* is also out with Routledge (2006).

Rhoda MacRae is Research Fellow at the Department of Applied Social Science, University of Stirling. Rhoda's PhD explored how young people identified and affliated with particular club scenes, and looked at the processes and resources required to 'become' a clubber over time. It argued that developing and maintaining a clubbing life-style required competency, skills and dispositons: it was a process that transmitted privilege and disadvantage. Rhoda's post doctoral research interests have concerned young people and criminal justice, service provision for substance misusing prisoners and child protection training for social workers.

Norma Mendoza-Denton is Assistant Professor in the Department of Anthropology at the University of Arizona, where she is also affiliated faculty in Linguistics, Cognitive Science, Women's Studies, and Mexican-American Studies. She received her PhD from Stanford University in 1997. Her main interests are sociophonetic variation, probabilistic sociolinguistics, language contact, gender and ethnicity, gesture analysis, and linguistic/ethnographic/videographic methods. She is author of *Homegirls:*

Language and Symbolic Practices in the Making of Latina Youth Styles (forthcoming Blackwell) and a variety of book chapters and journal articles on language, identity and gender.

Stewart Varner is a PhD candidate in the Institute of the Liberal Arts at Emory University. He earned an MA from the Department of Popular Culture at Bowling Green State University. His research focuses on the impact of globalisation on identity and culture.

Peter Webb is Lecturer in Media Studies in the Department of Sociology at the University of Birmingham. Prior to this he was a research fellow at the University of Bristol working on an ESRC project looking at the impact of e-commerce on the music, fashion and financial services industries. His research interests are popular culture, music industry and popular music, media, globalisation, social theory, politics. He has published work on the music industry, music networks and the Internet. He is also a musician and has released a number of acclaimed albums and singles under the name of Statik Sound System.

Index

Page numbers in italics refer to Figures or Tables.

Lightning Source UK Ltd.
Milton Keynes UK
08 September 2010

159616UK00001B/13/P